TECHNICAL
MANPOWER PLANNING

TECHNICAL MANPOWER PLANNING

Edited by

Dr. M. Sudhir Reddy
Project Officer,
NTMIS Nodal Centre,
JNTU,
Hyderabad (A.P.)

Dr. P. Murali Krishna
Associate Professor,
SKIM, SK University
Anantapur (A.P.)

Dr. K. Ramakrishna Reddy
Professor
Management & Member
Executive Council
SK University
Anantapur (A.P.)

Dr. K. Lal Kishore
Director
Academic & Planning
JNTU
Hyderabad (A.P.)

DISCOVERY PUBLISHING HOUSE
NEW DELHI-110002

First Published-2005

ISBN 81-8356-035-0

Published by

DISCOVERY PUBLISHING HOUSE

4831/24, Ansari Road, Prahlad Street,
Darya Ganj, New Delhi-110002 (India)
Phone: 23279245 • Fax: 91-11-23253475
E-mail:dphtemp@indiatimes.com

Printed at:
Amit Enterprises

DEDICATED

TO

GREAT TEACHER

SARVEPALLI RADHAKRISHNAN

September 5, 1888-1975

"We must remain sensitive to the prevailing currents of thought and be prepared to translate the universal truth into terms intelligible to our audience, without distorting their meaning."

Preface

In this vast Country, India, with huge population of 106 millions, it is difficult to know and assess the existing Manpower and its requirement for the India's Economic development. Towards this end the Government of India set up the National Technical Manpower Information System (NTMIS) Under the Ministry of Education and Culture in 1983, to review the status of the nation's needs and to suggest reorientation and improvements to the existing programmes, the government has set up 21 Nodal Centres at 17 reputed academic institutions/directorate of technical training and 4 regional Boards of Apprenticeship training across the nation. The NTMIS also has a lead Centre at New Delhi which Co-ordinates the working of Nodal Centres.

The Planning of Technical Manpower is the main function of NTMIS. The Manpower is mainly generated by different Technical Institutions, Universities, professional bodies and industries. The need for Technical Manpower is wide spread across the nation in this technologically influenced society. The beneficiaries of this Technical Manpower are the State and Central government organisations, private sector enterprises, NGOs and a few Local bodies in the Country. On the other side, the number of aspirants with technical competence seeks better opportunities in India and abroad. In the past, NTMIS scope was confined to post-graduates, graduates and diploma holders in Engineering and Technology only. At present the equally sought after disciplines such as Management, Pharmacy, Computer Sciences and Hotel Management and catering Technology are also included with in the scope of NTMIS.

The NTMIS organises several Seminars and conferences across the country every year through its Nodal Centres. This book is an outcome of contribution by participants of national seminar on "Technical Manpower Planning in India-Issues and Concerns" held between 5-7, September, 2004. The seminar was organised jointly by the NTMIS, Delhi and JNTU, Hyderabad at JNTU, Hyderabad. This was the second national seminar and first held in the southern region of NTMIS. The seminar was inaugurated by Prof. R. Natarajan, Chairman, AICTE, New Delhi on the most auspicious "Teachers Day". Hence, the book is dedicated to the **Great Teacher Dr. Sarvepalli Radhakrishnan.**

The Book is compilation of the articles contributed by the authors across the country. The authors own the responsibility for their respective articles. The articles have thoroughly edited and included in this book. This exercise of conducting seminar and publishing the book has been possible due to many people.

We express on sincere thanks to Prof. H. Ramachandran, Director, IAMR, Delhi for Choosing AP Nodal Centre at JNTU for organising the seminar we are sincerely thankful to Prof. Y. Venkatrami Reddy, VC, JNTU for his constant support and encouragement Er. Anil Kumar, Chief, NTMIS, IAMR has been a source of support and motivation to us in conducting the seminar. We thank him for the same. We are extremely thankful to Mr. Tilak Wasan of Discovery Publishing House, New Delhi for publishing this book within a reasonable time. Our thanks are also due to all participants, resource persons authors and the staff that made this publication possible.

M. Sudhir Reddy
P. Murali Krishna
K. Ramakrishna Reddy
K. Lal Kishore

Contents

1

The Knowledge Economy and its Requirements

The Type of Technical Manpower We Need

Manas Bhunia[*]

Anindya Bhattacharya[**]

ABSTRACT

The emergence of a 'knowledge economy' is the most significant phenomenon over the last ten years in the Indian socio-economic profile. The 'knowledge economy' deserves a new category of technical manpower, now-a-days often termed as 'knowledge workers' in popular parlance. This is the arena where the economy is expanding in the real sense and an actual demand-supply mechanism of newer technical manpower seems more pertinent here. This chapter examines the scope of technical manpower requirement in this area and also the implied structural changes which need to be considered in any major policy implications on technical manpower assessment.

Key Words: Knowledge Economy, Knowledge Worker, Structural Changes.

---

* **NTMIS Nodal Centre, Board of Practical Training (ER), Kolkata– 700 064, Email: ntmiskol@yahoo.com**

** **NTMIS Nodal Centre, Board of Practical Training (ER), Kolkata– 700 064, Email: ntmiskol@yahoo.com**

INTRODUCTION

The present world is passing through a phase of unprecedented changes. A rapid technological revolution over the last 20 years has drastically altered the face of the society. The economy has taken a new turn and in no way we can turn back from the inevitability of an emerging 'global village'. We are gradually entering into the era of a 'knowledge economy', where knowledge (albeit, information array) is the order of the day. This information array, in a way, is inducing a paradigm shift to the entire understanding. In this backdrop, we need to conceive the essence of 'knowledge worker' and its pattern of emergence, which would help us to estimate the real technical manpower requirement, the dominant force in the new economy.

The term 'knowledge worker' we first used by Peter F. Drucker in the year 1959[1] when the possibility of emerging of such a knowledge economy was too far off. Drucker conceived of a future society which would have a bigger domain of a service sector; and the traditional sectors like agriculture, manufacturing would be gradually reduced to a small space in the overall socio-economic arena. That has evolved as a reality today, though in a different sense, and so, the term 'knowledge worker' has found its right place in this context. Here in this chapter we would focus on the requirements of knowledge worker, or to put in traditional terms, the technical manpower, in both quantitative and qualitative terms.

ASSESSMENT AND DIFFERENT STUDIES

There have been a lot of studies on the emergence of this knowledge economy. An overview of this economy and its trends along with the manpower engaged can be understood from the facts summed up by NASSCOM: *From a base of 6,800 knowledge workers in 1985-86, the number increased to 522,000 software and services professionals by the end of 2001-02. It is estimated that out of these 522,000 knowledge workers, almost 170,000 are working in the IT software and services export industry; nearly 106,000 are working in the IT enabled services and over 220,000 in user organisations.*[2]

In another report prepared by NASSCOM-McKinsey, as given below, we get a magnitude of the manpower requirements (knowledge workers) in the evolving knowledge economy:

- Fresh jobs in India in year 2001-2002—1.82 million and replacement jobs-over 250,000;
- Requirement of 2.2 million knowledge workers by 2008;
- Attrition rate of knowledge workers is 14 per cent currently—down from 17 per cent in 1998 and 25 per cent in 1992;
- Nearly 1 in 5 fortune 500 companies have sourced knowledge workers from India.

Source: NASSCOM-McKinsey Report.[3]

Now, to have an understanding of the knowledge economy we should take into account the overall changing socio-economic scenario. Considering the changes, it can be described as an upsurge towards an Information Age. Some relevant data are furnished here below to have a view on the present situation. The data here below depict a very interesting picture. We have taken data for 5 countries to have a comparative understanding. The countries like Japan and USA fall in the category of high income group of countries whereas India, Brazil and Argentina fall in the categories of low income, lower middle income and upper middle income group of countries respectively. The categories are of the World Bank benchmarks.

Table—1.1 Comparative study of different sectors

	Agriculture		Industry				Services	
	% of GDP		Total % of GDP		Manufacturing % of GDP		% of GDP	
Countries	**1990**	**2002**	**1990**	**2002**	**1990**	**2002**	**1990**	**2002**
India	31	23	28	27	17	16	41	51
Japan	2	1	39	31	27	21	58	68
Brazil	8	6	39	21	25	13	53	73
Argentina	8	11	36	32	27	21	56	57
USA	2	2	28	23	19	15	70	75

Source: 2004 World Development Indicators, The World Bank.[4]

Though India has a high per cent of GDP in agriculture due to its position in the low income group, the pertinent point to note is that the major increasing shift in the per cent of GDP over the 12 years has been in the sector of services. In case of all other countries (except Argentina) there has been a fall in the per cent of GDP in agricultural sector. But the services sector in all of the countries had a steady rise over the last decade. This is indicative of the emergence of the knowledge and its prominent place in the overall economic domain. Interestingly, the industry, especially the manufacturing sector had a steady decline over the years which also indicate the end of the old-pattern industrial age.

STRUCTURAL CHANGES AND ITS CONSEQUENCES

The sweeping revolutions in the overall profile of the technology itself have brought some significant changes in the economy as a whole. As the technology is researched and nourished in the laboratories of the big corporations, and moreover, the huge fund necessary for it is provided by the big brands, so these big houses possess an advantage over the use of newer technology. But as a historical consequence, some areas of technology have freed themselves from the exclusive clutches of the big houses and have become more user-friendly with a wider access. This has happened due to prevalence of hard-core competition among the corporations producing technology or direct technology related products where the rule of the game is to be consumer-friendly and have an expansive market. As a result, such technology has become cheaper, widely usable and movable. Examples can be given in regard to computers, interent, entertainment and electronic produces, and to some extent in the field of communications. The dimensions of this change of the economy can be understood from a survey of the Price Waterhouse Coopers. The survey has revealed as estimate of $ 1.2 trillion business in the field of media and entertainment by the year 2005 which would have a 7.2 per cent yearly growth rate.[5] Besides, the bio-tech industry is coming in a major way which is all set to cross the $ 1-billion mark turnover, in India alone, this fiscal year.[6]

The more significant of this is the disintegration of the organised, assembly-line based disposition of working class. The conquering of the economy by a virtual world has created a mass of unorganised knowledge worker in the new fields of TV serials, script writing, web designing, content writing, sales promotion, call centres, decoding of genome technology, internet, share market and what not. This is moving towards a slow demise of the old-patterned work traditions (like 10am-5pm office duty). And more interestingly, the big houses now-a-days talk about 'core competence' where they prefer to outsource the technical work keeping in their hands the core policy strategy. So, an innumerable number of small firms, home businesses are cropping up in the form of self-entrepreneurship, taking up the work released from the big firms, thus changing the structure of the economy in a substantive way. Moreover, the capacity of dispersion of modern technology i.e. splitting of technology according to different functions has enabled a common man to take up a particular function easily as his work. The scope of self-entrepreneurship has thus widened a lot and is now the reality of the day. This is the overall perspective of the new economy that is emerging and we need to posit out technical manpower planning in this background. Otherwise, all exercises would prove to be futile.

INDIA AS A SUPER POWER

India has taken a lot of advantage of this knowledge economy. The IIT's and technical colleges of our country have produced a vast number of well-versed and competent manpower, who have successfully faced the international challenges and have rightly fitted themselves into the domain of the knowledge economy. Now the challenge is whether the knowledge power of our country can overtake the international competition and emerge as a super power on its own. We have excellent manpower resources and a useful utility of them can place us in a leading position. But that deserves an updated knowledge of our own resources, as estimate of the requirement of technical manpower and a proper imparting of modern technical education. First of all, we need to know the dynamics of the emerging knowledge economy, where the scopes are being created and which are the areas where we are equipped enough to perform at the level best in terms of international standard.

THE FUTURE

The scope of forecasting the requirements of technical manpower in this new area becomes more complicated. This is due to the fact that we have no comprehensive idea about the nature of the new knowledge economy. Moreover, it has a vast element of uncertainty where the changes are very rapid. So, the process of evolving a methodology is too intricate and we need to incorporate a lot of parameters. At the first hand, if we do not take into account the structural changes it incorporates and the relative dynamism that it engineers, we would not be able to understand its basic logic. For that matter, a continuous and integrated study considering a large network of data is of urgent need. An online information system where the changes are needed to be incorporated almost on a daily basis is the prerequisite condition to have a futuristic trend in the pattern of the demand and supply of technical manpower requirements. Besides, the logic of the economy is also to be understood at the same time. It is of no doubt that the economy has taken a new face with lots of new dimensions evolving into the scene. So, it is of utmost importance to grasp the logically of the economy itself, basing on which we may determine the modalities of ascertaining the requirements of its manpower, obviously the technical manpower.

Our attempting here is to emphasise on the structural changes that are sweeping the world economy. As we have mentioned, on the one hand, there is the every possibility of an emerging 'global village' implying unification of the world economy and on the other, there is a process of dispersion where the technology becomes more usable and accessible to a wide range of users. This has expanded the horizon of the economic activity as a whole with lots of scopes and uncertainties, thus, creating an opportunity to work out elaborate intricacies of manpower requirements. This, obviously, deserves an online mechanism of supply and demand and also a detailed a parametric inputs where every turn (at least the major ones) can be counted to have an almost accurate futuristic assessment.

A major shift in the thinking of the academic world is also necessary in a similar way. As our world economy gets more and more dynamic and prone to change so there must be a thought to assign a common thread to every stream of engineering discipline. It is very unreliable to predict on the future prospects of a particular discipline considering the fuzzy content embedded in the over all present socio-economic perspective. So, a student opting for a particular discipline considering its bright future at the beginning of his study may end up frustratingly at the end after 4 years when that discipline seemed to be of no hopeful career prospect. So, if there is a common thread and swapping elements among the disciplines, the requirements may thus be compensated.

So, what is needed is to review the entire exercise of manpower planning in the context of the newly emerging knowledge economy. We have tried in this chapter to set the perspective. The detailed modalities are of urgent necessity.

REFERENCES

1. Drucker F. Peter, *Landmarks of Tomorrow*, Transaction Publishers, 1959.
2. *Knowledge Professionals*. http://www.tatatelecom.com/experienceindia/Advantage/knowledge.asp.
3. *The Indian Job Scenario*, http://www.careermosaicindia.com
4. *2004 World Development Indicators*, First Printing, The World Bank, Washington, 2004.
5. Bhattacharya Anindya, Jagotik-Virtual Bastobotar Porikotha, *EKAK MATRA*, Vol. 2, No. 3, 2001, pp. 24-27.
6. Special Correspondent, Biotech Boom Imminent, *The Telegraph*, Dated 12 August, 2004.

2

Technical Education
Challenges Ahead

*K. V. Subbarao**
*CH. Subbarao***

ABSTRACT

The pyramidal structure of technical education of I.T.I.s, Polytechnics, Engineering Colleges and the higher education and research in technology is to be strengthened with each arm extending its contribution for the technical manpower requirements. In view of the employability and the availability of the technicians, this branch of education assumes significance. But, the demands of the industry are undergoing changes in succession in view of technological upgradation and the output of these technical institutions also must be thoroughly recast yielding place to more hands-on knowledge rather than bookish theory, so that the industry as well as the country look ahead towards economic growth and prosperity in this changing global scenario.

Key Words: Engineering Colleges, Industrial Training Institutes, Modernisation, multidisciplinary. Polytechnics, Revamping of syllabi.

* **Sr. Lecturer in CCP, Government of Polytechnic for Women, Nellore - 524 003, E-mail: rao_kvs2000@yahoo.co.uk**

** **Head of CCP, S.G.M. Government Polytechnic, Abdullapurmet, RR District, E-mail: srilakshmirao2004@yahoo.co.in**

INTRODUCTION

Education is not only the provider of bread and butter for an individual but more importantly the enhancer of the knowledge and vision. Role of education in nation building is not merely a question of social equality and equipping persons for securing employment. Education would remain one of the basic services to be organised by the State and human resources development through a multi-layered broad based pyramidal system of education would be an important strategy of nation building in our country. The technical manpower requirements are addressed to by the Industrial Training Institutes, Polytechnics and Engineering Colleges. Though our country has been mostly agrarian, the returns from this sector have been mostly erratic due to various factors and it is but natural for the economy to look to manufacturing and services sectors for its growth. Thus, industrial development received priority in our planning process. We need technically competent manpower for efficient and effective use of the resources. The vision of the Government both at Macro and Micro level is inarguably to produce quality products marketable anywhere in the world. In this context, every area of governance is subject to paradigm shift and technical education is no exception.

We are proud to register higher literacy rate in recent years, of course with immense support from various governmental and non-governmental agencies. The universities and technical institutions have registered phenomenal growth, no doubt, in their number but also in the number of graduates. But the industrial growth over the last decade or so, has not been matching with the pace of such educational growth, leaving thousands, and in some cases, lakhs of technically qualified persons unemployed. Industry, facing cutthroat competition in the light of liberalisation, globalisation and privatisation, is fighting to control the costs just to keep its head above water. Although the number of universities has expanded, and many of the u:niversities continue to maintain high standards of education, it is a matter of serious concern that the expansion in quantity has been accompanied by a fall in quality. Modernization of syllabi, examination reforms and greater attention to issues of governance of universities and colleges, all require urgent attention. Assertion of the dignity of labour and vocationalisation of curricula are essential to ensure that a disjunction does not take place between the educational system and the work place.[1] In order to be globally competitive we have to refurbish the pattern, structure and content of technical education.

PRESENT SCENARIO

As is natural with a growing economy, the country witnessed growth not only in educational institutions but also in the out-turn of the students. From secondary education onwards, the plans enabled education to include vocational training as well. Education was increasingly sought to be made relevant to work, to enhance employment opportunities. Even the technical training imparted was to be increasingly related to industry. Quality in education, along with the necessary focus on vocational training, was expected to solve the twin problems of the need for manpower and of unemployment. Tables 2.1 and 2.2 show the glimpse of the number of students admitted, passed out of the educational institutions and the available stock during the period 1951-1997. But, this growth could not add much to the country's economy. With regard to employment in factories the total number of workers remained stagnant during the period 1995-96 and 2000-01. The number of industrial workers increased only from 8,23,979 to 8,25,827 during the same period recording only a marginal increase. It is argued that whatever the industrial growth taking place in the State, it is without additional jobs. The number of notified vacancies decreased from 53,431 in 1980-81 to 10,919 in 2000-01.[2] The percentage expenditure on University and Higher Education to GDP, which was 0.77 per cent in 1990-91 shows a gradual decrease to 0.62 per cent during 1997-98 and rises to 0.88 per cent in 2000-2001.

Table—2.1 Progress of admission and out-turn of engineering candidates on all India basis

Year	Engineering			
	Degree Level		Diploma Level	
	Admission	Out-turn	Admission	Out-turn
1951	4788	2893	6216	2626
1961	15497	7026	26525	10349
1971	18207	18223	33154	17699
1981	34835	19012	61114	35487
1986	36328	29291	94728	50390
1987	55508	30078	102525	56560
1988	56867	33864	104113	
1989	62603	37615	112899	
1990	66686	41464	111262	63794
1991	70481	44724	117835	65325
1992	73018	44144	119465	63888
1996	103933	60749	161125	95283
1997	138450	59311		

Sources: Ministry of Human Resource Development, Technical Education in India Survey of Facilities.

Craftsmen Training is imparted to young men and women of the age group of 15-25 in 42 engineering and 18 non-engineering trades. For this purpose, Industrial Training Institutes (ITIs) have been set up all-over the country. Till the end of 1998, 4,086 such institutes had already been functioning. The training imparted is useful for getting employment, especially in the local industries.

Table—2.2 Estimated Stock of engineers in the working age group *all India*

Year	Degree holders	Diploma holders	Total
1	2	3	4
1955	350	440	790
1961	640	840	1480
1971	1745	2304	4049

(Contd...)

1	2	3	4
	3049	4258	7307
			9922
1987	4129		10587
1988	4360		11319
1989	4624		12076
1990	4922		12900
1991	5196		13789
1992	5530		14654
1993			15489
1994		197	16431
1995		791	17423
1996			18430
1997		11973	19492
1998	7004	12555	20539

Source: NTMIS, AICTE, Govt. of India.

With such huge manpower at hand, why is the Industry unable to absorb the mass of resources? The absence of interaction between the industry and the educational institutions is one of the major causes for the failure. Inarguably, the educational institutions are not producing what the industry requires. With information technology driving the present day world and most of the tasks being monitored by the computers, the industry wants multifaceted individuals who can fit into any kind of situation—be it pure engineering or management or both—so that it can reduce the costs. If the curriculum is so designed as to produce such multi-dimensional intelligentsia removing some of the redundant and obsolete technology, not only the industry's requirements are fulfilled but also the employability is improved to a great extent. These considerations apply with even greater force to the technical educational system. Both technical and management education need to be managed strategically in order to provide broad-based, multi-disciplinary education incorporating composite skills and knowledge to meet the challenges posed by globalisation. Organisation of any new course/diversification at one or the other levels has to take into consideration a systematic study of the manpower requirement and utilisation, linked with the occupational structure of the various employing sectors. It is, therefore, necessary to keep this in mind while organising any new course/diversification at any level right from the craftsmen to the post-graduate so that the entire spectrum of activities in the employing fields is kept in mind.

SUGGESTIONS

In view of the changing requirements, the following suggestions are offered which can be considered:

1. The curriculum basically at every stage of technical education, no doubt, should be revamped. The association of the industry at the time of curricula preparation is not the only solution. Besides adopting some of the technical educational institutions in their areas of operation, the industry can visualise the future. The redundant topics have to be dropped altogether, giving credence to the latest science and technology.

2. In the highest plane of the technological advancement i.e. the post graduation and research, there must be innovation and quality in place of routine and quantity. Though there has been a vociferous appeal that qualitative research is needed for the country's economic growth, it remains a dream and it is a sad testimony that the universities are mute spectators to the large number of degrees churned out by them. Unless the definition of research stresses on innovation or something new, everyone in this system is a culprit for the deceleration in this regard.

3. It is a common belief that engineering is much sought after because it provides better opportunities for admission into Management Education in premier institutions. Though it is not proved to the hilt, the Engineering graduate after spending considerable part of valuable life has to spend again two more years for obtaining the Management Degree so that his services

can be best utilised. If the premier Universities offer an integrated course which offers a combination of quality technical and managerial education at least to a limited talented group, then such talent would certainly drive the industry forward. This multidisciplinary specialisation will be of a great response to the myriad problems facing the economy at present.

4. Polytechnics, which have been producing diploma holders, provide the input for not only to the industry but also to the Engineering colleges. The motto of polytechnic education is to offer a technically competent person who can act as supervisor and an intermediary between the craftsman and the junior-level management. The polytechnics have not witnessed rapid changes in their curricula incorporating the latest techniques of either the management or the handling of equipment and are lethargic imparting the conventional theoretical knowledge. It is imperative that there should be a thorough holocaust of the syllabi and the methodology of instruction in polytechnics with much of the emphasis on practical and hands-on-training on modern machinery, without compromising on the quality for which the diploma holder is trusted for years and in some cases decades.

5. Having realised the significance of vocational education, the Government of India has taken up large-scale modernisation of Industrial Training Institutes during the next few years. This is an important issue, which is overlooked, perhaps, for obvious reasons. Further, the craftsman, after undergoing the training mostly in vernacular languages of the various states, has to answer a test in English, which becomes highly difficult for him. What is to be tested is not the theoretical knowledge presented in an altogether higher language, but the practical application in real life situations. With the modernisation in the offing, the I.T .I.s must rise up to the occasion for providing suitably qualified technicians for the lower strata of the industry.

REFERENCES

1 Approach Paper on Tenth Five Year Plan, 2002-2007, Planning Commission, Government of India, New Delhi, p. 37.

2 Pattern of Development in India—A Study of Andhra Pradesh—SER Division—Planning Commission—Government of India.

3

Status of Technical Manpower in North-Eastern States

*Debabrata Maji**
*Manabjyoti Hazarika***

ABSTRACT

Technical Education play an important role in the socio-economic growth and development in North Eastern States of the country and ready to face the challenges in pursuance with globalisation and liberalization and in the context of new economic policies. The present status of the Technical Education with its subsequent development in last few years has been elaborated in this chapter. In-depth study, analysis, scope of technical education and subsequent employment has been presented in this chapter based on published data from different ATMRs, NTMIS and census report of the year 2001.

INTRODUCTION

Information, Finance, Manpower and Infrastructure are the basic key elements of any developed country. To make India, a developed Nation by 2020 the similar elements may require highly

* **North-Eastern Regional Institute of Science and Technology, Nirjuli (Itanagar)– 791 109, Papum Pare District, Arunachal Pradesh, E-mail: dmaji2004@Yahoo.co.in**

** **North Eastern Regional Institute of Science and Technology, Nirjuli (Itanagar)– 791 109, Papum Pare District, Arunachal Pradesh, E-mail: manab_tez@Indiatimes.com**

as input for such realistic pledges. In India, out of total Human resources, there are only 15 per cent is the Technical manpower, which is not sufficient for a developed nation. To make India as developed nation, efforts are going on in all respect including increasing the Technical manpower. Resulted, in 1983, the Government of India has set up an information system to review the position of Technical manpower time to time in our country named National Technical Manpower Information System (NTMIS) under control of Institute of Applied Manpower Research (IAMR) for proper planning and management of Technical manpower in our country. Presently, 21 Nodal Centres across the country are actively engaged to collect various data pertaining Technical Educational Centres, passed out students and their engagements in different sectors such as Govt., Private, undertakings, Enterprises, local bodies etc and to analyses.

TECHNICAL EDUCATION IN NORTH-EAST INDIA

During pre-independence period access of Technical education was limited in a few pockets only where Assam Textile Institute was established in 1920 and Prince of Wales Institute of Engineering and Technology in 1927. During the first two decades after independence also, Technical education did not its importance as it shared have been. Emphasis on Technical education was not given when the National Policy of Education was formulated in 1968 and 1986. Technical Education in North-East India is also starved of proper attention probably due to its remoteness and general nature of habitat. During the last two/three decades Technical education at Diploma, Degree and Post graduate level has improved at a much faster rate than the country average. Significantly this improvement is not limited to urban area only. Rural educational centres are emphasizing of small training centres to promote entrepreneurship among the rural mass. Training centers are developed to train the rural mass in craft technology, such as arts and crafts, carpets, wood carving, necklaces, weaving, cane and bamboo works apart from Automobile, Mechanical, Electrical machinery and Machine tools etc. for encouraging development of small scale industries based on locally available resources.

The North-Eastern Regional Institute of Science and Technology (NERIST) was set up by the Government of India, conceived as a project of the North-Eastern Council (Ministry of Home affairs) as an innovation for providing efficient technical education on modular pattern to create technical manpower at various levels for the development of the seven sisters viz., Arunachal Pradesh, Assam, Manipur, Meghalaya, Mizoram, Nagaland, and Tripura i.e., North-Eastern region (NE region) of the country. Thus, NERIST is endeavouring, with its existence as a unique and leading Institute of Technical Education in the field of technology and Applied Science not only in the NE region but also in India by its unconventional and innovative academic structure. In its existence (Established on 1986), it is pursuing the policy of educating the whole man. But, the technical and social sciences are emphasized in its unconventional and innovative academic programmes which help the students to perform equally well as educationists, Scientists, Leaders in Industry, trained Engineers and Technicians.

During the laying foundation stone of the Sixth Indian Institute of Technology (IIT) on July 4, 1992, the then Prime Minister of India, Shri P.V. Narasimha Rao told that IIT at Guwahati must be an Institution with a difference with something special and new subjects oriented distinctive Institution especially suited to the needs of the NE Region both in its working and its conceptualization and a challenging Institute and should not be a replicate of other IITs in India, because, we made a special case which felt a strong need for the development of North East India when everybody was referring to the decision to have no further IITs. In general practice, it has seem that the IITs have become the main channels of brain drain and other developing countries like Chicago, San Francisco are catching our talent graduates before passed out students from this Institutions and resulted we didn't find them when we are wanted. Sir Galbraith has written one of his famous book that a source of wealth to America is the brain that comes from other countries. A committee examined and found that the IITs had become so elite that other engineering colleges, Regional Engineering Colleges (presently NITs) etc., which needed attention somehow lost their elan and they were not being given the same care which the IITs enjoyed which is absolute favourites and it was decided not to have any more IITs. Table 3.1 (see on page 22) and Table 3.2 (see on page 23) are shown the list of Engineering and Technological Institutions in North East India.

SCENARIO OF EMPLOYMENT

The students passed out from the Technological Institutions of NE Region are serving in prestigious Industries and organisations such as: ABB (Asia Brown Boveri); APTECH; AT&T; Bells Laboratory; Texas Instruments, Ericsson (USA); CDC; C-DOT; CMC Ltd.; Crompton Greaves; Fujitsu: HCL-HP Ltd., Hero Cycles; Hewlett-Packard (Hong Kong); Hindustan Cables; Hindustan Paper Corporation; Indian Railways; Modi; Motorola; NIC; NIIT; Oil India; PDL; Philips India; Reliance Industries; Shipping Corporation of India Ltd.; Siemens; Steel Authority of India Ltd.; Tata Telecom; TCS; Videocon; Wipro Ltd.; MICO; Hindustan Motor; Lucas-TVs; Paper Mills; NEEPCO; NTPC; HPCL; Indian Army; BHEL; BRPL; CEERI; Escorts; IDPL; Indian Airlines; ISRO; ITI; L&T Ltd.; Metro Railways; NBCC; ONGC; Praga Tools; TELCO; NAL etc. etc.

A good number of students go for higher studies, viz., M. Tech., ME, MBA in premier Institutions like IITs and IIMs and some of them go to Institutes abroad. Table 3.3 (see on page 25) and Table 3.4 (see on page 26) have shown the passed out student's scenario in different level in North East Region.

STATUS OF TECHNICAL MANPOWER IN NORTH EAST INDIA

Table 3.5 and Table 3.6 (see on page 27 & 28) are shown the different level activity status of Technical manpower in NorthEast India. In the seven N.E states, near about 60 per cent of technical manpower got absorbed after completion of their study. Year-wise break-up is presented in Table—3.5. The technical manpower engaged through self-employment scheme was very poor during the period of study.

In case of diploma holders, the percentage of employment varied from 31 in 1997 and 1999 to 42 in 1994 for all the seven North-Eastern states.

STATUS OF TECHNICAL MANPOWER IN SECTOR-WISE

The employment scenario in terms of the sector of employment is analyzed for the last eight years (1993-2000) at both degree and diploma levels. The information are furnished in Tables—3.7 & 3.8 (see on pages 29 and 30). It is observed from the Table—3.7 that absorption of graduate engineers in Central Govt. departments is still very low. The main employer of graduate engineers in the N.E. states is either state Govt departments or private sector undertakings. The rate of absorption varied from 11 per cent to 28 per cent in public sector, 24 per cent to 52 per cent in private sector and18 per cent to 36 per cent in state Govt. departments during the period of study. The rate of absorption in public and private sectors in N.E. states are comparatively low to the other parts of the country. Table—3.8 shows that the employment scope for diploma holders in the state Govt. departments is far better than the graduate engineers. About 69 per cent of diploma engineers were employed in state govt departments in 1995, followed by 58 per cent in 1996, 56 per cent in 1993, 55 per cent in 1999, 52 per cent in 1994, 48 per cent in 1997 and 39 per cent in 1998. Interestingly, public and private sectors showed lower number of employment of diploma engineers as compared to graduate engineers.

STATUS OF TECHNICAL MANPOWER IN FUNCTIONARIES

Table—3.9 and Table—3.10 (see on pages 31 & 32) are shown the main functions performed by the Technical Manpower in different level. Table shows that the functions like Technical Supervisions, Design and Planning, Production/Operations. The engagement of graduate engineers in the functions namely Research and Development, Administration, Management were very low during the period 1993-2000. Similarly, at the Diploma level, absorption of engineers in the function related to Management, Administration, Research & Development, Imparting Training was negligible.

UNEMPLOYMENT SCENARIO IN NORTH EAST INDIA

The size of unemployment at the end of 1997-1998..., 2004 are estimated according to their absorption rates and are presented in Table—3.11(see on page 33). Though fluctuation exists in the estimated size of un-employment for the years 1997-2000, a decreasing trend has been reflected from the year 2001 onwards for both degree and diploma level. The highest number of unemployment at degree level is estimated to 722 for the year 2001 and 2016 at diploma level for the year 1999.

CONCLUSION

The different aspect of technical manpower based on outturn survey report for the years 1997-2000 has been analysed in respect of information about status of the technical manpower, the nature of job, nature of establishment, source of employment and it may help in the planning and management of technical manpower in the North-Eastern States.

To analyse of the labour market in the North-Eastern States reveals that there is huge potential for employment in the area of Hydropower and natural resources but presently it is extremely grim. Due to absence of heavy industries except few refineries and proper infrastructure, the North-Eastern States are deprived to trapped its own resources and increase the pressure on unemployment. Natural calamities and insurgency problems are the main hurdle and force the development very slow in the region.

To solve the unemployment problem in the North-Eastern States and to reduce the gap between the demand and supply, few suggestive measures may be taken up shortly:

1. Rapid growth of Industries in relevant with resources in the region;
2. Introduction of specialised courses in the technical education related to local resources;
3. Compulsory Industrial Training outside NE-Region during summer vacation in all level and every year;
4. Entrepreneurship park and development;
5. Modification/improvement of existing infrastructure with latest technology.

In the era of rapid Liberalisation and Globalisation policy and competitive world market scenario, it is the peak time to mould our engineers to face the challenge with the rest of the part of our country particularly and the world as a whole.

Table—3.1 Degree level technological and engineering institutions in North-East India

Sl. No.	Name of Institutions	Degree Course Offered	P.G. Course Offered
1.	Assam Engineering College, Jalukbari, Guwahati-13	Civil, Mechanical, Electrical, E&T, Engineering, Production Engineering, Instrumentation Chemical, Computer, Science	Flood Control, Watershed management, Soil Mechanics, MCA
2.	Jorhat Engineering College, Jorhat-1	Civil, Mechanical, Electrical, E&T, Instrumentation, Computer Science	MCA
3.	National Institute of Technology, Silchar	Civil, Mechanical, Electrical, E&T Engineering, Computer Science	
4.	Indian Institute of Technology, North Guwahati, Guwahati-30	Civil, Mechanical, Computer Sc. & Engg., B. Designing	Computer Sc., E&T, Mechanical
5.	School of Art & Crafts	Art & Crafts	
6.	Tripura Engineering college Tripura (west)- 799055	Civil, Electrical, Mechanical	
7.	North-Eastern Regional Institute of Science & Technology, Itanagar, Arunachal Pradesh -791109	Civil, Electrical, Mechanical, Electronics Computer Science & Engg., Agri. Engg.	
8.	Govt. College of Technology, Takyelpat, Imphal, West Manipur	Civil, Computer Sc. & Technology, Electronics & Communication.	
9.	Regional Institute of Pharmaceutical Science & Technology, Abhoynagar, Agartala, Tripura	Pharmacy	

Table—3.2 Diploma level technological and engineering institutions in North-East India

Sl. No.	Name of Institutions	Year of Establishment	Courses Offered
1	2	3	4
1.	Assam Engineering Institute, Chandmari, Guwahati-3	1948	Civil, Electrical, Mechanical, Chemical, Electronics & Tele Comm. Engg., Computer Engg.
2.	The Prince of Wales Institute, Jorhat-1	1927	Civil, Electrical, Mechanical, Agriculture Engineering, Automobile Engineering, Instrumentation, E&T Engineering
3.	Bongaigaon Polytechnic, Bongaigaon -783380	1986	Civil, Electrical, Automobile
4.	Dibrugarh Polytechnic, Lahowal, Dibrugarh-10	1965	Civil, Electrical, Mechanical
5.	Nagaon Polytechnic, Nowgaon-782001	1961	Civil, Electrical, Mechanical, Computer Engineering
6.	Silchar Polytechnic, Silchar	1960	Civil, Electrical, Mechanical, E&T Engineering
7.	Girls' Polytechnic, Bamunimaidan, Guwahati-21	1964	Modern Office Management, Architectural Assistantship
8.	Assam Textile Institute, Ambari, Guwahati-1	1920	Textile Technology
9.	Indian Institute of Handloom Technology, Khanapara	1982	Handloom Technology
10.	Residential Girls' Polytechnic, Golaghat	1988	Electronics & Telecommunication, Textile Chemistry & Design
11.	Govt. Polytechnic, Imphal, Manipur	1960	Civil Engg., Electrical Engg., Mechanical Engg., Electronics

(Contd...)

1	2	3	4
12.	Shillong Polytechnic, Mawlai, Shillong-8, Meghalaya	1965	Civil. Engg., Electrical Engg., Mechanical Engg., Electronics
13.	Mizoram Polytechnic, Hrangchalkawn, Lunglei, Mizoram-796701	1981	Civil Engg., Electrical Engg., Mechanical Engg.
14.	Kelhose Polytechnic, Atoizoo, Zunheboto, Nagaland-798619	1972	Civil Engg., Electrical Engg., Mechanical Engg.
15.	Tripura Polytechnic Institute, Narsingarh, Tripura (West)	1958	Civil Engg., Electrical Engg., Mechanical Engg.
16.	North-Eastern Regional Institute of Science & Technology, Itanagar, Arunachal Pradesh-791109	1985	Civil. Engg., Electrical Engg., Mechanical Engg., Electronics, Comp. Sc., Agri. Engg.
17.	Centre for Electronics Design & Technology of India, Manipur	1988	Electronics Engg.
18.	Women Polytechnic Kohima, Nagaland-797001	1998	Modern Office Practice
19.	Women Polytechnic Zarkawat, Aizawl, Mizoram-796001	1998	Modern Office Practice, Electronics & Telecommunication
20.	Centre for Electronics Design & Technology of India Aizawl, Mizoram	2001	Electronics Engg.
21.	Arunachal Polytechnic, Itanagar Arunachal Pradesh– 791 111	2002	Information Technology, Travel Tourism & Hotel Management
22.	Regional Institute of Paramedical and Nursing Aizwal, Mizoram	1997	Pharmacy
23.	Regional Institute of Pharmaceutical Science and Technology, Abhoynagar, Agartala, Tripura	1997	Pharmacy

Table—3.3 Degree level passed out students in North Eastern region

	1993	**1994**	**1995**	**1996**	**1997**	**1998**	**1999**	**2000**	**2001**	**2002**
Arunachal	173	128	151	168	148	147	182	187	167	179
Tripura	114	124	87	104	95	123	111	111	112	108
Assam	443	363	459	407	487	525	534	560	577	563
Total	**730**	**615**	**697**	**679**	**730**	**795**	**827**	**858**	**856**	**843**

Table—3.4 Diploma level passed out students in North-Eastern region

	1993	1994	1995	1996	1997	1998	1999	2000	2001	2002
Arunachal	115	122	97	92	118	113	100	122	101	124
Manipur	55	52	70	73	87	90	129	144	116	134
Meghalaya	86	150	89	93	46	32	43	61	57	47
Mizoram	77	104	51	79	29	28	44	40	52	NA
Nagaland	45	47	85	95	134	70	70	49	50	30
Assam	671	491	420	624	813	485	313	290	344	366
Total	**1100**	**1042**	**814**	**1114**	**1261**	**867**	**799**	**806**	**497**	**NA**

Table—3.5 Activity status of technical manpower in North-East India at degree level

Year	Activity in percentage					
	Employed	Self employed	Studying	Apprenticeship	Unemployed	Others
1993	55	1	1	3	40	–
1994	61	2	2		33	2
1995	53	6	8	3	28	2
1996	60	3	8	1	27	1
1997	54	6	5	3	31	1
1998	58	1	11	4	25	1
1999	58	1	7	10	23	1
2000	56	3	6	5	28	2
Total	**455**	**23**	**48**	**29**	**235**	**10**

Table—3.6 Activity status of technical manpower in North East India at diploma level

	Activity in percentage					
Year	Employed	Self employed	Studying	Apprenticeship	Unemployed	Other activity
1993	41	3	6	4	46	–
1994	42	5	6	6	40	1
1995	37	4	10	6	42	1
1996	35	2	9	7	46	1
1997	31	3	7	18	40	1
1998	32	2	15	7	41	3
1999	31	1	23	8	36	1
2000	32	2	20	7	37	2
Total	**281**	**22**	**96**	**63**	**328**	**10**

Table—3.7 Sector-wise technical manpower at degree level

Years	Distribution of technical manpower (%) in various sectors						
	Central Govt.	State Govt.	Local body	Public sector	Private sector	Co-operative Society	Other
1993	8	36	2	23	24	1	6
1994	6	32	3	19	24	4	12
1995	5	19	6	28	36	1	5
1996	3	18	2	23	45	3	6
1997	6	14	2	32	41	1	4
1998	7	20	3	11	52	–	7
1999	8	20	3	11	56	–	2
2000	7	21	2	19	47	1	3
Total	**50**	**180**	**23**	**166**	**325**	**11**	**45**

Table—3.8 Sector-wise technical manpower at diploma level

Year	Distribution of technical manpower (%) in various sectors						
	Central Govt.	State Govt.	Local body	Public sector	Private sector	Co-operative Society	Other
1993	2	56	4	9	17	4	8
1994	6	52	2	11	22	3	4
1995	4	69	4	9	10	1	3
1996	4	58	5	10	12	5	6
1997	4	48	2	10	32	1	3
1998	8	39	4	14	31	1	3
1999	10	55	2	7	16	7	3
2000	9	53	4	9	18	5	2
Total	**47**	**430**	**27**	**79**	**158**	**27**	**32**

Table—3.9 Degree level technical manpower in main functions

Sl. No.	Main Functions	1993	1994	1995	1996	1997	1998	1999	2000
1.	Undergoing Training	9	21	1	11	11	12	15	7
2.	Management	4	4	6	4	3	5	6	3
3.	Design/Planning	4	12	4	5	13	11	14	16
4.	Teaching	20	7	1	5	11	7	8	5
5.	Production/Operation	6	6	20	12	17	10	7	6
6.	Service	11	5	8	6	2	4	6	9
7.	Sales/Purchase/Publicity	4	5	12	4	4	8	5	8
8.	Technical Supervision	18	16	18	25	15	18	11	19
9.	Maintenance	12	7	8	8	7	6	9	10
10.	Imparting Training	1	2	–	10	1	4	5	7
11.	Testing Quality Control	–	1	–	2	0	-	2	3
12.	Administration	6	2	3	-	4	3	2	1
13.	Research & Development	–	1	–	6	9	4	5	3
14.	Store Management	5	5	6	–	3	6	3	2
15.	Other Function	–	6	13	2	–	2	2	1
	Total	**100**	**100**	**100**	**100**	**100**	**100**	**100**	**100**

Table—3.10 Diploma level technical manpower in main functions

Sl. No.	Main Functions	1993	1994	1995	1996	1997	1998	1999	2000
1.	Undergoing Training	8	8	21	11	4	6	7	12
2.	Management	2	–	2	–	1	2	–	–
3.	Design/Planning	7	5	7	8	8	7	6	4
4.	Teaching	2	12	4	4	2	2	3	2
5.	Production/Operation	5	8	16	14	4	2	4	6
6.	Service	10	9	10	14	11	10	13	12
7.	Sales/Purchase/Publicity	10	1	2	5	3	4	2	4
8.	Technical Supervision	34	36	19	15	46	38	40	35
9.	Maintenance	5	4	9	6	14	7	6	4
10.	Imparting Training	–	–	–	4	1	3	–	–
11.	Testing Quality Control	5	–	2	1	2	3	2	–
12.	Administration	1	4	3	–	–	2	–	4
13.	Research & Development	–	–	–	8	2	7	6	5
14.	Store Management	2	7	3	2	1	2	6	8
15.	Other Function	9	6	2	8	1	5	5	4
	Total	**100**	**100**	**100**	**100**	**100**	**100**	**100**	**100**

Table—3.11 Unemployment senario in-North East India

At the end of the Year	Estimated size of unemployment	
	Degree	Diploma
1997	470	1243
1998	691	1707
1999	588	2016
2000	574	1984
2001	722	1779
2002	686	1341
2003	463	535
Total	**4194**	**10605**

REFERENCES

1. Sharma, S. P., M. J. Hazarika, N. Khargharia, *A Study of Labour Market for Graduate Engineers and Diploma Holders in the North-Eastern States* NTMIS, Nodal Centre, NERIST, Itanagar.
2. *Present Status of Engineering Education in Assam,* NTMIS Bulletin, Vol-IX, No. 3, Oct-Dec, 2003.
3. *Technical Manpower Profile,* Institute of Applied Manpower Research, New Delhi.
4. *Annual Technical Manpower Review for N.E. States*—1997 to 2004, Institute of Applied Manpower Research, New Delhi.
5. Information Brochure of NERIST.
6. *DAVP Publication* "Speech of the Prime Minister, Shri P. V. Narasimha Rao".

4

Technical Manpower Employment Potential in India

Analysis and Policy Implications

*Santanu Roy**

*Sunita Sharma***

ABSTRACT

Human resources development poses a serious challenge to any developing country like India to achieve economic growth. Like any resources, human resources are amenable to research-based policy, management and planning interventions for productive and effective use. The present study probes into the question of employment potential of technical manpower in the country in light of the economic liberalisation processes currently underway and the advent of information technology related economic activities like Business Process Outsourcing (BPO) and information technology enabled services (ITeS). It analyses the picture of Indian talent pool of students enrolled in different streams (science, commerce, and arts) from 1971 to 1998. Further down, it probes into the number of engineering admissions in the degree level from 1997 to 2003, and this data is used to simulate these figures up to the year 2008. Based

* **National Institute of Science, Technology and Development Studies, K.S. Krishnan Marg, Pusa, New Delhi 110 012, Email: rsan58@yahoo.co.uk; santanu@nistads.res.in**

** **School of Future Studies and Planning, Devi Ahilya University, Indore, Email: ruby_sonu@yahoo.com**

on these and other such analysis of skill availability and job openings for the technical manpower, this chapter looks into the policy implications of different technical manpower related initiatives of the government and the impact of such policies on the technical manpower employment potential in India.

Keywords: Technical manpower, BPO, IT, ITeS, knowledge professionals.

INTRODUCTION

A remarkable achievement in the global economy in recent years has been the continued healthy growth in developing countries as a whole and in those of Asia in particular. Indeed, the success achieved, especially by the countries of East and South East Asia, in terms of economic growth during the last two-and-a-half decades is quite well-known.

An important development in the Indian economy since the early 1990s has been the introduction of economic reforms aimed at moving towards more liberalized or deregulated market-based economic regimes. This has opened up new areas for investment but at the same time has also resulted in the downsizing of certain traditional sectors.

In order to maintain, sustain and improve upon the rate of economic growth of a developing country like India, proper management of its human resources is vital. Indeed, the development of a country's human resource is the key to its progress. These resources are amenable to research-based policy, management and planning interventions for productive and effective use. The most visible of this is the growth of technical manpower in the new economy sectors, notably the Information Technology (IT) and the biotechnology sectors. Availability of a sufficient number of high quality manpower is a key requirement to ensure the ongoing and sustainable growth of India's IT industry. And more importantly, to make sure that India moves up in the IT job value chain, to move up from the low end of the IT industry segment to the high-valued segment of the IT industry.

JOB MARKET AND TECHNICAL MANPOWER IN INDIA

India has one of the largest higher education systems in the world and offers a range of world class professionally skilled manpower especially in the new economy sectors. The most important new economy sector is that of the Information, Communication and Telecommunications (ICT) sector. The importance of this sector stems from the fact that the Indian IT industry has grown impressively in the last 10 years from a US$ 150 million in 1991 to US$ 17.6 billion in 2002-03[1]. In 2002-03 the software and services exports were approximately US$ 9.6 billion and the domestic software and services market was approximately US$ 2.2 billion. It is estimated that the Indian software industry employs nearly 550,000 employees, a third of which is employed in software exports. India is expected to have a headcount of around 4 million IT professionals by 2008. The Indian IT industry is approximately 2.8 per cent of India's GDP and is expected to become 7 per cent by 2008. India is the fourth largest telecom market in Asia after China, Japan and South Korea.

Most of the jobs requiring technical skills in this new economy sector are in the Business Processes (BP). BP refers to white collar processes required to service employees, vendors and customers: human resources, auditing, accounting, customer-care, telemarketing, tax preparation, claims processing, payroll, benefits management and document management. It may be noted that over 90 per cent of new job creation since the year 2000 has been in services. Further, 'Business services' is the largest growth segment among service growth areas.

IT and ITeS: Potentialities in India

The reasons why India continues to remain a preferred hub for offshore IT/ITeS sectors are many. A report jointly brought out by benchmark-it.co.uk Ltd. and Netscribes (India) Pvt. Ltd. entitled 'benchmark IT performance'[2] on the trend to outsource a range of business processes and the role that India has to play in this global market, has highlighted the following reasons for this:

- Large talent pool of English speaking skilled graduates;
- Low cost and high education levels of staff;

- Lower attrition rate;
- Relatively well developed software and call centre industry;
- Strong existing customer base of blue-chip companies;
- Powerful venture capital interest in investing in growth opportunity;
- Developing track record of proven delivery and systems/processes.

According to Vales[3], India's BPO prominence is based on several factors that includes India's client relationship with its Y2K conversion work with North American and European vendors and global organizations and the fact that India benefited from the marketing buzz of favourable reports by the National Association of Software and Service Companies for India (NASSCOM), Gartner Group, International Data Corporation (IDC), McKinsey & Company, and PricewaterhouseCoopers. A recent study by Roy and Sharma[4] has probed deeply into these issues—the reasons why India continues to remain a preferred off-shore hub, what these trend portent for traditional higher technical education that remains essentially cut-off from this stream (except for a small percentage of BPO/ITeS jobs), and the dynamics of career options in BPO/ITeS activities in India.

According to another study carried out by Dossani[5], India's capabilities in software offshoring are in no small measure due to the following reasons:

- Low labour costs ($300-500/m) for high quality technical manpower;
- Adequate supply of English speaking programmers and systems analysts in urban areas;
- Availability of project management skills;
- Good communication systems and other infrastructure;
- Strong flow of global venture capital, and technological sophistication;

- All-in costs of \$10-25/hour, compared with US costs of \$40-120/hour;
- Strong focus on applications development for banking and telecom.

For this very important new economy sector, we can expect a 20 per cent growth in labour deployment per annum from current base of 230,000 persons[5]. We can also expect a continued focus on applications development for financial services industry, with emphasis on vertical growth in telecom and IT, and horizontal growth in engineering services and system integration.

TECHNICAL MANPOWER POOL IN INDIA

The trends in higher education have changed over the past few decades in India. Table 4.1 presents a graphic picture of Indian talent pool of students enrolled in different streams from 1971 till 2000 (data has been taken from the websites of Institute of Applied Manpower Research and the University Grants Commission). The corresponding plotted curves for science, commerce and arts streams are shown in Figure 4.1. It is observed from Table 4.1 and Figure 4.1 that in India as elsewhere, the enrolment in the arts stream were always the maximum in number. However, in the year 1971, the students enrolled in science streams were more than double the number of students enrolled in commerce streams and compared not too unfavourably with those enrolled in arts streams. However, the enrolment in science streams decreased over the next ten years in real terms and the number of students enrolled in commerce and arts streams increased during the same period so that by 1981, the students enrolled in commerce stream were more in number than those enrolled in science streams. The next ten years (1981-1991) saw an increase in enrolment in all streams but the rate of this increase was much more for students enrolled in the arts and commerce. During the period 1991-1998, the number of students enrolled in all streams increased. However, the rate of increase in commerce enrolment was marginal and that in science was moderate. It was the arts stream that had suddenly taken a big leap (an increase of 82% over a period of seven years) as if everybody had taken a sudden liking for these courses.

Table—4.1 The Indian talent pool of enrolled students

Stream	1971	1981	1991	1998	2002
Science	4,95,285	4,89,415	7,56,896	11,42,724	18,34,493
Commerce	2,32,404	5,36,217	9,94,532	12,02,570	16,60,238
Arts	7,64,387	10,16,036	15,34,348	27,90,889	41,58,606

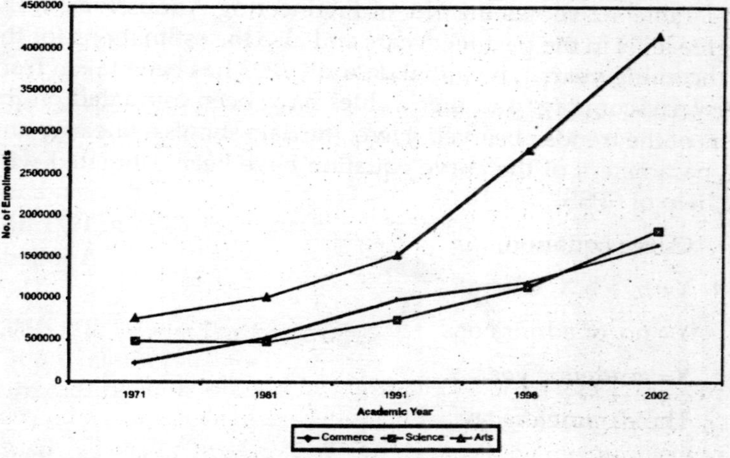

Fig. 4.1: Indian talent pool 1971-2002

One of the possible reasons for the above could be that the era of economic liberalization in India started in the year 1991. The economy started opening up, and multinational corporations started their operations in India on a much larger scale. The trend has continued ever since. Successive governments in the Centre have initiated measures to push up reforms in various sectors of the economy. The number of job openings in soft skills rather than in hard technical skills increased manifold opening up new job avenues for arts graduates not existing earlier.

Trends in Engineering Admissions

India is the leader in the global market for offshore outsourcing with a market share of 40-60 per cent. India has one of the largest pool of technically qualified people from its over 250 universities (>900 colleges) and engineering colleges that produce trained manpower at the degree/diploma level. Educational institutions and polytechnics, as well as the prestigious Indian Institutes of Technology (IITs) along with National Institutes of Technology (earlier known as Regional Engineering Colleges) along with many other Science and Technology Institutes are the principal sources of newly qualified graduates/post-graduates.

Table 4.2 shows the No. of Engineering Admissions in the degree level in the past few years and also the estimations for the forthcoming years. The initial data till 2003 has been taken from www.nasscom.org[6] and then values have been estimated on the basis of the trends observed. Here, the data shows a linearity and the parameters of the curve equation have been estimated with the help of SPSS.

Curve equation,

$Y = b_0 + b_1X$, where

Y= no. of admissions

X= academic year

The parameters are

$b_0 = 101$

$b_1 = 30$

Figure 4.2 shows the curve of all the values including projections for the coming years.

Table—4.2 Trends in degree level engineering admissions

Academic Year	No. of Admissions (in thousands)
1	2
1997	138
1998	157
1999	179
2000	233
2001	257
2002	282

(Contd...)

1	2
2003	310
2004	341
2005	371
2006	401
2007	431
2008	461

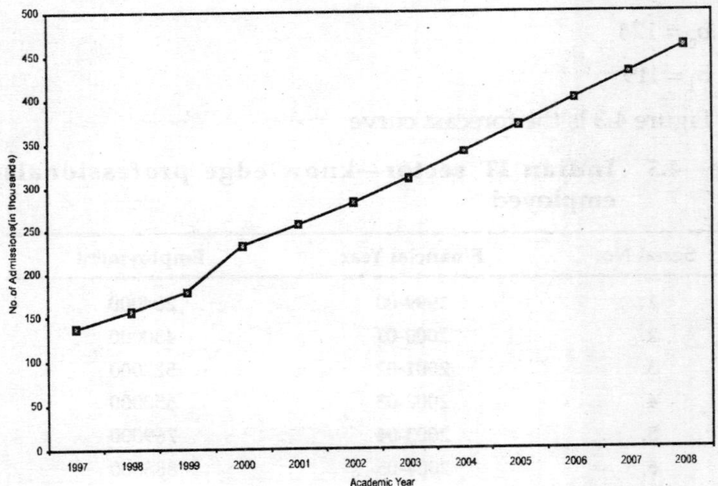

Fig. 4.2: Degree level engineering admissions

INDIAN KNOWLEDGE PROFESSIONALS

There has been a steady growth in the number of India's IT professionals over the last decade. Table 4.3 presents the no. of Knowledge Professionals employed in India, annually. The initial data from 1999-00 to 2001-02 has been taken from www.nasscom.org[6] and the projections have been done up to 2007-08. In this context, the Knowledge Professionals are a combination of manpower from Software Exports sector, Software Domestic sector, Software-captive in user organisations and IT enabled services. The trends show a linear behaviour.

We have used the Statistical Package for Social Sciences (SPSS) package to analyse the initial data. The curve equation and the estimated parameters are as follows:

$Y = b_0 + b_1X$, where

Y = no. of people employed

X = financial year

The parameters are

$b_0 = 174$

$b_1 = 119$

Figure 4.3 is the forecast curve.

Table—4.3 Indian IT sector—knowledge professionals employed

Serial No.	Financial Year	Employment
1.	1999-00	284000
2.	2000-01	430000
3.	2001-02	522000
4.	2002-03	650000
5.	2003-04	769000
6.	2004-05	888000
7.	2005-06	1007000
8.	2006-07	1126000
9.	2007-08	1245000

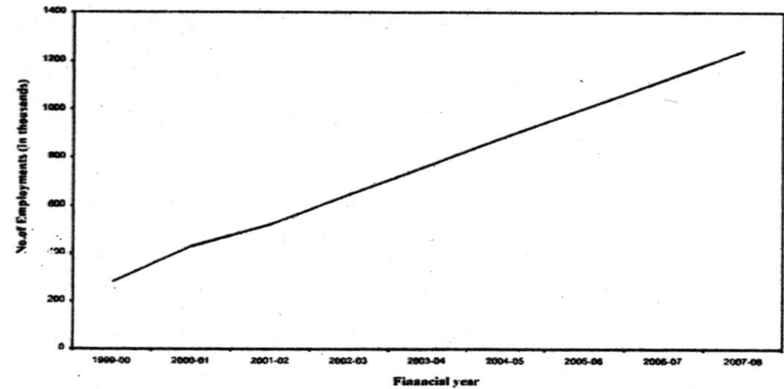

Fig. 4.3: Indian IT sector: knowledge professionals employed

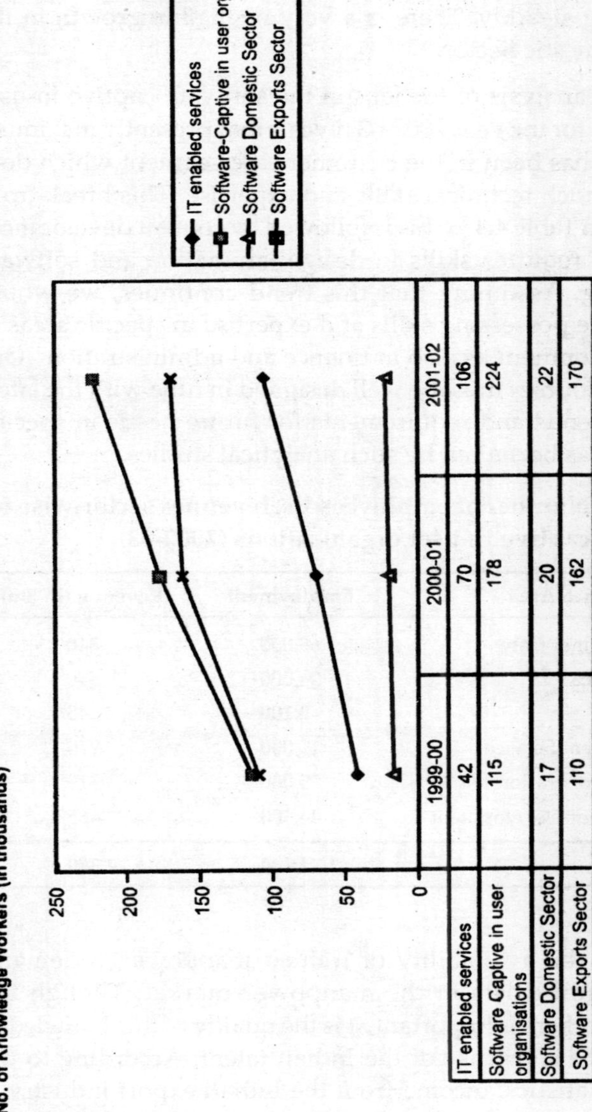

	1999-00	2000-01	2001-02
IT enabled services	42	70	106
Software Captive in user organisations	115	178	224
Software Domestic Sector	17	20	22
Software Exports Sector	110	162	170

Fig. 4.4: Break-up of knowledge professionals

Figure 4.4 gives a segment-wise break up of the knowledge professionals represented in Table 4.3 (up to the year 2001-02). It is apparent from the graph that the software captive in-user business, IT enabled services and software export segments have been growing steadily. There is a very negligible growth in the Software Domestic Sector.

Further analysis of the jobs in the software captive in-user organisations for the year 2002-03 reveals that presently maximum employment has been in the customer care segment which does not require much technical skills and expertise. This break-up is represented in Table 4.4 [7]. This is followed by content development segment that requires skills in design, animation and software programming. Assuming that this trend continues, we would require people possessing skills and expertise in specific areas in content development as also in finance and administration . Our professional courses must be well designed in tune with the latest technology trends and requirements for future needs in specific job segments as borne out by such analytical studies.

Table—4.4 Number of employees Vs. revenues sector-wise for captive in user organisations (2002-03)

Service Area	Employment	Revenue (in $m)
Customer Care	65,000	810
Finance	24,000	510
HR	2,100	45
Payment Service	11,000	210
Administration	25,000	310
Content Development	44,000	465
Total	**1,71,100**	**2,350**

Source: Nasscom

Despite the availability of trained manpower, a demand supply gap still exists in the manpower market. Though the quantity of workers is important, it is the quality of this knowledge base that is the showcase of the Indian talent. According to the NASSCOM statistics, income from the Indian export industry is higher than from the domestic market. On the technical front, the skills in demand are in the areas of R&D, Software engineering/ programmers/analyst, Internet and e-commerce applications, Database administrators, Network specialists and communication engineers, Digital media, Business applications of software development, Web based applications, Networking applications, Java, Data warehousing, Client-networking, Project management, Quality assurance and technical writing, Legacy systems, etc. Thus, there's ample scope for professional specialized in these skill areas.

CONCLUSION

The offshore centres in India have utilised the Indian talent pool for their services. Initially, such centres were set-up for jobs that do not require any specialised skills but in the present scenario, the trends are different. The technical job market is rising and offshore models are the talk of the day. Overseas clients have discovered India as a huge source of manpower catering to their specific service demands. This analysis puts forth a picture for the employment of knowledge professionals in the years to come. The study highlights those sectors that would require technical manpower with specific skills and expertise catering to the newly emerging areas.

However, there are certain constraints that should be kept in view in this discussion on this new economy sector. There are existing negatives in this sector like shortage of vertical expertise in IT-intensive areas such as insurance, logistics and health care, and shortage of horizontal expertise in strategic consulting, engineering services, market research, product development, sales, packaging and product quality assurance[4]. Moreover, the presence of multinational corporations (MNC) that play a crucial role in this sector is still very low (13% of employment) and this directly affects the prospects of a further growth in higher-end IT jobs and significant value additions in project assignments. This is also borne out by the fact that product development is still negligible whereas services make up 96 per cent of the total revenue of the sector.

REFERENCES

1. www.embassyofindia.com/IndiaNewsJuly2003
2. benchmark-it.co.uk Ltd. and Netscribes (India) Pvt. Ltd., benchmark-it performance. January, 2003, *www.benchmark-it.co.uk.*
3. Vales, J. India's Offshoring BPO Model: The Upcoming Transformation *HRD Today*, May, 2003, pp. 58-60.
4. Roy, S. and Sharma, S., Alternatives to Higher Technical Education: Career Prospects in Business Process Outsourcing, in Singh, T.P. and Bawa, H.S. (eds.), *Proceedings of the Second TIET Foresight Symposium on Higher Technical Education: Issues of Access and Delivery (TFS-II)*, November 22-23, Thapar Institute of Engineering & Technology (Deemed University), Patiala, 2003, pp. 135-147.
5. Dossani, R., Software and Business Process Offshoring, 2003, *http://asia.stanford.edu/events/fall03/slides/dossaniSlides.pdf*
6. *www.nasscom.org*
7. *www.bpoindia.org/knowledgeBase*

5

Technical Manpower and Self-Employment in Jammu and Kashmir

B.L. Koul[*]
Naresh Dubey[**]
D.L. Verma[***]

ABSTRACT

The basics for the development of a state is its technical manpower. The agencies that utilize technical manpower are in general government, semi-government or private concerns. A healthy state needs a healthy mixture of all the three sectors for all round development of the state.

In this chapter contribution of self employment with respect to technical manpower in the state has been analyzed and in view of the present scenario need of a healthy component of self- employment stressed so that the state develops an industrial base and there are also avenues for the self-employment for the qualified engineers and other technical persons in the state.

* **NTMIS-Nodal Centre, National Institute of Technology(Srinagar), Camp Classes, Jammu, Email: jktmis@sancharnet.in**

** **NTMIS-Nodal Centre, National Institute of Technology(Srinagar), Camp Classes, Jammu, Email: jktmis@sancharnet.in**

*** **NTMIS-Nodal Centre, National Institute of Technology(Srinagar), Camp Classes, Jammu, Email: jktmis@sancharnet.in**

Key Words: Technical Manpower, State, Self-employment, Industry, Engineers

INTRODUCTION

The National Technical Manpower Information System(NTMIS)[1] provides information about the employment profile of engineering graduates and diploma holders year after year. This information includes information regarding number of graduates and diploma holders who get self-employed through enterprises of their own or their family, secured employment within or outside India and information about those who go for higher studies etc. This piece of information about the state of Jammu and Kashmir is presented in Table 5.1. It is observed that from 1982 to 1987, there has been a component of self employment for the absorption of graduates engineers and after 1987 this component has reduced to zero. At diploma level there has been no component of self employment at all.

Table—5.1 Employment status of engineering graduates and diploma engineers of Jammu and Kashmir state (1982- 2001)

Level/Year	Paid Employment	Self Employment	Studying	Unemployed	Total
Degree					
1982	213(97.3%)	3(1.4%)	1(0.5%)	2(0.9%)	219(100%)
1983	200(80.0%)	15(6%)	3(1.2%)	27(10.8%)	250(100%)
1984	132(63%)	8(4%)	3(1.4%)	61(29.0%)	210(100%)
1985	342(65.1%)	15(3.8%)	8(1.5%)	143(27.2%)	525(100%)
1987	239(73.1%)	16(5.0%)	12(3.7%)	46(14.1%)	327(100%)
1993	10(12.8)	-	-	-	78(100%)
1994	16(33.3%)	-	-	32(66.7%)	48(100%)
1996	24(46.2%)	-	-	22(42.3%)	52(100%)
1997	30(44.1%)	-	-	27(55.9%)	57(100%)
1998	14(30.4%)	-	-	32(69.6%)	46(100%)
1999	65(52.0%)	-	-	60(48.0%)	125(100%)
2000	70(52.6%)	-	-	63(47.7%)	133(100%)
2001	74(46.8%)	-	-	84(53.2%)	158(100%)

The expenditures incurred by the state government[2] on industrial and other sectors over the period 1982 to 2000, are presented in Table 5.2. It is observed that the state's expenditure on the development of industrial infrastructure varies from 2 to 7 per cent of the total expenditure on six major heads (for details see Annexure 5.1), when expenditure on tourism and communication varies from 3 per cent to 14 per cent, agriculture from 65 to 20 per cent and irrigation and power from 28 per cent to 77 per cent.

Table—5.2 Expenditures on various sectors in J & K

Year	Expagrc	Expcdc	Expirrpc	Expindc	Exptcomc	Expssc
1982	2750.47	219.02	34466.47	973.72	1756.07	4501.06
1983	2497.97	198.92	31302.35	884.33	1594.86	4087.85
1984	2326.59	185.27	29154.81	823.66	1485.44	3807.40
1985	4366.26	227.95	6658.27	1269.35	3224.28	7762.70
1986	3998.46	208.75	6097.41	1162.43	2952.68	7108.81
1987	3643.00	190.19	5555.34	1059.09	2690.19	6476.83
1988	3380.68	176.50	5155.33	982.83	2496.48	6010.46
1989	3274.52	170.95	4993.44	951.96	2418.08	5821.72
1990	4696.85	214.72	8598.23	1656.71	3176.71	9560.17
1991	4896.39	301.17	10286.24	2244.14	3980.70	11217.28
1992	4565.07	421.61	11728.64	1656.71	4390.55	10160.15
1993	4336.48	400.49	11141.34	1592.54	4170.70	9651.40
1994	4150.47	383.32	10663.45	1524.23	3991.80	9237.41
1995	3750.44	346.37	9635.68	1377.32	3607.06	8347.09
1996	3491.59	322.47	8970.65	1282.27	3358.11	7771.00
1997	5136.11	855.63	8357.78	1211.48	1373.33	12729.97
1998	5364.98	530.01	7257.60	1008.74	859.62	11103.94
1999	5605.21	935.03	8626.90	1231.19	1078.79	12738.03
2000	5422.22	554.61	8239.66	1016.13	913.52	11306.29

There is, therefore, need to analyze the inputs of the state government with regard to the development of the industrial infrastructure and other related sectors for the development of a sound industrial base in the state.

SELF-EMPLOYMENT IN JAMMU AND KASHMIR

In Jammu and Kashmir during eighties there was a component of self-employment present in the employment of graduate engineers. This component varied from 2 per cent to 5 per cent of the total engineers employed. Diploma engineers did not go for self employment. Over the years this component instead of increasing has decreased and from nineties till date there is no component of self employment in the employment profile of graduates as well as diploma engineers of the state. There could be two main reasons for the same, firstly either we have not been supportive to those who endeavoured to venture into self-employment, with the result these ventures instead of becoming a success story have since been closed. The other aspect being lack of proper motivation and aptitude among the aspiring engineering graduates and diploma holders, besides difficulties in getting financial assistance for setting up of viable ventures in the state.

A look at the industrial scenario[2] provides proper background about the present industrial set up in the state. Table 5.3A presents year-wise number of registered (reported) factories with employment. From 1981 to 1995 the number of registered factories has varied between 293 units in 1982 to 422 units in 1985. The employment has also varied from 11681 in 1993 to 44715 in 1987. Table 5.3B gives number of medium scale units in public sector from 1980 to 2001. There is hardly any change in this sector over the years. The information on Small Scale Industrial units is presented in Table 5.3C. It is this sector that has had some success as is shown in the Fig. 5.1(see on page 52). The number of units have steadily grown from 8428 in 1980 to 42716 in 2000 and the employment has likewise increased from 42,992 in 1980 to 1,87,800 in 2000. However SSI units do not employ either graduate or diploma engineers instead they utilize skilled people mostly from ITI's . It is the factories and medium scale units that have the potential of utilizing the graduate and diploma engineers.

Table—5.3A Employment in registered factories

Year	No. of Units Reported	Total Workers
1981	293	27707
1984	404	34469
1985	422	42348
1986	405	33515
1987	378	44715
1988	264	16278
1989	212	12528
1993	265	11681
1994	NA	19754
1995	309	23898
1997	NA	4300
1998	NA	NA

Table—5.3B Medium scale industries in the state public sector

Year	No. of Units	Employment
1980	25	5249
1981	31	7034
1985	31	6932
1989	28	6052
1990	28	5994
1994	31	6538
1995	30	6001
1996	31	5673
1997	26	5554
1998	45	5760
1999	16	3597
2000	27	5148
2001	25	4427

Table—5.3C No. of small scale industrial units registered with directorate of industries and commerce J & K government

Year	Units	Employment
1980	8428	42992
1985	18520	84821
1988	26322	115243
1989	28168	123472
1990	29963	131164
1995	36821	159671
1996	38029	165064
1997	39436	171962
1998	40627	178004
1999	41950	183698
2000	42716	187800

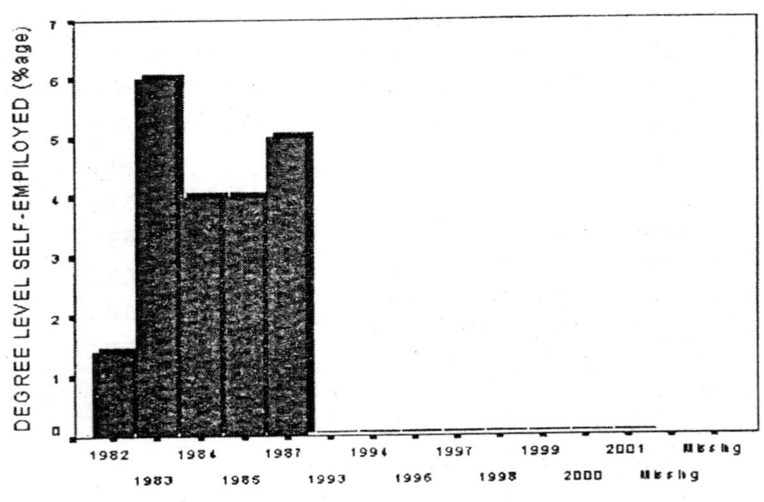

Fig. 5.1

We have therefore, got to analyze the expenditures incurred on development of industrial infrastructure by the government. At present the state does not have any major industries. Obviously, the state needs some more inputs for the development of the necessary infrastructure and other related facilities for the proper development of the atmosphere of self-employment in the state.

The per cent of expenditures on various developmental activities over the period 1982 to 2001 is:

Agriculture	:	6 to 20%
CD	:	0.5 to 2%
Irrigation and Power	:	28 to 77%
Industries	:	2 to 7% and
Transport and communication	:	3 to 14%

The percentage distribution of Net State Domestic product by industry of origin at constant (1980-1981) prices is presented in Table 5.4. The component of secondary sector that includes industrial sector varies between 13 per cent to 19 per cent only as compared to primary sector (36% to 47%) and tertiary sector (49% to 39%). In Table—5.4a is presented the break up of the secondary sector in terms of its constituents and it is seen that the contribution of manufacturing is less than half of the total value of the secondary sector.

Table—5.5 presents a comparison of four parameters i.e. power generated, per capita power consumption, number of factories and employment in factories in the states of J & K and Karnataka, Kerala and M.P. The power generated is minimum in Jammu & Kashmir. It is less than the power generated in Kerala, per capita power consumption is minimum in Jammu and Kashmir and number of factories is maximum (9386) whereas employment in factories is the lowest(36000).

There are other indicators as well that indicate lack of industrial policy in the state of Jammu and Kashmir, for instance Table—5.6 presents road length per 1000 sq. km area (as on 31.3.1997) which is 127 km in J & K as compared to All India level of 779 km, number of motor vehicles per 100 sq. km. (1997-98) of

Table—5.4 Percentage distribution on net state domestic product by industry of origin at constant (1980-81) prices

Sector/Year	1980-81	1983-84	1984-85	1985-86	1986-87	1987-88	1990-91	1992-93	1993-94	1995-96	1996-97	1997-98	1998-99	1999-00
1. Primary	47.4	45.52	44.47	44.84	41.68	36.61	38.49	36.6	37.52	39.98	40.31	36.74	36.52	36.4
2. Secondary	12.9	13.84	15.12	15.00	17.19	19.05	16.81	16.12	17.59	14.18	13.35	14.69	14.89	14.41
3. Tertiary Sector	39.70	40.64	40.32	40.16	41.13	43.94	44.70	47.28	44.89	45.84	46.34	48.57	48.59	49.19
Total Net State Domestic Product	100	100	100	100	100	100	100	100	100	100	100	100	100	100

Table—5.4A Percentage distribution of net state domestic product by industry of origin at constant (1980-81) prices, secondary sector

Sector/Year	1980-81	1983-84	1984-85	1985-86	1986-87	1987-88	1990-91	1992-93	1993-94	1995-96	1996-97	1997-98	1998-99	1999-00
Manufacturing (registered sector)	1.34	2.14	3.82	2.62	2.46	4.33	2.95	2.80	3.33	2.03	1.94	1.80	2.01	1.93
Manufacturing (un-registered sector)	3.30	3.46	3.50	3.62	4.15	4.89	4.20	3.60	5.33	4.94	4.36	4.25	4.11	4.73
Construction	7.66	7.66	7.26	7.79	9.48	8.44	8.01	8.00	12.95	13.57	13.06	13.15	12.47	12.09
Electricity/gas & water supply	0.60	0.58	0.63	0.97	1.10	1.39	1.65	1.72	-4.02	-6.36	-6.01	-4.51	-3.70	-4.34
Total	**12.9**	**13.84**	**15.12**	**15.00**	**17.19**	**19.05**	**16.81**	**16.12**	**17.59**	**14.18**	**13.35**	**14.69**	**14.89**	**14.41**

Table—5.5 Comparison of power generated, per capita power consumption, No. of factories and employment in factories

State	In Four States			
	Power generated (Crore K WHr.) 1998-99	Per capita power (KWHr.) consumption 1998-99	Factories (Nos.) 1997-98	Employment in factories (000') Nos. 1997-98
J&K	580.02	255	9386	36
Karnataka	1715.00	349	6955	628
Kerala	760.10	305	4897	360
MP	2056.30	398	4234	467

Table—5.6

	Av. Rd. Length per 1000 sq. kms. area 31.3.1997	Reg. Motor vehicles per 100 sq. kms of area (00) 1997-98	No. of Trucks per lakh pop. 1997-98	Motor Veh. per lakh population (1997-98)
1. J & K	127	325	257	3281
2. All India	779	1293	261	4216

area is 32500 as compared to All India figure of 129300, the number of trucks per lakh of population (1997-98) is 257 as compared to All India figure of 261 and number of motor vehicles per lakh population (1997-98) is 3281 when the All India figure is 4216.

Thus there is lot more that needs to be done so that Jammu and Kashmir becomes an industrial state as well. A proper strategy is needed so that the state's natural as well as human resources are used optimally for the betterment of the state as a whole. We therefore need to address these issues in terms of:

1. Proper inputs by the state for the development of infrastructure for a healthy industrial base;
2. Facilities with regard to financial assistance to aspiring entrepreneurs; and
3. Proper motivation and development of aptitude at the final semester level to the aspiring graduate/diploma engineers for setting up of viable industrial units in the state.

ANNEXURE—5.1

Definitions of parameters used in Table 5.2.

These represent expenditures incurred on various heads a s defined in the following:

1. expagrc:
   (1) Agriculture
   (2) Animal Husbandry
   (3) Forest
   (4) Fisheries
2. expcdc:
   (1) CD & NES
   (2) C-operation
3. expindc:
   (1) Large & Medium Industries
   (2) Mining & Metallurgical Industries

(3) Village & Small Sale Industrial Units

4. exptcomc:

   (1) Roads, road transport

   (2) Tourism

5. expssc:

   (1) Education

   (2) Health/Medical Education

   (3) Housing, Urban Dev.

   (4) Water supply

   (5) Social Welfare

   (6) Labour Welfare

6. expirrpc:

   (1) Irrigation and Power

ANNEXURE—5.2

1. Primary Sector

   (1) Agriculture

   (2) Forestry

   (3) Fishing

   (4) Mining & Quarrying

2. Secondary Sector

   (1) Manufacturing

   (2) Construction

   (3) Electricity, gas and water supply

3. Tertiary Sector

   (1) Transport, communication

   (2) Trade, hotels, restaurants

   (3) Banking & Insurance

   (4) Real Estate

   (5) Public Administration

   (6) Other Services

REFERENCES

1. *Annual Technical Manpower Reviews, Jammu and Kashmir, Institute of Applied Manpower Research,* New Delhi, 1982-2000.

2. *Digest of Statistics, Government of Jammu and Kashmir,* Directorate of Economics and Statistics, Planning and Development Department 1999-2000.

6

Profile of Technical Manpower in Karnataka State

A. H. Sequeira[*]

ABSTRACT

The National Technical Manpower Information System (NTMIS)–Nodal Centre for Karnataka State started functioning at National Institute of Technology Karnataka, Surathkal, during the year 1985 with a view to generate and maintain an up-to-date databank for providing reliable information on technical manpower of the State. During these 20 years of its existence, the Nodal Centre has generated the Annual Technical Manpower Review (ATMR) reports for the batches of students passed during the year 1985 to year 2001 in the Karnataka State. To extend the coverage of database on Technical Manpower, disciplines related to Management, Hotel Management and Catering Technology and Pharmacy courses were also added during the year 2000. This chapter discusses some important highlights of ATMR 2001-2005, and feature issues related to employment prospects, unemployment, potential market for emerging branches in engineering and technology.

GROWTH OF TECHNICAL EDUCATIONAL FACILITIES IN KARNATAKA STATE

Technical educational facilities in Karnataka State has been growing significantly since last two decades. At the time of

* **Project Officer, NTMIS–Nodal Centre, National Institute of Technology Karnataka, Surathkal, Email: aloysiushs@yahoo.co.in**

independence, only 4 engineering colleges and 2 polytechnics existed. After a span of 57 years after independence, the number of technical institutions have increased to 118 degree colleges and 186 polytechnics in the state during the year 2003. The growth of institutions imparting technical education in Karnataka State is shown in Figure 6.1.

The educational facilities in Karnataka State for engineering Post-graduate Degree, Master in Business Administration (MBA), Master of Computer Application (MCA), Hotel Management and Catering Technology (HMCT) and Pharmacy courses (degree, diploma, and post-graduate) for the year 2003 are shown in Figure 6.2. During the year 2003, the colleges imparting education in engineering Post-graduate were 28, Post-graduate institutions in Management were 71, MCA 82, colleges in HMCT 20, degree colleges in Pharmacy 48 and 76 diploma institutions in Pharmacy in the state.

INTAKE AND OUTTURN

The sanctioned intake and outturn for engineering degree, diploma , post graduate and MBA, MCA, HMCT and Pharmacy for the years 1998 to 2003 is shown in figure 6.3, figure 6.4, figure 6.5, figure 6.6 respectively.

(a) *Engineering Degree*: The total sanctioned intake for various disciplines was 38897 during year 2003 when compared to 24384 is year 1998. The annual outturn increased from 12036 in 1998 to 14450 during 2003, an increase of nearly 21 per cent during the span of 5 years. The outturn increased in some branches like Computer Science, Electronics and Communication, Information Science and Mechanical Engineering disciplines.

(b) *Engineering Diploma:* There is marginal increase in sanctioned intake for various disciplines. The sanctioned intake decreased from 32,488 to 32,068 during the year 1998 to 2003. The annual outturn increased 8971 to 11463 during the years 1998 to 2003, an increase of 18 per cent in five years.

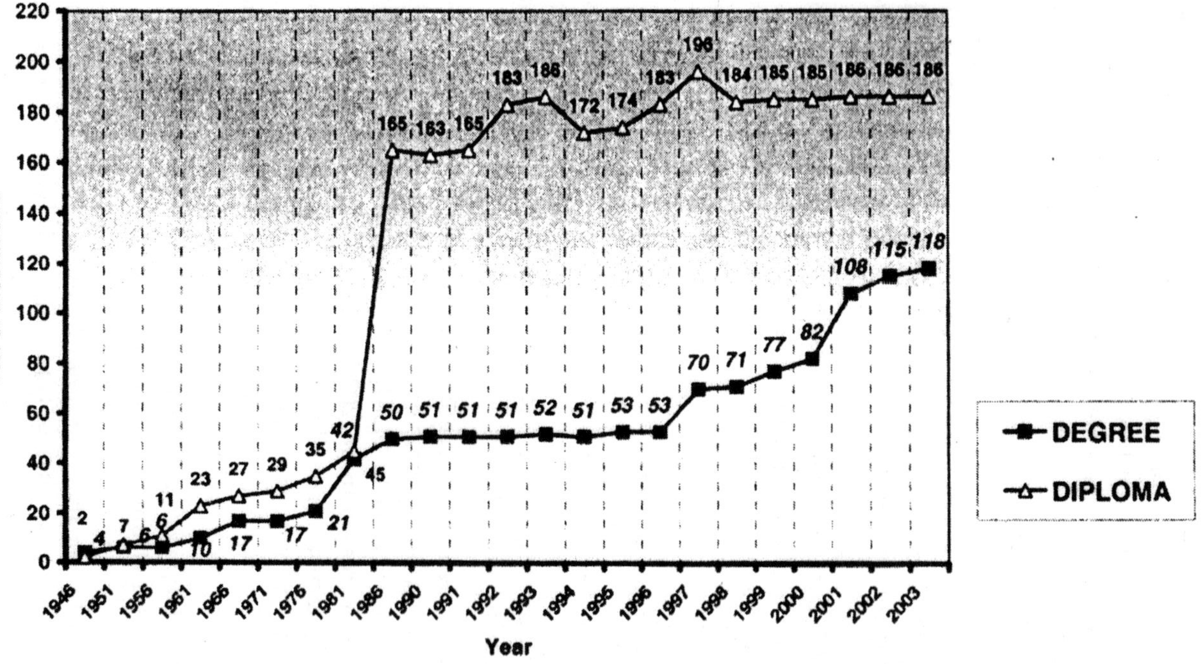

Fig. 6.1: Growth of technical educational facilities in Karnataka (1946-2003)

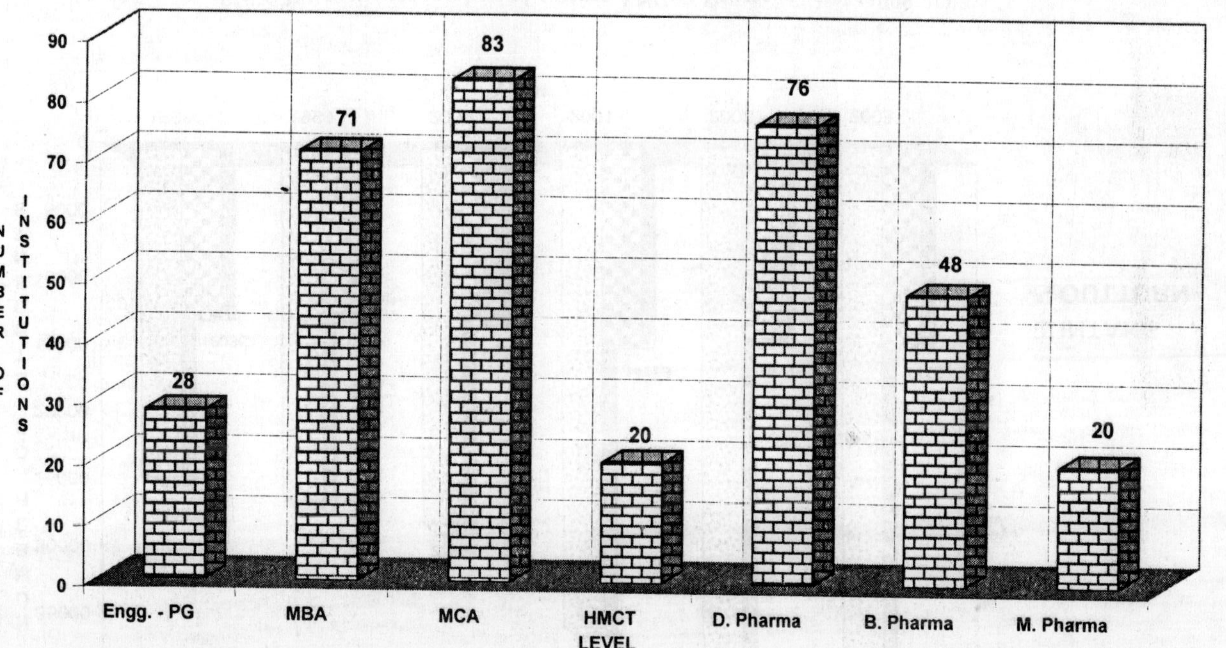

Fig. 6.2: Number of technical/management/pharmacy/HMCT institutions in Karnataka state during 2003

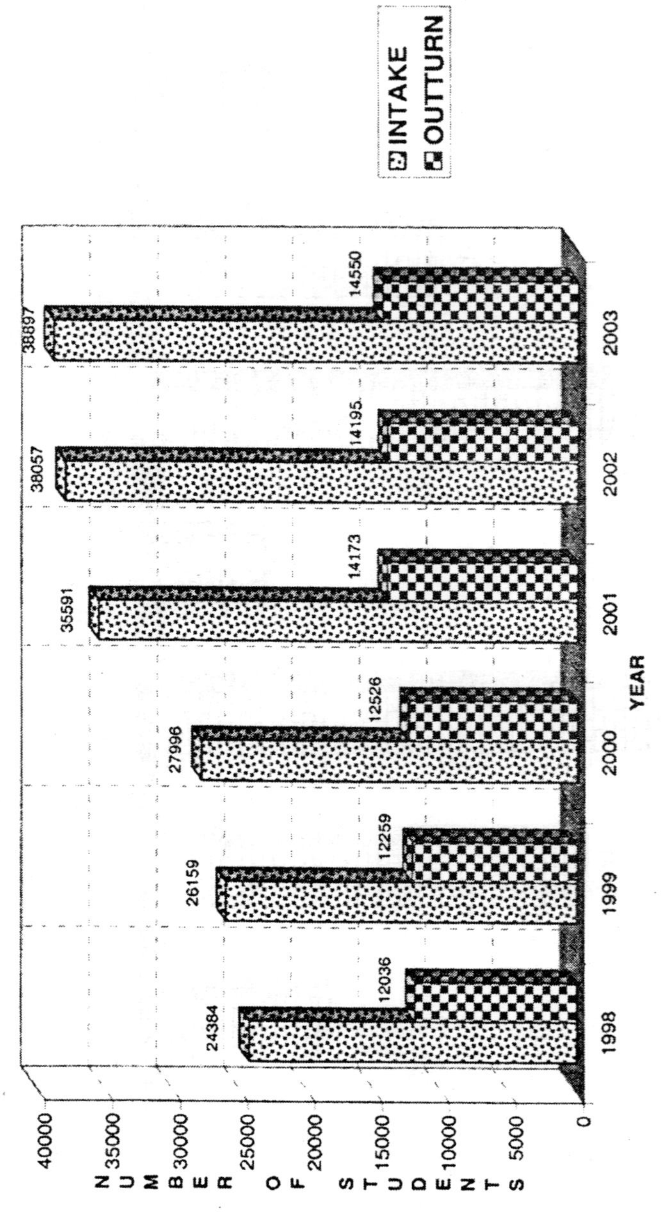

Fig. 6.3: Sanctioned intake and outturn ENGG: Degree courses (1998-2003)

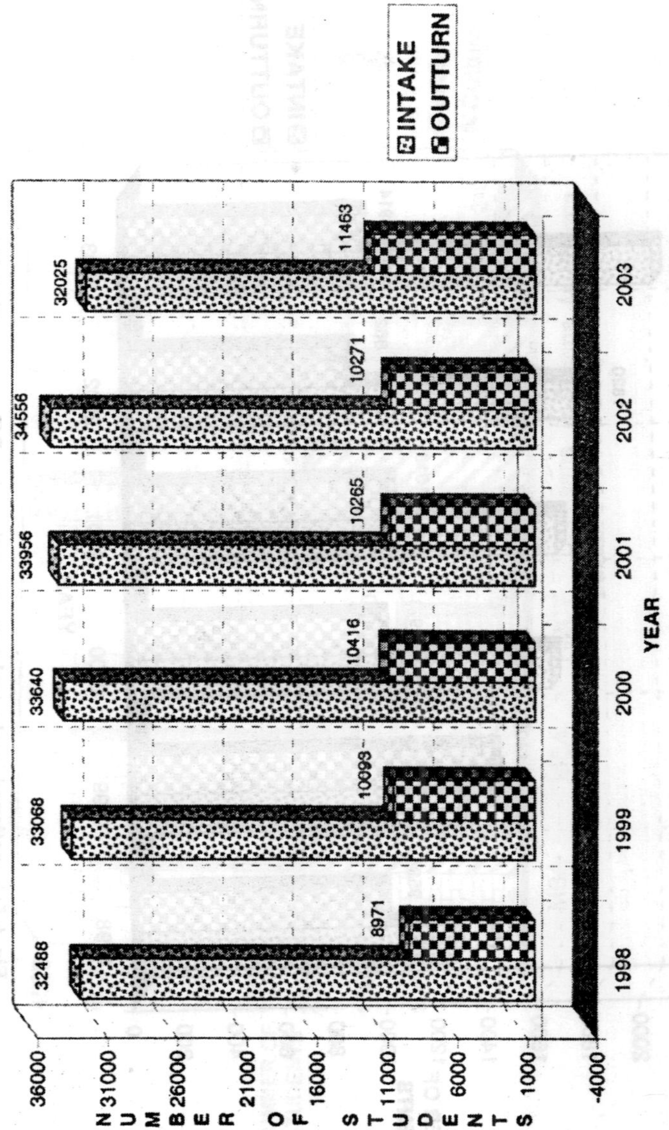

Fig. 6.4: Sanctioned intake and outturn engineering diploma courses (1998-2003)

(c) *Engineering Post-graduate*: The growth of sanctioned intake and the annual outturn during the year 1998 to year 2003 were shown in figure 6.5. The intake increased from 1245 to 2060 during the years 1998 to 2003, an increase of 65 per cent in five years. The outturn increased from 959 to 1431 during the years 1998 to 2003, an increase of 49 per cent in five years.

(d) *MBA, MCA, HMCT and Pharmacy:* The sanctioned intake for the year 2003 was 4071 in MBA, 4115 in MCA ,1100 in HMCT, 4324 at diploma in pharmacy, 2560 at degree in pharmacy and 445 at post graduate degree in pharmacy courses. The annual outturn for the year 2003 was 1650 in MBA, 1820 in MCA, 628 in HMCT, 3599 at diploma in pharmacy, 849 at degree in pharmacy and 240 at post-graduate degree in pharmacy courses.

GENDER DISTRIBUTION

The gender-wise distribution at degree, diploma and post graduate level is indicated in figure 6.7 and figure 6.8 for the year 2001.

(a) *Engineering Degree:* Among the degree holders, 77 per cent were male and 23 per cent were female and the ratio of male to female was 1: 0.30

(b) *Engineering Diploma:* Among the diploma holders, 77 per cent were male and 23 per cent were female and the ratio of male to female was 1: 0.30

(c) *Engineering Post-graduate*: Among the post graduates, 86 per cent were male and 14 per cent were female and the ratio between male and female was 1: 0.26

(d) *MBA, MCA, HMCT and Pharmacy*: Among MBA degree holders, 76 per cent were male and 24 per cent were female. In MCA 75 per cent were male and 25 per cent were female. In HMCT 88 per cent were male and 12 per cent were female. In Pharmacy discipline the male students comprised of 75 per cent, 89 per cent and 82 per cent at degree, diploma, and post graduate level respectively. Similarly in the same discipline the female students comprised of 25 per cent, 11 per cent and 18 per cent at degree, diploma, and post-graduate level respectively.

DISTRIBUTION OF STUDENTS BY AREA OF RESIDENCE

The distribution of degree, diploma and post-graduate holders who belongs to urban and rural areas are shown in figure 6.9 and figure 6.10.

(a) *Engineering Degree:* About 76 per cent of the students belonged to urban area and remaining 24 per cent belonged to rural area. The students who joined for degree course from urban area were about three times more than rural area students.

(b) *Engineering Diploma:* About 57 per cent of the students belonged to urban area and remaining 43 per cent belonged to rural area. The students who joined for diploma course from rural area were more when compared to degree holders.

(c) *Engineering Post-graduate*: About 61 per cent of the students belonged to urban area and remaining 39 per cent belonged to rural area of their residence location.

(d) *MBA, MCA, HMCT and Pharmacy:* About 73 per cent of the MBA degree holders belonged to urban area and remaining 27 per cent belonged to rural area. Among MCA, 62 per cent belonged to urban area and remaining 38 per cent belonged to rural area of their residence location. Among HMCT, 80 per cent belonged to urban area and 20 per cent belonged to rural area. Among Pharmacy, 63 per cent belonged to urban area and 37 per cent belonged to rural area at degree level and 44 per cent belonged to urban area and 56 per cent belonged to rural area of their residence location at diploma level. Among post-graduate level, 79 per cent belonged to urban area and 21 per cent belonged to rural area.

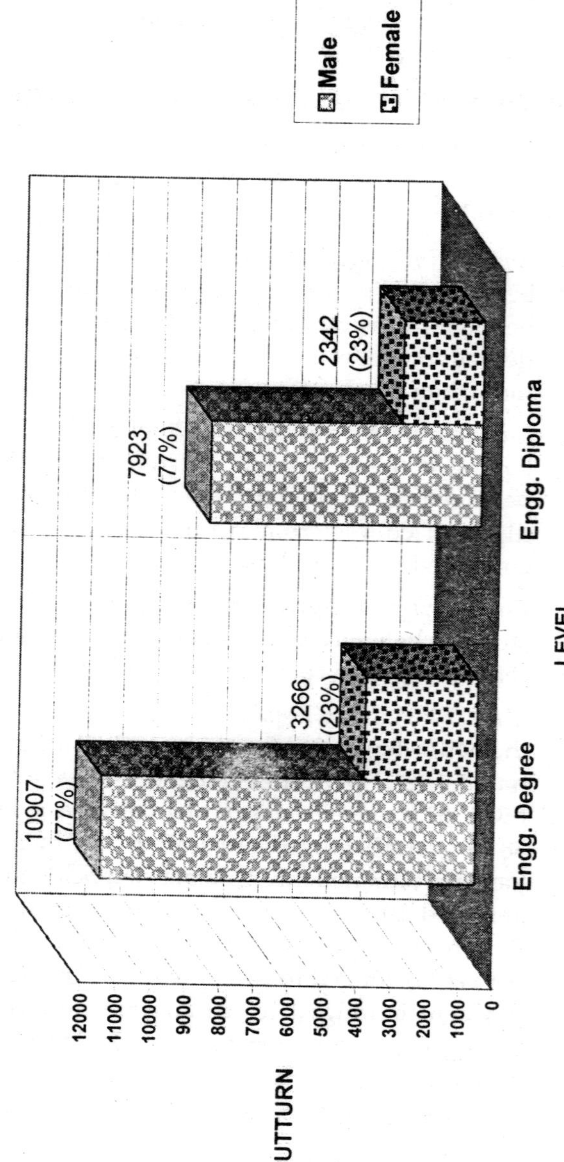

Fig. 6.7: Distribution of students gender-wise—2001 Batch

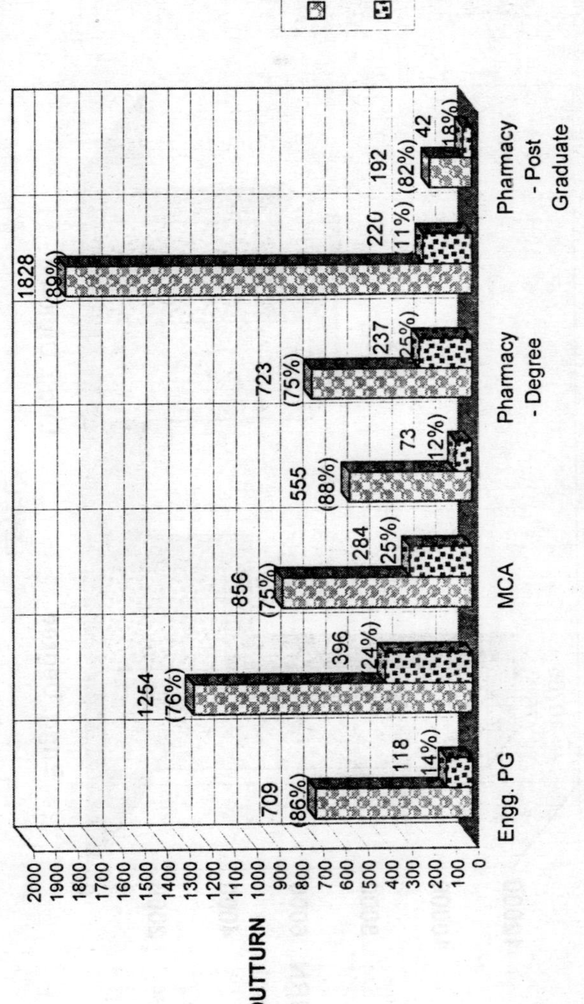

Fig. 6.8: Distribution of students gender-wise—2001 Batch

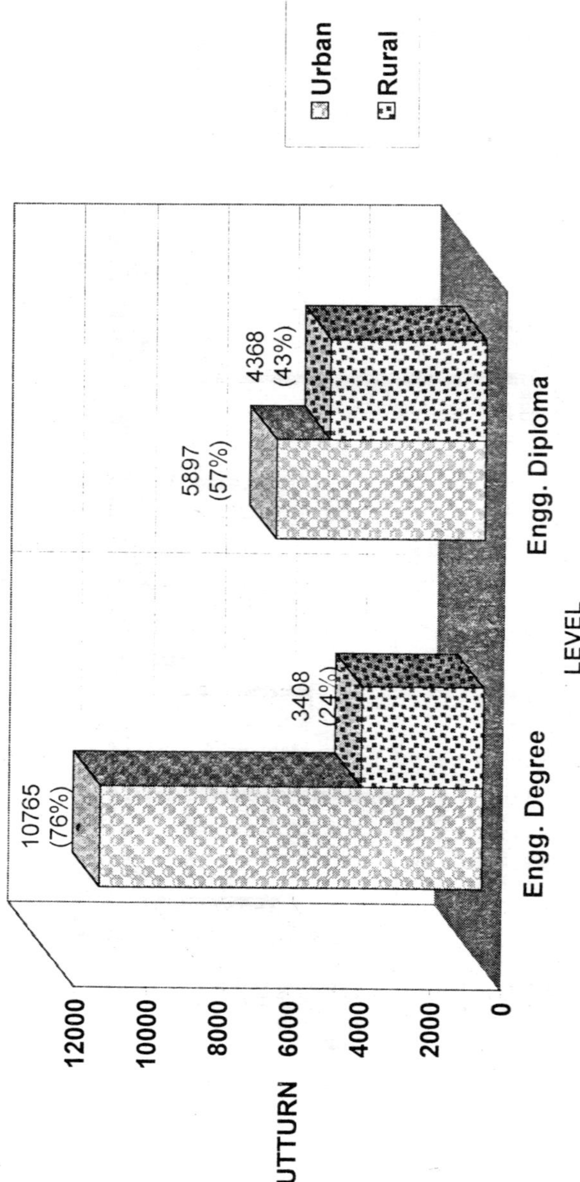

Fig. 6.9: Distribution of students area-wise—2001 Batch

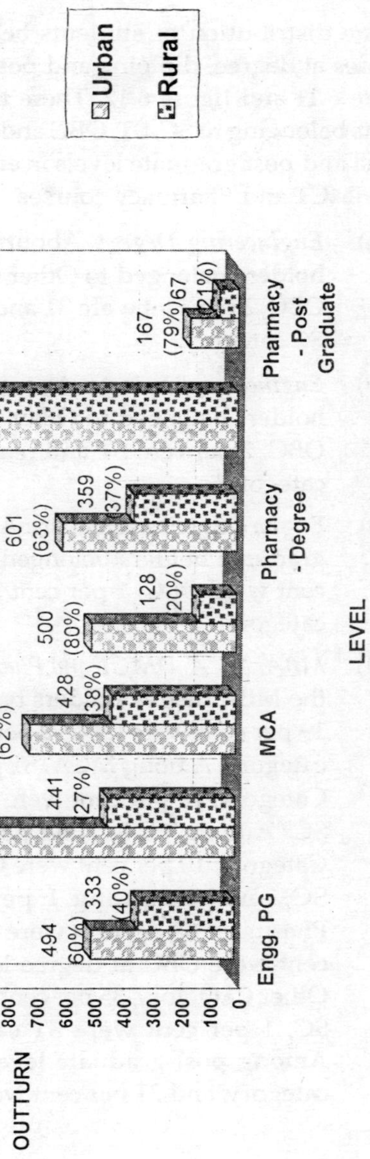

Fig. 6.10: Distribution of students area-wise—2001 Batch

DISTRIBUTION OF STUDENTS BY SOCIAL CATEGORY

The distribution of students belonging to different social categories at degree, diploma and post-graduate levels is shown in figure 6.11 and figure 6.12. There is sufficient involvement of students belonging to SC, ST, OBC and Other categories at degree, diploma and post graduate levels in engineering as well as MCA, MBA, HMCT and Pharmacy courses.

(a) *Engineering Degree:* About 74 per cent of the degree holders belonged to Other Category, 17 per cent were OBC, 2 per cent were ST and remaining 7 per cent were SC category.

(b) *Engineering Diploma:* About 58 per cent of the diploma holders belonged to Other Category, 33 per cent were OBC, 2 per cent ST and remaining 7 per cent were SC category.

(c) *Engineering Post-graduate:* About 76 per cent of the post graduate holders belonged to Other Category, 16 per cent were OBC, 1 per cent ST and 6 per cent were SC category.

(d) *MBA, MCA, HMCT and Pharmacy:* About 73 per cent of the MBA degree holders belonged to Other Category, 19 per cent were OBC, 2 per cent ST and 6 per cent SC category. Among MCA, 81 per cent belonged to Other Category, 16 per cent were OBC, and 3 per cent were SC. Among HMCT, 84 per cent belonged to Other Category, 10 per cent were OBC category, 6 per cent in SC, and remaining 1 per cent were ST. Among Pharmacy, 83 per cent were Other Category, and 17 per cent were OBC at degree level and 61 per cent were Other Categtory, 35 per cent were OBC, 3 per cent were SC, 1 per cent were ST category at diploma level. Among post-graduate level, 79 per cent were other category, and 21 per cent were in OBC Category.

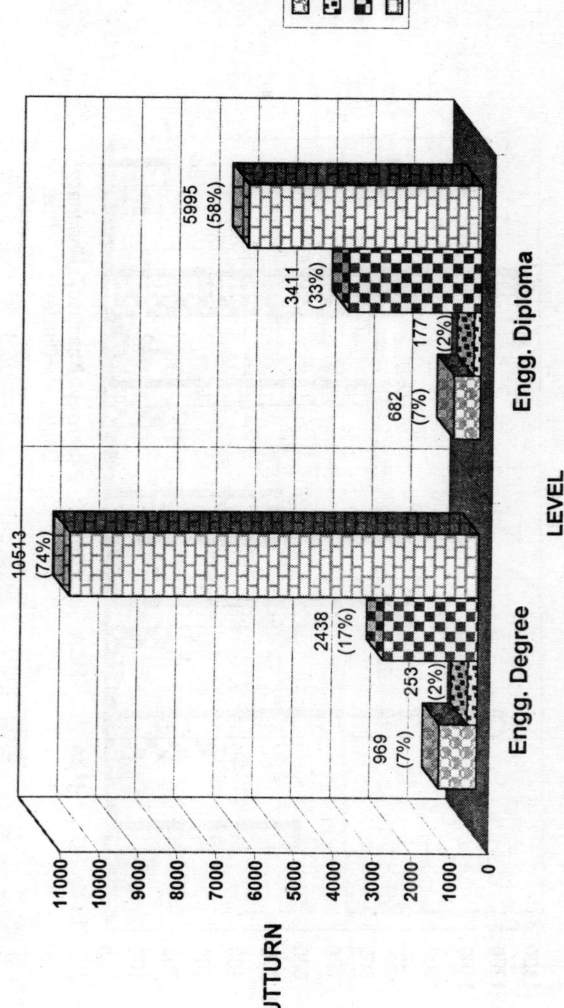

Fig. 6.11: Distribution of students social category—2001 Batch

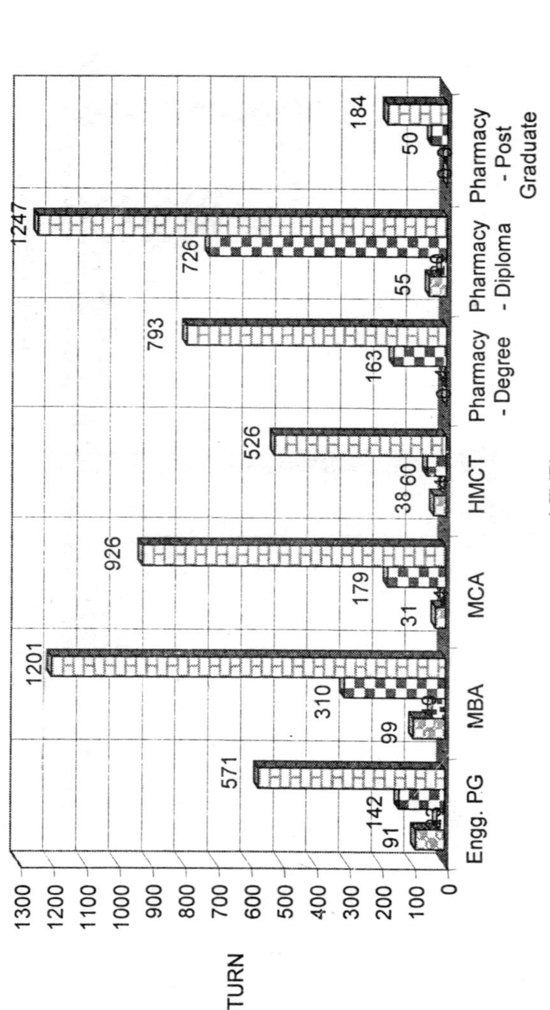

Fig. 6.12: Distribution of students social category-wise—2001 Batch

ACTIVITY STATUS

The distribution of students activity as on 30th June 2003 and who passed during the year 2001(i.e. two years after passing degree, diploma and post graduate) is shown in figure 6.13 and figure 6.14.

(a) *Engineering Degree*: About 50 per cent of graduates were having paid job in India and nearly 1 per cent were employed abroad. About 1per cent were engaged in self employment and about 15 per cent were continuing higher studies both at India and abroad. About 26 per cent of the total outturn were unemployed and only 1 per cent of were engaged on other activities. Percentage of unemployment was comparatively higher in branches like Printing Technology (48%), and Automobile (36%).

(b) *Engineering Diploma:* About 40 per cent were having paid job in India and abroad, about 1 per cent were engaged on self family enterprises. Nearly, 25 per cent were continuing their studies in India. The unemployment percentage was about 25 per cent. It is interesting to observe that the percentage of students continuing higher studies was relatively high when compared to degree level. The percentage of students paid job in India and Abroad was encouraging in certain branches like Textile Technology (63%), Sugar and Paper (65%) and Metallurgy (50%). Percentage of unemployment was higher in Architectural Assistantship (52%) compared to other branches.

(c) *Engineering Post-graduate:* About 65 per cent were in paid job, 27 per cent were unemployed and remaining were studying and involved in other activity.

(d) *MBA, MCA, HMCT and Pharmacy:* Among MBA outturn, 74 per cent were having paid job, 15 per cent were unemployed and remaining were studying and involved in other activities. Among MCA outturn, 51 per cent were having paid job, 39 per cent were unemployed and remaining 10 per cent were studying and involved in other activities. Among HMCT outturn,

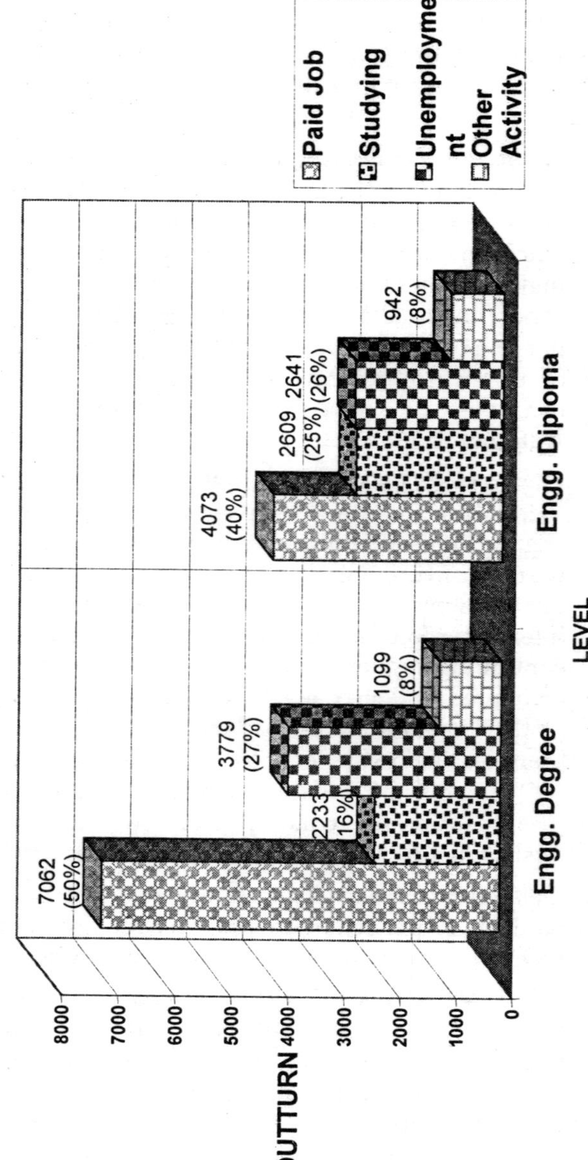

Fig. 6.13: Distribution of students activity as on 30th June 2003—2001 Batch

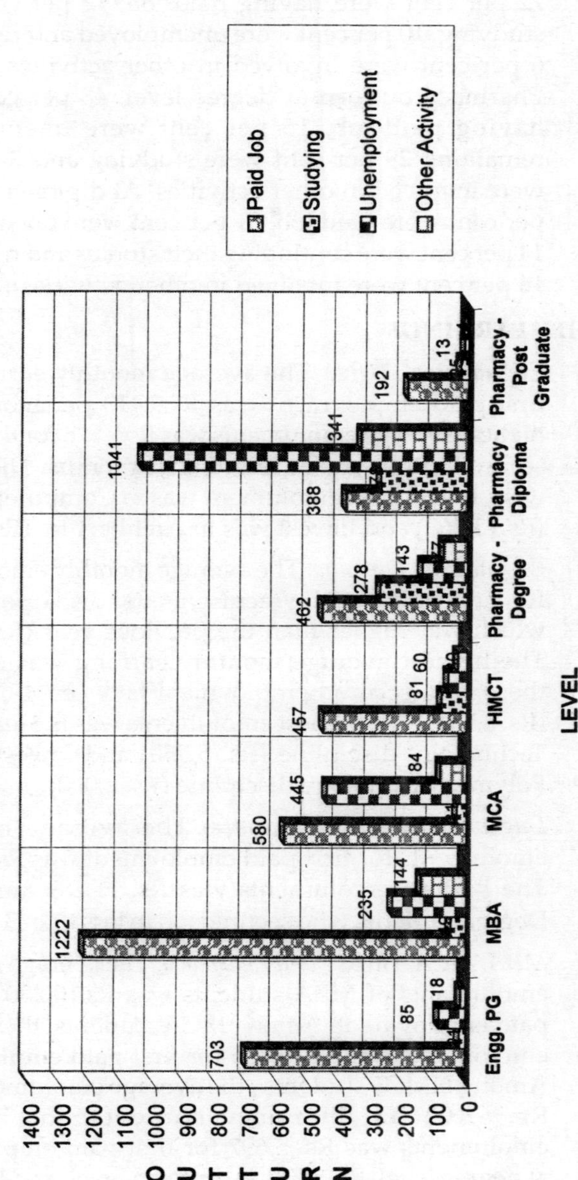

Fig. 6.14: Distribution of students activity as on 30th June 2003—2001 Batch

72 per cent were having paid job, 12 per cent were studying, 10 per cent were unemployed and remaining 6 per cent were involved in other activities. Among Pharmacy outturn at degree level, 48 per cent were having paid job, 15 per cent were unemployed, remaining 29 per cent were studying and 8 per cent were involved in other activities. At diploma level, 19 per cent were paid job, 51 per cent were unemployed, 14 per cent were continuing their studies and remaining 16 per cent were involved in other activities.

MONTHLY EARNINGS

(a) *Engineering Degree:* The average monthly earnings for first paid employment was Rs.9,413 per month. The highest average emoluments was Rs.9,776 for those who secured employment less than 3 months. Discipline-wise, the highest emolument was in Computer Science (Rs.13,062) and lowest was in Architecture (Rs. 4416).

(b) *Engineering Diploma:* The average monthly emoluments for first paid employment was Rs. 3,454 per month which was higher than the previous year (Rs. 3,227). The highest average monthly earning was amongst those who secured employment between 4-6 months (Rs. 3,581). The highest emoluments was in Heat Power Technology discipline (Rs. 5,550) and lowest was in Polymer Technology discipline (Rs. 2,000).

(c) *Engineering Post-graduate:* The average monthly emoluments for first paid employment was Rs. 11,692. The highest emoluments was Rs. 11,289 among PG Degree students who secured job in less than 3 months.

(d) *MBA, MCA, HMCT and Pharmacy:* The average monthly emoluments of MBA students was Rs.10,230 for first paid employment. Among MCA students, the average emoluments was Rs. 9,785 for first paid employment. Among HMCT students , the average emoluments was Rs. 6,102. In Pharmacy students, the average emoluments was Rs. 5,697 for first paid employment at degree level, Rs. 3,751 at diploma level, and Rs. 9,645 at post-graduate level.

UNEMPLOYMENT STATUS

The estimation of gap between supply and demand of engineers was worked out on the basis of estimation of total outturn and total engineers absorbed for employment during the year 2005. The difference between supply and demand gives the estimated gap between two parameters. The estimated gap between supply and demand is presented in Table 6.1 to Table 6.4.

Table—6.1 Estimated gap between supply and demand at degree level at the end of year 2005 by discipline

Discipline	Estimated stock of Engineers available for employment at the end of 2005	Estimate of Engineers Absorbed during 2005	Estimated Gap of Excess of Supply over Demand
Agriculture Technology	66	31	35
Automobile	358	141	217
Architecture	370	247	123
Bio Medical Medical Electronics	306	98	208
Ceramic & Cement	12	14	-2
Civil Engg.	2420	1173	1247
Chemical Engg.	590	295	295
Computer Science	5965	3032	2933
Electronics & Communication	6517	3001	3516
Electrical & Electronics	2457	1199	1258
Environmental Engg.	146	70	76
Instrumentation Tech.	835	494	341
Industrial Production	1395	770	625
Information Science	505	364	141
Mechanical	4422	3177	1245
Metallurgy	52	28	24
Mining Engg.	77	44	33
Polymer Technology	35	25	10
Textile Technology	249	140	109
Telecommunication	555	276	279
Transportation	14	11	3
Total	**27346**	**14630**	**12716**

Table—6.2 Estimated gap between supply and demand at diploma level at the end of year 2005 by discipline

Discipline	Estimated stock of diploma engineers available for employment at the end of 2005	Estimate of diploma engineers absorbed during 2005	Estimated gap of excess of supply over demand
Automobile	1758	792	966
Architectural Assistantship	210	52	158
Business Management	96	11	85
Cement & Ceramics	11	10	1
Civil	1785	862	923
Chemical	91	47	44
Commercial Practice	1500	590	910
Costume Design & Dress Making	463	158	305
Computer Science	4403	1686	2717
Civil Draughtsmenship	86	35	51
Electronics & Telecommunication	5201	2436	2765
Electrical	2101	933	1168
Heat Power Tech.	16	10	6
Instrumentation Tech.	477	171	306
Library Science	167	60	107
Mechanical	5301	2460	2841
Metallurgy	79	41	38
Mining Mine Surveying	72	35	37
Machine Tool Tech.	160	80	80
Printing Tech.	89	25	64
Polymer Technology	39	12	27
Sugar & Paper	14	10	4
Textile	88	59	29
Welding & Sheet Metal	49	13	36
Others (Leather Tech. Cinemautography/ Sound & TV)	39	18	21
Total	**24256**	**10588**	**13668**

Table—6.3 Estimated gap between supply and demand at post graduate level at the end of year 2005 by discipline

Discipline	Estimated stock of PG Engineers available for employment at the end of 2005	Estimate of PG Engineers Absorbed during 2005	Estimated Gap of Excess of Supply over Demand
1	2	3	4
Agriculture Technology	8	4	4
Bio-Medical Engg.	46	32	14
Construction Technology/ Mgt. Prestressed Concrete	32	30	2
Computer Science & Engg./ Software Technology	144	177	-33
Chemical Plant & Design Chemical	17	11	6
Environmental Engg. Industrial Water Pollution Control	48	41	7
Thermal/Heat Power Engg.	76	32	44
Industrial Structures/Geo Tech.	23	20	3
Industrial/Power Electronics	103	89	14
Lighting Science & Engg/ Illumination Tech.	30	17	13
Machine Design Design Engg.	46	35	11
Engg Management	87	36	51
Production & Management/ Maintenance Engg/.	69	49	20
Materials/Tools Engg.	20	11	9
Systems Analysis & Comp. Application	17	17	0
Adv. Mfr. Engg./ Prod.Engg. & System Tech.	53	37	16
Digital Electronics/Commn Engg./Adv. Communication	86	68	18
Master of Computer Application	3005	1266	1739
Power Energy Systems	44	43	1

(Contd...)

1	2	3	4
Process Metallurgy	16	5	11
Structural Engg./ Computer Aided Design & Structure Highway Engg.	246	137	109
Textile Technology	16	10	6
Hydraulics & Water Resources Engg./Marine Structures	20	20	0
Total	**4252**	**2187**	**2065**

Table—6.4 Estimated gap between supply and demand at the end of year 2005 by level

Courses	Estimated stock of Professional available for employment at the end of 2005	Estimate of Professionals Absorbed during 2005	Estimated Gap of Excess of Supply over Demand
Master of Business Management	3282	2029	1253
Bachelor in Hotel Management & Catering Technology	1335	651	684
Bachelor in Pharmacy	1391	848	543
Diploma in Pharmacy	6904	686	6218
Master in Pharmacy	350	261	89

(a) *Engineering Degree:* There has been an excess of technical manpower in all the disciplines. The estimated stock of engineers at degree level was 27,346 and estimated absorption of engineers was 14,630, thus creating an excess of 12,716 engineers. This excess was maximum in disciplines like Electronics and Communication (3,516) and Computer Science (2933).

(b) *Engineering Diploma*: There has been an excess of diploma engineers at the end of year 2005 in all the disciplines. The estimated stock of diploma engineers at the end of year 2005 was 24,256 and estimated absorption was 10,588. The estimated gap of excess of supply over demand was 13,668.

(c) *Engineering Post-graduate:* There has been excess of PG Degree holders in engineering at the end of year 2005 in all the disciplines. The estimated excess would be 326 PG Degree holders at the end of year 2005.

(d) *MBA, MCA, HMCT and Pharmacy*: The total MBA students passed during the year 2001 who would likely to be absorbed during year 2005 are estimated to be 2029. Among MCA students, the estimated stock was 3005, estimated absorption was 1266 and unemployed were 1739 at the end of year 2005. Among HMCT students, the size of unemployment at the end of year 2005 was estimated to be 1391. Among Pharmacy degree and diploma students, the total number who would be employed during year 2004 are estimated to be 848 and 685 respectively. The unemployment size at degree, diploma and post graduate level for students passed during year 2001, would be 543, 6218 and 89 respectively.

PROFILE OF FACILITIES

A comparative study of facilities and variations between the years 1994 and 2003 is indicated in the Table 6.5. The percentage variations for some of the facilities is significant.

Table—6.5 Summary on facilities for technical education in the state

Parameter	1994	2003	Percentage Variations
Total Number of Diploma Institutions	172	186	8
Total Number of Degree Institutions	51	118	131
Total Sanctioned Intake into diploma courses	28450	33956	19
Total Sanctioned Intake into degree courses	19331	38897	101
Total Outturn of Diploma Courses	9871	11463	16
Total Outturn of Degree Courses	11494	14550	27
Total Outturn of 10th Level	263501	338615	29
Total Outturn of 10+2 Level	112814	167053	48
Overall Teacher Student Ratio—Degree Level	1: 16	1: 22 (2001)	38
Overall Teacher Student Ratio—Diploma Level	1: 11	1: 13 (2001)	18

CONCLUSION

It is observed the number of institutes imparting technical education have steadily increased over the last decade. Similarly, the total intake and annual outturn of students these institutions have also shown increasing trend. However, trend in employment opportunities has not been encouraging. Overall, it may be concluded that considerable growth in technical education has taken place in the state.

7

Technical Manpower and its Utilisation in Jammu and Kashmir

B.L. Koul[*]

Naresh Dubey[**]

D.L. Verma[***]

ABSTRACT

Since independence, there has been phenomenal expansion in the higher educational system, higher engineering and technical education is an important component of higher education, which is essential for the overall industrial and economic growth of the country.

This chapter reviews present status of higher education in general and engineering and technical education in particular in the state and an effort has been made to analyze the causes at the root of the present unemployment in Jammu and Kashmir and possible remedial measures that could be taken not only to reduce the unemployment in the state, but produce a quality product that could contribute significantly for the development of the state in particular and the country in general.

* **NTMIS-Nodal Centre, National Institute of Technology(Srinagar), Camp Classes, Jammu, Email: jktmis@sancharnet.in**

** **NTMIS-Nodal Centre, National Institute of Technology(Srinagar), Camp Classes, Jammu, Email: jktmis@sancharnet.in**

*** **NTMIS-Nodal Centre, National Institute of Technology(Srinagar), Camp Classes, Jammu, Email: jktmis@sancharnet.in**

Key Words: Higher Education, Technical Education, Primary Education, Economy, Technical Manpower, Skill, GDP, Educated, Industry, Courses

INTRODUCTION

India is a democratic country, implemented economic developmental programmes from 1951 onwards and started undergoing changes from the middle of 1980s. Soviet model started yielding to market forces, closed economy gradually started opening up to the outside world. This trend of Liberalization, Privatization and Globalization (LPG) started from mid 1991. The country has since been implementing a programme of economic reforms called Structured Adjustment Programmes (SAP).

Education was in the state list earlier, but after 1976 is in the concurrent list. Thus federal government has a dominant role in higher and technical education in country.

In this chapter a review of the status of Higher and Technical Education in the country has been presented. Since the Higher Education is in the concurrent list , it is the federal government that matters in the decision making and implementation of policies and programmes framed from time to time. Being a vast country, there are pockets which are economically developed and there are others which are economically under developed. There is rural and urban divide in the economic development of the state. We, therefore, review the policies and programmes of the government for Higher and Technical Education and analyze various causes for the poor quality, unemployment, lack of motivation among the educated young engineers and possible remedial measures that could be taken so that we have a quality product that is well motivated to meet any future challenges in the society.

HIGHER EDUCATION IN INDIA

Since mid 1980s' new theories of economic growth have emphasized the role human capital as the hey of economic growth and development. It is the higher education that enriches the quality of manpower. This has been borne from a recent study of 190 countries by the World Bank. Thus higher education is a basic investment necessary to improve the over all quality of life. In

India 6-7% of the eligible group (18-22years) are getting the benefit of higher education. The World Bank document (1994) states ," The development of higher education is correlated with the economic development." Enrolment ratio in higher education averages 51 per cent in the countries that belong to high-income group, compared with 21 per cent in middle-income group and 6 per cent in low-income group. Therefore, the first and foremost task for India is to expand its higher education system further in a planned way so as to cover as large a portion of the eligible age group as possible otherwise it will become difficult for India to survive as a major nation.

The quality and social relevance of higher education imparted in our institutions remains quite low and deteriorating due to paucity of funds. The lack of training given to teachers and inadequate training during their service have led to deterioration in quality. Salaries of teachers are being raised periodically but with long time gaps. The gulf between the industry remuneration and the salary of teachers is very wide. The Indian academic system does not provide for paying differential salaries to different disciplines taking into account the market demand for professionals. A vast majority of the students who face uncertainties with regard to employment are also not highly motivated. The poor quality of education imparted and the out moded pedagogical practices do not place many demands on the students. Divesting research from teaching has been another reason for the poor quality of education. India is a developing nation, it should develop its higher education system. The development of HES requires funds and even more for its maintenance. Over the nine five-year plans has not shown noticeable improvement, rather in relative terms it has been declining continuously. Moreover the department of economic affairs (GOI) has recently classified HES as non-merit service and has recommended that the subsidy must be reduced. This viewpoint is completely ill informed and has in it, potential for disastrous consequences.

There are genuine concerns if HE is a vehicle for upward social mobility of the poor. As HE is considered as a social service, it is highly subsidized by the government,. However, a survey conducted by UGC in 1970s' revealed that 70 per cent of the university students came from top 20 per cent of the income groups. On the other hand 70 per cent of the government revenue came from the indirect taxes paid by all the citizens of which 60 per cent were living in poverty. Thus poor people who are deprived of HE are forced to pay for the education of well to do through subsidy. This justifies reduction of subsidy and enhancement of fees.

There are several committees, which have deliberated on the issue of various aspects of HE from time to time, and some genuine concerns have been projected about the HES in India. Ambani-Birla report for instance states, " Curriculum are not in tune with needs of the society resulting in increasing levels of educated unemployment".

The country's education system suffers today not due to lack of policy recommendations or programmes of action but due to the failure in their implementations. The review committee report 1992, confessed "much of what is contained in this report has already been dealt with by commissions and committees that were called upon to go into the education policy from time to time from the 19th century onwards. Implementation was the only problem." Part of the reason for this failure in implementation lies in the fact that they did not take into account the strength of resistance to institutional change from well entrenched internal groups. There were also no concrete suggestions for the mobilization of resources. The lack of political will is clearly evident from the present status of education in the country.

During present days of fields of human activities including education has been influenced by the process of globalization. Presently HE is not at all different from any other commodity or commercial product that can be bought and sold at the market place.

As per reports of UNESCO and World Bank, social and private returns of the higher educations are less than those of primary and secondary education. It is estimated that social return of primary education is 25 per cent while that of HE is only 1 per cent. This has led to the thinking that the returns of HE are largely personal/private and therefore, subsidy on this should be reduced. The GOI started implementation of this agenda by reducing the share of allocation for higher education. Therefore, in future, universities will have to be self-supporting by searching out alternative means of finance and generating funds from internal resources.

Privatization of HE is inevitable. India's school education is already partially privatized with large number of higher-fee charging public schools functioning all over the country. The dual system of school education, has already caused considerable damage to the social fabric of the nation. If private universities proposed to be set up also follow the policy of public schools, the social gulf between the rich and poor will further widen and damage thus caused will be irreparable. Thus we have to safeguard the interests of the poor people through an adequate state policy.

The present educational system is characterized by considerable disparities among regions (rural/urban divide), states (developed and backward) disciplines(science and humanities versus professional courses) etc. In research, applied research, evaluative studies , monitoring and feasibility surveys have gained over pure academic studies and basic research.

The universities have to redesign their programmers so as to make them flexible, cost-effective and relevant to the market economy. If our universities have to survive in the global market, we have to abandon the traditional mindset of making compromises in curricular reforms, conduct of examinations, admission of students and selection of teachers.

The strong linkage between the economy and education was never so clearly visible as now. It is the availability of employment in the market that makes the learners choose their areas of study. Thus a package of reforms in school level science curriculum is needed in the present days.

It is necessary for us to ensure that higher education is accessible to all, at least to all those who desire and deserve it. If we fail to do so, the existing gap between rich and poor will further widen. For achieving this target within the shortest possible time, we must expand distant Education System by way of establishing a network of Open Universities in India.

We need a proactive leadership in HE at the Central and State Government levels for formulating appropriate policy and practices in developing the potential of the future generation through an efficient and relevant higher education with accountability. HE is a futuristic investment in social, political and economic sense of term. It deserves a better attention than that it gets at the present.

TECHNICAL EDUCATION IN INDIA

Despite all national education commissions from 1964 onwards recommending and all political; parties agreeing to, the need for setting apart six per cent of the GNP for education, under-funding of education remains a major constraint of educational development in the country. There has been massive increases in enrolment at all stages, but funding never reached anywhere near the target. In 1990s', the ratio came down from 4.1 per cent in 1991 to 3.2 per cent in 1997. the cause of Higher Technical education suffered further as its share in the educational budgets of the federal and state governments dropped from 18.1 per cent in 1991 to 16.7 per cent in 1995-96. The already low share of capital expenditure in the total educational expenditure came down from 1.3 per cent in 1990-91 to 0.8 per cent in 1995-96. The expenditure per student in HE came down from Rs. 551 to Rs. 429 during this period. The decline in relative share of expenditure is partly the result of the decline in total public expenditure consequent to the fiscal compression effected under Structured Adjustment Programmes (SAP). The ratio of public expenditure to GDP came down from 30.6 per cent in 1991 to 27.1 per cent in 1998-99. The under funding of education in 1990s' is not entirely due to SAP. It is also due to lower priority assigned to this and other social sectors under the new policy environment. The cause of higher technical education suffered partly because of the cuts in the share of educational expenditure in GDP. These sub-sectors suffered further , because it was argued that the social rate of return from Higher and technical education was much less than primary and secondary education (earlier World Bank thinking). The subsequent thinking of the World Bank on " Knowledge for Development" has not yet percolated down to Indian policy makers. The votaries of liberalization in India have also not taken into cognizance the large role of actually being played by governments in social sectors in the most market driven societies.

The great productiveness of a country like America is due less to possession of natural resources than the development of wide range of skills. Thus three basic types of engineering have developed into numerous new technologies, which have tended to become independent fields.

The engineer should be alert for any fundamental discovery which may be turned to practical use and for betterment of the processes he is using. The structure of the engineering education should be such that when opportunities occur it will be possible for the country or the industries to collect requisite personnel from technicians to execute technical jobs to turn the discovery to use within as short a period as possible. Such a set up of engineering education existed in Germany and exists in USA, but not in United Kingdom, of which the Indian system was too long a bad and obsolete copy. Thus though many of the great and fundamental discoveries which led to the Radar and Atomic Energy utilization were made by British physicists, their large scale utilization was possible only in America, where the requisite personnel of all types could be made available and set to work. The British recognized this defect in their structure of engineering and technology education during the course of the last war. Their ministry of education set up a committee under Lord Eustace Percy, " to advise the Ministry on the needs of the technical education in England and Wales, with particular attention for the means required for maintaining appropriate co-operation between universities and technical colleges."

PROBLEMS AND PERSPECTIVES

The technical education system has been more or less inward looking, the impact of the system on the other elements of the economy is yet to be objectively assessed. The technologist is not a solitary individual unconnected with the happenings in the other spheres of the system. Of immediate concern, perhaps for the professionals is no doubt, the chosen field of his profession but the interaction with the allied professionals, as also the neighbouring community has also to be taken into account to determine the professionals place in the whole system.

Wastage in Technical Education

The wastage in the technical institutions as per a report is 30 per cent at degree level and 52 per cent at diploma level and at IIT level it is marginal. Therefore any effort to reduce wastage would contribute to the efficiency of the system.

Unemployment of Engineers

In a growing economy like India why should an educated person, especially in the field of technology, be unemployed? There could be several reasons, two main possibilities are:

1. Those claiming unemployment are people listed on the government employment exchanges, such people invariably are after government jobs, even if they hold jobs elsewhere;
2. Some people are unwilling to try something different, for economic or social status reasons. They lack direction, motivation, aptitude and flexibility.

A person having a technical qualification is first and foremost an educated person, with the ability to think and apply his mind to different tasks. It is often better students who become engineers and who should therefore, have less difficulty earning a living employed in a different profession. Therefore many engineers who are thriving in non-engineering professions. An education is never wasted if the person so desires. India has a huge unemployment problem and it has to be addressed seriously, but the solution does not lie in reducing educational seats but in increasing employment opportunities.

Many technical institutes lack equipment and facilities to train our students properly. It is a grave problem with India's education system and needs urgent rectification. "Education is the key for that it makes you flexible" has been well said by an expert.

Need to Review of Course Content

It is necessary to have a good look at the courses being offered now not merely for the organisational purposes of 'graded' facilities. Mere accumulation of information is not knowledge and complete knowledge by itself does not give the necessary wisdom. The purpose of education is not to produce "educated " individual at one stretch by putting all the information and knowledge into course at one time, but, on the other hand it is to take the individual to progressive stages where he could be in a position to acquire what further information and knowledge he wants for his future activities. It we accept this philosophy it is to be conceded that what is important is not to "load" the curriculum but arrange it in such a way that different requirements and needs of the individual's calling are provided in the process of life-long education. The credit system no doubt can go quite some way in this regard. But a deliberate attempt is to be made to recognize the fact that many of those who pursue these courses of studies will remain as technologists whereas quite a few of them might end up as managers. Further even a technologist has to have sufficient insight into the marginal areas of allied fields, if not in-depth study in that field itself. The course content, therefore, should be so modified as to allow the technologist to have an over all view in addition to his core discipline, e.g., the professional may have to have managerial training in addition to his professional calling. The education in our institution campuses should break away from the rigid stand of a unidisciplinary approach and a fixed framework but cater to a larger interest to acquaint and give an insight in various fields of expertise of which the institutional faculty and facilities are capable of, by offering on a massive scale refresher courses, study programmers, etc.

Sisterhood Programmes

While there is no doubt that certain segments of Technical Education System have built up strong potential (IITs'. Univ. Departments, some state colleges..), there are others which are rather weak. It is here that practicable and effective systems of cooperation programmes between institutions of different types at different levels are to be organised. Desirable are the programmes of exchange of teachers on short-term and long-term, on massive scale planned in relation to specific levels and goals of development, providing opportunities and appropriate programmes for making available at specific and for known periods the facilities available at the better institutions for the use of the staff of the not-so-well off institutions.

Industry-Institute Collaboration

For the improvement and further development of the system it is necessary that there is interaction between technical institutions and industries and other field organisations. The Employing sector should go all out to associate and involve itself in all matters and at all levels of technical education, planning and implementation. A stage has been reached where purely academic consideration in a system of professional education should not be the criteria in determining about suitability of personnel for technical education. Schemes such as adoption of institutions by industry etc., which have been initiated, should be encouraged totally by the industry.

Resource Bank of Technical Manpower (Domestic and International)

The potential for technical education system both in terms of human and physical resources are so large that it is worthwhile for us now to think from a national stand-point to have a pooled bank for technical expertise and aid, both for domestic and external purposes. A well organized and processed pool of such resources would be of great advantage for any need in any sector of the economy of the country including the technical education system itself for delivering many of the responsibilities for which now outside help is sought. This will also ensure job satisfaction to those who have expertise and higher attainments in sophisticated technology and thus prevent brain drain from the country.

8

Perspective of Technical Manpower Requirements and Demands

B.L. Koul[*]

Naresh Dubey[**]

D.L. Verma[***]

ABSTRACT

One of the important parameters for the development of a state is the technical manpower. The environment keeps on changing and so does the requirement of the technical manpower for the stability of the system. The changes in the basic parameters of the system thus demand regular updating of the technical manpower. A case study is presented and the component of the technical manpower that need to be fine tuned for a stable and viable system discussed. The need for change in the focus like discipline, sector and function etc. are emphasized for a better quality of the product.

Key Words: State, Development, Technical Manpower, Sector, Discipline.

* **NTMIS-Nodal Centre, National Institute of Technology(Srinagar), Camp Classes, Jammu, Email: jktmis@sancharnet.in**

** **NTMIS-Nodal Centre, National Institute of Technology(Srinagar), Camp Classes, Jammu, Email: jktmis@sancharnet.in**

*** **NTMIS-Nodal Centre, National Institute of Technology(Srinagar), Camp Classes, Jammu, Email: jktmis@sancharnet.in**

INTRODUCTION

It is imperative that for a system to be stable, the changes taking place in environment over time demand changes in technical manpower requirement too. Thus over the years after independence the dynamics of the system has changed, the extent of resources available, the scope of technical manpower requirement and the needs of the society have taken different dimensions. Technical manpower which is one of the most important components for the progress and development of a state in particular in the age of open market and electronic commerce has to be as good a product as an electronic gadget we are using. The gadget is regularly being updated and made more efficient so that its utility becomes more and more user friendly. In the same manner, the technical manpower has to be regularly updated, so that it caters the needs of this dynamic system.[1]

The NTMIS data of Jammu and Kashmir state for the period 1982 to 2001 provides information about the following vital parameters[2], i.e:

1. Facilities for technical education in Jammu & Kashmir;
2. Employment pattern within and outside the state;
3. Sector-wise pattern of absorption; and
4. Staff strength in technical institution in the state.

These parameters have been analyzed in this chapter and the findings there of have been reported here.

FACILITIES FOR TECHNICAL EDUCATION

Since 1982 facilities for technical education have increased in all the states and so in the state of Jammu and Kashmir also. Table—8.1 presents information about graduate students qualified from the institutions in the state and those qualified from institutions in other states over the period 1982 to 2001. The total number of graduates qualifying every year is tending to increase. In eighties it was around 200 and now it is above 300. The number of students that used to qualify from other states was less than 25 per cent during eighties and this is now above 50 per cent. In Table—8.2 is presented the corresponding information about diploma engineers. The total number that is qualifying is showing a decreasing trend. The number that qualifies from other states is varying from year to year, but is not more than 25 per cent. Thus at graduate level more students qualify from institutions in other states compared to those from institutes within the state. There are two possible explanations for this trend:

1. Better exposure and facilities outside the state in comparison to within the state;
2. Optimal usage of time in institution outside the state.

Table—8.1 Migration of students for education at degree level

Year	Qualified from J & K State	Qualified from other States	Total
1982	175 (85%)	31 (15.0%)	206
1983	165 (84.1%)	31 (15.8%)	196
1984	192 (83.1%)	39 (16.9%)	231
1985	361 (94.1%)	23 (5.9%)	384
1986	221 (91.7%)	20 (8.2%)	241
1987	214 (97.2%)	6 (2.7%)	220
1993	79 (48.76%)	83 (51.2%)	162
1994	258 (85.1%)	45 (14.85%)	303
1996	49 (36.8%)	84 (63.1%)	133
1997	57 (27.1%)	154 (72.9%)	211
1998	46 (23.1%)	152 (76.7%)	198
1999	124 (32.97%)	252 (67.03 %)	376
2000	133 (45.7%)	158 (54.2 %)	291
2001	158 (51.5%)	149 (48.5%)	307

Table—8.2 Migration of students for education at diploma level

Year	Qualified from State	Qualified from other States	Total
1	2	3	4
1982	274 (95.8%)	12 (4.2%)	286
1983	207 (86.9%)	31(13.1%)	238
1984	184 (85.6%)	31(14.4%)	215
1985	219 (98.6%)	3 (1.4%)	222

(Contd...)

1	2	3	4
1986	130 (100.0%)	–	130
1987	21 (100.0%)	–	21
1993	79 (48.8%)	83(51.2%)	162
1994	258 (85.1%)	45(14.9%)	303
1996	474 (90.1%)	52 (9.9%)	526
1997	322 (77.1%)	92(22.2%)	414
1998	427 (99.2%)	36 (7.8%)	463
1999	369 (88.9%)	47(11.2%)	416
2000	106 (70.7%)	44(29.3%)	150
2001	158 (85.9%)	26(14.1%)	184

EMPLOYMENT PATTERN

More then 50 per cent of the graduate engineers were employed within the state since 1982 and this trend has nearly remained the same (Table—8.3). However, the absolute figure of employment has decreased. Now lesser jobs are available within the state in comparison to eighties. At diploma level since 1982 to 2001 more than 80 per cent (Table—8.4) of the employed diploma engineers were employed within the state and rest outside the state. Thus diploma engineers still have a better chance of getting a job within the state in comparison to degree engineers. In the absence any industries in the state degree engineers find it more and more difficult to get employed within the state as the main agency for there employment is the state government departments only. Diploma engineers, however manage to get into sectors other than government as skilled persons and manage to get some jobs within the state.

Table—8.3 Distribution of employed engineers by place of work for first paid employment at degree level

Year	Within the State	Outside the State	Total
1	2	3	4
1982	119(55.09%)	97(44.9%)	216
1983	137 (68.5%)	63(31.5%)	200
1984	49 (49.5%)	50(50.5%)	99

(Contd...)

1	2	3	4
1985	79(48.76%)	83(51.2%)	162
1986	53 (48.1%)	57(51.8%)	110
1987	168 (61.9%)	103(30.0%)	271
1993	8 (44.4%)	10(55.5%)	18
1994	19 (82.6%)	4(17.3%)	23
1996	18 (66.7%)	9(33.3%)	27
1997	28 (93.3%)	2 (6.7%)	30
1998	12 (85.7%)	2(14.3%)	14
1999	40(61.05%)	25(38.4%)	65
2000	42(60.01%)	28(40.0%)	70
2001	47 (63.5%)	27(36.5%)	74

Table—8.4 Distribution of employed engineers by place of work for first paid employment at diploma level

Year	Within the State	Outside the State	Total
1982	234 (99.1%)	2 (0.84%)	236
1983	127 (94.7%)	7 (5.2%)	134
1984	23 (74.1%)	8 (25.8%)	31
1985	37 (92.5%)	3 (7.5%)	40
1986	15 (88.2%)	2 (11.8%)	17
1987	17 (89.4%)	2 (10.6%)	19
1993	47 (72.3%)	18 (27.6%)	65
1994	57 (60.6%)	37 (39.3%)	94
1996	6 (60%)	4 (40%)	10
1997	46 (65.7%)	24 (34.3%)	70
1998	166 (89.2%)	20 (10.75%)	186
1999	108 (78.2%)	30 (21.7%)	138
2000	19 (79.2%)	5 (20.8%)	24
2001	19(100.0%)	–	19

SECTOR-WISE PATTERN OF EMPLOYMENT

During eighties state government was the main employer of graduate engineers (40% to 52%) (refer Table—8.5) when public and private sectors together employed about 25 per cent to 40 per cent of the employed graduates and the Central Government employed nearly 10 per cent of the employed graduates engineers.

This trend is changing now. The component of state government is decreasing and in 2000, the state government share was just 20 per cent . On the other hand the contribution of public and private sectors has started increasing (>50% in 2001) while the component of Central Government remains nearly unchanged. Obviously the state and Central Government departments seem to have reached a limit and we should not expect more than 20 per cent contribution from these sectors. These sectors are in fact the sectors envisaged for the development of necessary infrastructure for the development of other related activities. Therefore, the area of our focus now should be public and private establishments. There has been a steady growth in these establishments and young engineers should focus there energies accordingly.

At diploma level, during eighties 65 per cent to 90 per cent of diploma engineers employed were employed in state government departments, when public and private sectors undertakings employed more than 60 per cent of the employed diploma engineers (Table—8.6). Therefore, the graduate as well as diploma engineers should focus their energies towards these sectors, so that they get proper employment opportunities in these sectors.

REGARDING TECHNICAL TEACHING INSTITUTIONS

As years have passed not many opt for teaching as profession. Probably, because it is not adequately paid for. In 1982 there were hardly any positions vacant in technical institution in the state when in 2000 about 25 per cent positions were vacant at degree level as well as diploma institutions Table—8.7 (A) and 8.7 (B). Secondly, there is lack of qualified staff as well. Table—8.8 (A) and 8.8 (B). For example in 1982 at degree institutions 65 per cent were with Ph.D degrees when in 2001only 23 per cent were with Ph.D. degree. This has obviously effected the quality of teaching in the institutions and consequently the quality of the product.

Table—8.5 Distribution of employed graduate engineers by sector of employment

Year	Central Govt.	State Govt.	Local Body	Public Sector	Pvt. Sector	Co-op.	Others
1982	14(6.5%)	98(45.4%)	–	39(18.1%)	50(23.1%)	–	6.9(15%)
1983	17(8.4%)	105(52%)	1(2%)	34(16.8%)	23(11.4%)	1(0.5%)	9.9(20%)
1984	12(8.8%)	42(30.8%)	5(3.6%)	20(14.7%)	55(40.4%)	–	2(1.4%)
1985	26(11.8%)	103(47.0%)	2(0.9%)	14(6.3%)	49(22.3%)	1(0.4%)	3(1.3%)
1986	5(3.5%)	77(53.8%)	6(4.2%)	13(9.1%)	28(19.6%)	1(0.7%)	13(9.1%)
1987	18(6.6%)	104(38.4%)	9(3.3%)	32(11.8%)	93(34.3%)	–	15(5.5%)
1993	2(11.1%)	2(11.1%)	2(11.1%)	6(33.3%)	6(33.3%)		–
1994	4(17.4%)	2(8.7%)	–	6(26.1%)	10(43.5%)		1(4.3%)
1996	8(29.6%)	4(14.8%)	–	12(44.4%)	3(11.1%)		–
1997	2(6.7%)	16(53.3%)	–	8(26.7%)	2(6.7%)		2(6.7%)
1998	–	14(2%)	6(42.9%)	2(14.3%)	4(28.6%)		–
1999	3(4.6%)	6(9.2%)	1(1.1%)	9(13.8%)	45(69.2%)		1(1.5%)
2000	15(21.4%)	15(21.4%)	–	11(25.7%)	21(30%)		1(1.4%)
2001	6(8.1%)	6(8.7%)	5(6.8%)	18(24.3%)	34(45.9%)	5(6.7%)	3(15.7%)

Table—8.6 Distribution of employed diploma engineers by sector of employment

Year	Central Govt.	State Govt.	Local Body	Public Sector	Pvt. Sector	Co-op.	Others
1982	26(11%)	177(75%)	13(5.5%)	11(4.7%)	9(3.8%)	–	
1983	9(6.7%)	86(64.2%)	1(0.7%)	20(14.9%)	17(12.7%)	–	1(0.8%)
1984	1(2.9%)	4(11.7%)	2(5.8%)	10(29.4%)	10(29.4%)	–	7(20.5%)
1985	1(1.5%)	57(86.3%)	1(1.5%)	5(7.5%)	2(3.0%)	–	–
1986	–	29(84.9%)	1(3.0%)	1(3.0%)	1(3.0%)	–	2(6.1%)
1987	–	17(89.5%)	–	2(10.5%)	–	–	
1993	2(3.1%)	10(15.4%)	4(6.2%)	10(15.4%)	35(53.8%)		–
1994	8(8.6%)	11(11.8%)	3(3.2%)	21(22.6%)	45(48.4%)	5(5.4%)	
1996	6(4.5%)	41(30.8%)	4(3.0%)	41(30.8%)	38(28.6%)	1(0.8%)	2(1.5%)
1997	–	5(7.1%)	7(10.0%)	40(28%)	40(28%)		2(2.9%)
1998	–	3(1.6%)	4(2%)	19(10.2%)	144(77.4%)		16(8.6%)
1999	–	2(1.4%)	2(1.4%)	18(13%)	63(45.7%)		53(38.4%)
2000	–	2(8.3%)	2(8.3%)	12(50%)	8(33.3%)		–
2001	–	2(10.7%)	–	4(21.0%)	10(52.6%)		3(15.7%)

Table—8.7(A) Actual and sanctioned strength of teachers at degree level institutions

Year	Actual	Sanctioned	% A to S
1982	145	145	100.0
1983	135	138	97.8
1984	135	138	97.8
1985	135	138	97.8
1986	135	138	97.8
1987	135	138	97.8
1993	135	138	97.8
1994	135	138	97.8
1996	130	131	99.2
1997	142	204	69.6
1998	142	204	69.6
1999	322	445	80.6
2000	251	392	64.0
2001	242	309	78.3

Table—8.7(B) Actual and sanctioned strength of teachers at diploma level institutions

Year	Actual	Sanctioned	% A to S
1982	64	84	76.2
1983	70	88	79.5
1984	70	88	79.5
1985	70	88	79.5
1986	70	88	79.5
1987	70	88	79.5
1993	70	88	79.5
1994	70	88	79.5
1996	326	425	76.7
1997	345	469	73.5
1998	310	382	81.1
1999	359	445	80.0
2000	349	463	75.3
2001	292	374	78.07

Table—8.8(A) Distribution of teachers by highest qualifications at degree level institutions

Year	Ph.D.	Post graduate	Graduate	P.G. Diploma	Diploma	Total
1982	28(65%)	35(35%)	–	–	–	43
1983	21(22%)	33(35%)	40(43%)	–	–	94
1984	21(22%)	33(35%)	40(43%)	–	–	94
1985	21(22%)	33(35%)	40(43%)	–	–	94
1986	21(22%)	33(35%)	40(43%)	–	–	94
1987	21(22%)	33(35%)	40(43%)	–	–	94
1993	21(22%)	33(35%)	40(43%)	–	–	94
1994	21(22%)	33(35%)	40(43%)	–	–	94
1996	49(39%)	36(29%)	40(32%)	–	–	125
1997	68(55.7%)	14(11.1%)	40(32.5%)	–	–	122
1998	69(52.7%)	29(22.1%)	18(13.7%)	15(11.5%)		131
1999	46(40%)	26(22%)	39(34%)	4(3%)	1(1%)	116
2000	65(26%)	33(13%)	155(61%)	1(0.4%)		254
2001	54(23%)	71(30.3%)	105(44.8%)	4(1.7%)	–	234

Table—8.8(B) Distribution of teachers by highest qualifications at diploma level institutions

Year	Ph.D	Post Graduate	Graduate	P.G. Diploma	Diploma	Total
1982	–	–	14(24.5%)	–	43(75.5%)	57
1983	–	–	18(25.3%)	–	53(74.6%)	71
1984	–	–	18(25.3%)	–	53(74.6%)	71
1985	–	–	18(25.3%)	–	53(74.6%)	71
1986	–	–	18(25.3%)	–	53(74.6%)	71
1987	–	–	18(25.3%)	–	53(74.6%)	71
1993	–	–	18(25.3%)	–	53(74.6%)	71
1994	–	–	18(25.3%)	–	53(74.6%)	71
1996	2(1.18%)	16(9.4%)	120(7.1%)	31(18.3%)	–	169
1997	2(0.89%)	46(20.5%)	113(50.4%)	63(28.1%)	–	224
1998	2(0.87%)	21(9.2%)	141(61.8%)	64(28.07%)	–	228
1999	1(0.43%)	34(14.7%)	121(52.3%)	75(32.46%)	–	231
2000	1(0.42%)	46(17.4%)	152(57.7%)	64(24.3%)	–	263
2001	–	34(17.0%)	113(56.5%)	53(26.5%)	–	200

CONCLUSION

Facilities have increased for technical education in Jammu and Kashmir, but still at graduate level the number of students who graduate from institutions outside the state is more than those who graduate from institution in the state.

There is change in the sectors that provide employment to major fraction of the graduate and diploma engineers, presently public and private sectors are providing employment to substantial (50% at degree level and more than 80% at diploma level) fraction of the graduate and diploma engineers of the state. Earlier state government departments were the major employers. During eighties major fraction of graduate engineers was finding jobs within the state, this scenario has changed. Now number of jobs available within the state is lesser at graduate level, however at diploma level the pattern has not changed appreciably. In view of these findings, the focus of parents, students and teachers should not only be on the disciplines which are in demand but also on the fact that jobs are available outside the state and in public and private establishments. Thus there is need to look into these sectors and their requirements, so that our young engineers are properly geared for the same. There is, therefore, need of a cell in a technical institution, which could constantly update itself with the market requirements of such sectors that are potentially absorbing ones, so that the product of the institution is properly tuned to meet the expected challenges. Such cells would be parallel to Research and Development Cells in a factory, that are responsible for the technology update of the product produced by the factory that allows its product to stay competitive in the market. Such a cell in an institution should be in constant liaison with the concerns that are potential absorbers and there should be regular flow of to and fro information between the two, so that the product of the institution is a qualify product and hence has a potential market available. Since technology is changing fast, this demands that the programmes and recommendations of such a cell in a technical institution should be implemented immediately, so that procedural delays do not come in between such vital decisions, that may be responsible for making of carrier of our young engineers.

REFERENCES

1. K. K. George and Reji Raman, *Changes in Indian Higher Education—An Insiders's View.*

2. *Annual Technical Manpower Reviews, Jammu and Kashmir,* Institute of Applied Manpower Research, New Delhi, 1982-2000.

9

Employment Status of Engineering Students Belonging to Socially Backward Categories

A Case Study of Karnataka State

A. H. Sequeira[*]
T.G. Bhandary[**]
Arun Kumar Shetty[***]

ABSTRACT

The government has given special emphasis and encouragement to students belonging to socially backward categories to participate in education through the reservation policy. About fifteen per cent seats for Scheduled Caste(SC) and three per cent seats for Scheduled Tribe(ST) students are reserved for admission to courses at under-graduate and post-graduate levels in technical education. Although the Government has made provision for education to the underprivileged category students, there is dearth of information to explore and evaluate the extent to which these students have benefited. Only few studies are conducted on determining the status of the passed out students, their employability and their economic status. This chapter addresses some of the issues listed

* **Project Officer, NTMIS–Nodal Centre, NITK, Surathkal– 575025**

** **Research Associate, NTMIS Nodal Centre, NITK, Surathkal– 575 025**

*** **COCP, NTMIS Nodal Centre, NITK, Surathkal– 575 025, Email: ntmisnodal@yahoo.com**

above. The chapter also highlights the findings of the survey on such students conducted by the NTMIS – Nodal Centre for Karnataka State.

INTRODUCTION

In a democratic society like India, access to higher education necessarily results in social equality. After independence, efforts have been made by the Central and State Governments to provide reservations in the education institutions, including technical education institutions, for students from those social backward categories. Even though the Karnataka State has provided sufficient reserved seats for admission into technical institutions, the participation of social backward categories was not considerable for various reasons. The present study is taken up to trace the important issues like actual intake into engineering degree diploma institutions, annual outturn, activity status of the fresh engineers, average monthly emoluments and rate of absorption at degree and diploma levels. The study covered 3 batches of SC/ST category students passed out during the year 1999 to year 2001 from different colleges and polytechnics of the Karnataka State.

OBJECTIVES

The objectives of the study include:

1. To trace the trend in participation of students belonging to socially backward categories (i.e. Scheduled Caste and Scheduled Tribe) in technical education;
2. To analyze the essential indicators related to employment prospects for socially backward category students;
3. To highlight the opportunities for enhanced participation of students socially backward sections of the society.

METHODOLOGY

To achieve the above objectives, a pre-designed Student Follow-up Questionnaire was mailed to selected socially backward students who passed out from technical (degree and diploma) institutions located in the Karnataka State during the years 1999 to 2001 (two years after completion of the course). Efforts were

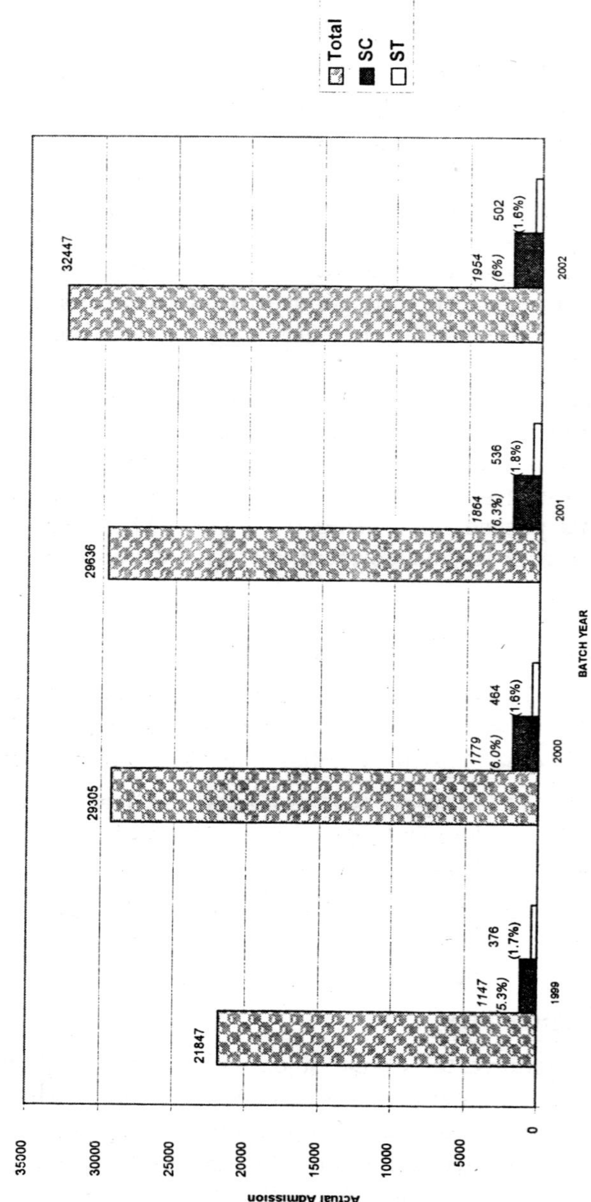

Fig. 9.1: Distribution of total admission and SC & ST students into engineering degree courses (1999-2002)

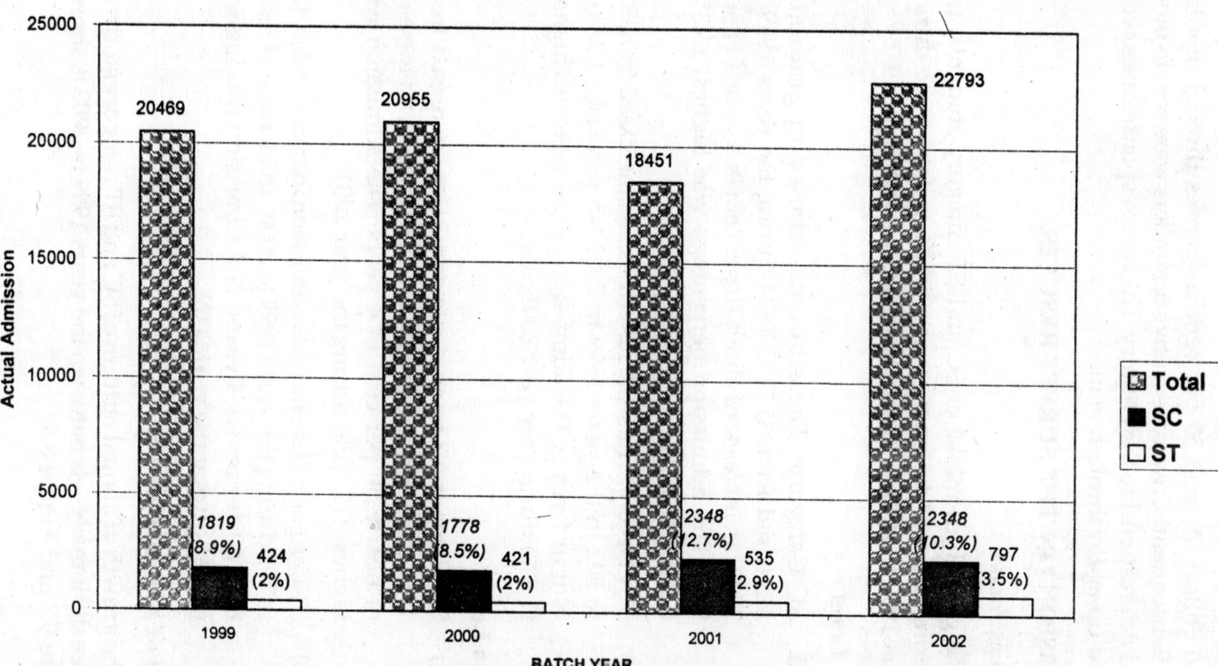

Fig. 9.2: Distribution of total admission and SC & ST students into engineering diploma courses (1999-2002)

made to collect at least 50 per cent responses through mailed survey. Subsequently, two consecutive reminders were sent to those who did not respond to the enquiry. The non-response cases were followed up again through mail.

DISCUSSION ON THE SURVEY RESULTS

Growth in Intake

The growth of intake of SC and ST category students into engineering degree/diploma courses in Karnataka State during the years 1999 to 2001 is shown in Figure 9.1 and Figure 9.2.

Degree Level

(a) *SC Category:* The students admission gradually increased from 1147 to 1954 during the years 1999 to 2002, an increase of about 70 per cent in 4 years (Figure 9.1). The admission percentage was highest (6.3%) during year 2001.

(b) *ST Category:* The students admission increased from 376 to 502 in the years 1999 to 2002, an increase of 36 per cent in 4 years. The admission percentage was highest (1.8%) during the year 2001.

Diploma Level

(a) SC Category: The students admission increased from 1819 to 2348 during the years 1999 to 2002, an increase of nearly 30 per cent in 4 years. The admission was highest (12.73%) during the year 2001.

(b) *ST Category:* The Students admission increased from 424 to 797 during the years 1999 to 2002, an increase of more than 80 per cent in 4 years. The admission was highest (3.5%) during the year 2002.

Growth of Annual Outturn

The growth of annual outturn of SC and ST category students at degree diploma levels between the years 1999 to 2002 is shown in Figure 9.3 and Figure 9.4.

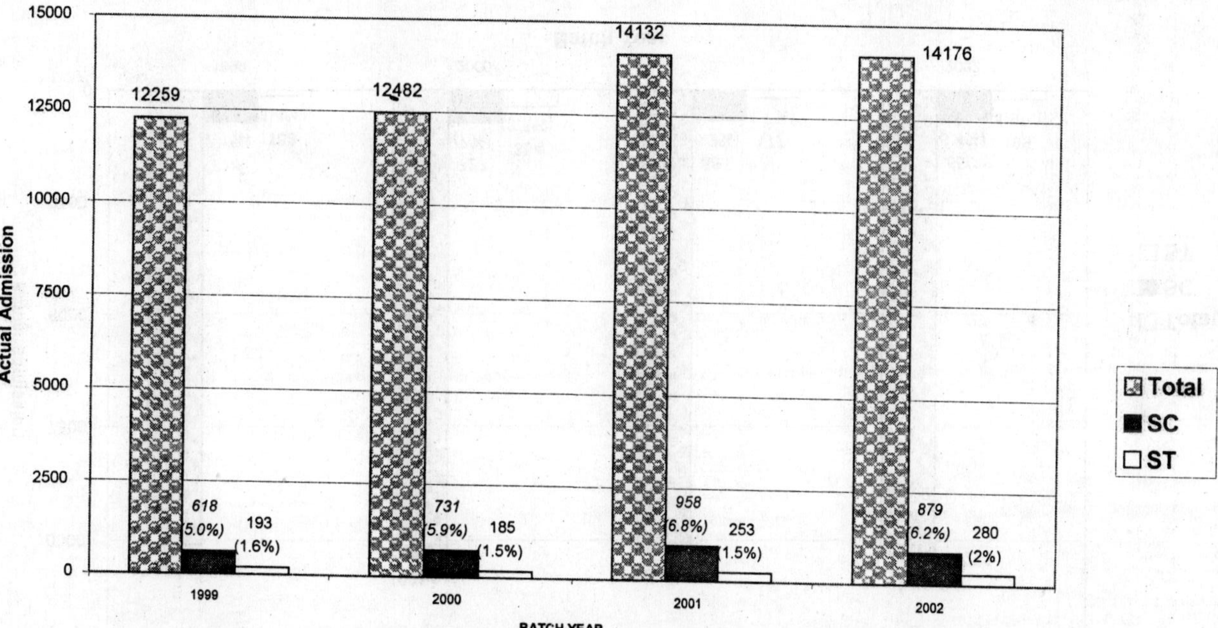

Fig. 9.3: Distribution of outturn of total, SC & ST students from engineering degree courses (1999-2002)

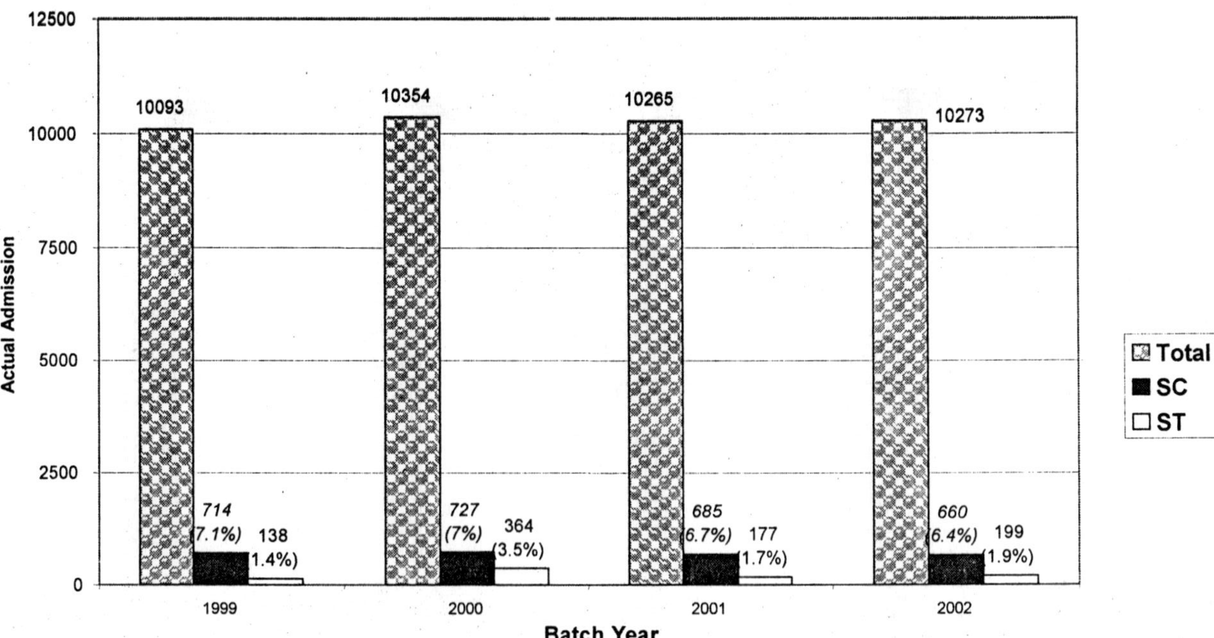

Fig. 9.4: Distribution of outturn of total, SC & ST students from engineering diploma courses (1999-2002)

Degree Level

(a) *SC Category:* The annual outturn of students increased from 618 to 958, an increase of 55 per cent, between the years 1999 to 2001. It again decreased to 879 in the year 2002 (Figure 9.3).

(b) *ST Category:* The annual outturn of students increased from 193 to 280, an increase of 45 per cent, between the years 1998 to 2002 (Figure 9.3).

Diploma Level

(a) *SC Category***:** The annual outturn of students decreased from 714 to 660, a decrease of 8 per cent, between the years 1999 to 2002 (Figure 9.4).

(b) *ST Category:* The annual outturn of students increased from 138 to 364, an increase of 163 per cent, between the years 1999 to 2000. It again decreased to 177 and 199 during the years 2001 and 2002 respectively (Figure 9.4).

Activity Status of Students

The activity status of SC and ST category students at degree/ diploma levels, passed during the years 1999 to 2001 is shown in Table—9.1. The activity was determined 24 months after students obtaining degree/diploma. The various types of activities considered for this study are mainly divided into: paid job (India/ Abroad); self-employment (own enterprises, family enterprises); studying (India/Abroad); and unemployed.

Degree Level

(a) *SC Category:* The percentage of students holding paid job was highest (36%) during year 1999 and lowest (26%) during the year 2000. The unemployed engineers were 46 per cent during year 1999 and 52 per cent during years 2000 and 2001. The students studying further were 17 per cent during 1999, about 8 per cent during year 2000 and 9 per cent during year 2001.

(b) *ST Category:* The percentage of engineers holding paid job was highest (42%) during the year 1999 and lowest

Table—9.1 Distribution of SC/ST Engineers by activity status by year-wise

Batch Year	Paid Job in		Self Employed in family/ own enterprises	Unemployed and interested in self employment	Studying in		Apprentice	Unemployed		Other activity	Total
	India	Abroad			India	Abroad		Looking for job	Not looking for job		
DEGREE – SC Category											
1999	225	7	3	11	41	2	42	284	3	0	618
	(36)	(1)	(0)	(2)	(7)	(0)	(7)	(46)	(0)	(0)	(100)
2000	191	0	8	17	47	12	55	380	0	22	732
	(26)	(0)	(1)	(2)	(6)	(2)	(8)	(52)	(0)	(3)	(100)
2001	269	0	13	14	66	16	55	506	16	14	969
	(28)	(0)	(1)	(1)	(7)	(2)	(6)	(52)	(2)	(1)	(100)
DEGREE–ST Category											
1999	82	0	0	3	4	0	15	89	0	0	193
	(42)	(0)	(0)	(2)	(2)	(0)	(8)	(46)	(0)	(0)	(100)
2000	59	0	0	3	24	0	10	94	0	0	190
	(31)	(0)	(0)	(2)	(13)	(0)	(5)	(49)	(0)	(0)	(100)
2001	98	0	4	4	23	0	7	117	0	0	253
	(39)	(0)	(2)	(2)	(9)	(0)	(3)	(46)	(0)	(0)	(100)

(Contd...)

1	2	3	4	5	6	7	8	9	10	11	12
DIPLOMA – SC Category											
1999	259	0	0	4	92	0	101	255	0	3	714
	(36)	(0)	(0)	(1)	(13)	(0)	(14)	(36)	(0)	(0)	(100)
2000	242	0	4	13	161	0	70	237	0	0	727
	(33)	(0)	(1)	(2)	(22)	(0)	(10)	(33)	(0)	(0)	(100)
2001	223	0	0	19	171	0	37	223	6	3	682
	(33)	(0)	(0)	(3)	(25)	(0)	(5)	(33)	(1)	(0)	(100)
DIPLOMA – ST Category											
1999	47	0	6	0	17	0	16	52	0	0	138
	(34)	(0)	(4)	(0)	(12)	(0)	(12)	(38)	(0)	(0)	(100)
2000	161	0	0	6	106	0	5	81	0	5	364
	(44)	(0)	(0)	(2)	(29)	(0)	(1)	(22)	(0)	(1)	(100)
2001	46	0	0	4	52	0	38	37	0	0	177
	(26)	(0)	(0)	(2)	(29)	(0)	(21)	(21)	(0)	(0)	(100)

Note: Figure in brackets shows the percentage.

(31%) during year 2000. The unemployed engineers were 46 per cent, 49 per cent, and 46 per cent during years 1999, 2000 and 2001 respectively. Those who continued studying were 13 per cent during year 2000. About 2 per cent students were self-employed during the year 2001.

Diploma Level

(a) *SC Category:* The percentage of students holding paid job was highest (36%) during year 1999 and lowest (33%) during the years 2000 and 2001. The unemployed engineers were 36 per cent during year 1999 and 33 per cent during years 2000 and 2001. Those who continued studying was 13 per cent, 22 per cent, and 25 per cent during years 1999, 2000 and 2001 respectively.

(b) *ST Category:* The percentage of engineers holding paid job was highest (44%) during the year 2000 and lowest (26%) during year 2001. About 38 per cent engineers were unemployed during 1999, and about 22 per cent and 21 per cent during years 2000 and 2001 respectively. Those who continued studying was 12 per cent, 29 per cent during years 1999, 2000, and 2001.

Average Emoluments

The average emoluments earned by SC and ST engineering graduates/diploma holders in their first paid employment is presented in Table—9.2.

Degree Level

(a) *SC Category*: The average monthly emoluments of engineers was Rs. 8,035 during the year 1999, Rs. 7,068 during year 2000 and Rs. 7,289 during the year 2001. The highest average emoluments earned (Rs. 18,750) was of those who secured job after 21 months during the year 1999 and lowest (Rs. 3,667)was of those who got job between 10-12 months during the year 2000.

(b) *ST Category:* The average monthly emoluments was Rs. 7,478, Rs. 7,858, Rs. 7,926 during the years 1999, 2000

Table—9.2 Average monthly emoluments (in rupees) of employed SC/ST engineers by time taken for first employment

Discipline	Waiting Period for First Paid Employments (in Months)								Overall Average
	<= 3	4-6	7-9	10-12	13-15	16-18	19-21	>21	
DEGREE – SC Category									
1999	6685	7996	6367	11028	7260	7447	5833	18750	8035
2000	7550	4833	4000	3667	4675	8500	7951	13529	7068
2001	8947	5417	6056	8314	6050	6200	6200	6981	7289
DEGREE – ST Category									
1999	7125	7500	8000	10027	7610	0	4031	12250	7478
2000	9886	6520	9625	6000	7933	6500	4000	2250	7858
2001	6818	3750	9033	5550	14883	10000	17838	10000	7926
DIPLOMA – SC Category									
1999	2818	3328	2650	3042	3029	2936	2350	2918	2922
2000	2793	2564	4375	3643	2833	3167	2740	2500	2932
2001	2984	2740	3000	3633	5243	3000	2539	3088	3128
DIPLOMA–ST Category									
1999	2760	3057	4400	0	3045	0	0	0	3223
2000	2642	3500	0	0	2300	0	1750	2975	2733
2001	2635	1900	2500	0	3333	3500	8400	0	2926

and 2001 respectively. The highest average emoluments earned (Rs. 17,838)was of those who secured job between 19-21 months during the year 2001 and lowest (Rs. 2,250) was of those who got job after 21 months during the year 2000.

Diploma Level

(a) *SC Category:* The average monthly emoluments were Rs. 2,922, Rs. 2,932, and Rs. 3,128 during years 1999, 2000, and 2001 respectively. The highest average emoluments earned (Rs. 5,243) was of those who secured employment between 13-15 months in the year 2001 and lowest (Rs. 2,350) was of those who got job between 19-21 months in the year 1999.

(b) *ST Category:* The average monthly emoluments was Rs. 3,223, Rs. 2,733, and Rs. 2,926 during years 1999, 2000 and 2001 respectively. The highest salary was Rs. 8,400 during the year 2001 and lowest was Rs. 1,750 during year 2000.

Rate of Absorption

The information collected through students follow-up questionnaire regarding the employment and the time taken by them in getting first paid employment has been compiled for various time intervals for working out the absorption rate. For estimating the absorption rate, following process has adopted:

1. Employed SC/ST category engineers were distributed discipline wise and time taken for getting first paid employment;
2. Number thus obtained was divided by the corresponding number of SC and ST category engineers for employment. This yielded the ratios of available engineers in economic activities at different time intervals;
3. The percentage of SC and ST category engineers absorbed in economic activities were accumulated with respect to time taken for obtaining first paid employment.

The percentage of absorption of SC and ST category engineers who passed during the years 1999 to 2001, both at degree and diploma levels is shown in Table 9.3.

Degree Level

(a) *SC Category:* The absorption in first year was highest (52%) for the year 1999 and lowest (29%) in year 2001. Nearly 82 per cent engineers could get the absorption within 3 years in year 1999. About 18 per cent engineers were unemployed beyond four years.

(b) *ST Category:* The absorption in first year was highest (48%) for the of year 2001 and lowest (38%) for 1999. Nearly 86 per cent of engineers could get absorbed within 3 years in the year 1999.

Table—9.3 Distribution of SC/ST engineers by absorption rate and year-wise

Batch Year	Percentage Absorption			
	I year	II Year	III Year	IV Year & More
	DEGREE–SC Category			
1999	52	13	17	18
2000	32	7	14	47
2001	29	23	14	34
	DEGREE–ST Category			
1999	38	29	19	14
2000	42	21	21	16
2001	48	11	12	29
	DIPLOMA–SC Category			
1999	50	15	22	13
2000	55	19	13	13
2001	28	30	24	18
	DIPLOMA–ST Category			
1999	46	23	18	13
2000	55	21	15	9
2001	56	14	17	13

Diploma Level

(a) *SC Category:* The percentage absorption was highest (55%) for the year 2000 and lowest (28%) for year 2001. The percentage absorption who took more than 3 years was highest (18%) in the year 2001.

(b) *ST Category:* The percentage absorption in first year was highest (56%) for the of year 2001 and lowest (46%) for the year 1999. Nearly 91 per cent of engineers could get absorbed within 3 years in the year 2000 and about 9 per cent engineers who took more than 3 years for absorption.

CONCLUSION

The study concludes that there has been adequate facility for enhanced participation of socially backward categories students in the technical education in Karnataka State. Although there is an increase in number of students admitted, the average percentage of actual admissions into degree and diploma institutions were much below the percentage reserved for such categories. The average percentage of unemployment was higher when compared to paid job activity at both degree and diploma levels. The average absorption rate was higher among ST category engineers while comparing to SC category engineers.

10

Engineering Manpower Challenges in Light of New Millennium Changes

*Nitin S. Gawhane**

ABSTRACT

Indian Universities and majority of engineering education institutions all these years were enjoying Sellers Market, internally, without much stiff competition from institutes and universities abroad. Apart from IITs and few RECs, mainly the focus was on Quantity. Talking in manufacturing sense, it was rather a PUSH type of system than PULL type. State Government and unaided institutes, which started merely two decades ago, have remained aloof from any radical changes and concrete improvements in terms of Quality. Bodies like Ministry of HRD, UGC, AICTE and ISTE are in search of excellence in their different activities, due to pressure of circumstances—Customer expectation on one hand, and resource utilization on another. Against this backdrop, this chapter is an attempt to identify few problems in current scenario with respect to engineering manpower. It deals with changing paradigm and speaks about operating constraints, in light of consumer awareness and qualitative requirements of Global Environment, which cannot be ignored. With brief about training component, vital in current dynamic

* **Assistant Professor, Department of Mechanical and Production Engineering, Yeshwantrao Chavan College of Engineering, Hingna Road, Nagpur– 441 110, Chairman, Indian Value Engineering Society. (INVEST)- Western Zonal Council, Nagpur Chapter, Email: gawhanen@rediffmail.com gawhanenitin@yahoo.co.in**

environment, it also tries to find why the training programmes fail? It concludes with, prescription of what should be done to enhance qualitative manpower.

PREAMBLE

Engineering education is seen as one of the prestigious programme for employment and betterment of life. By its inherent nature, it has to be blend of percept and practice. The recent changes of economic restructuring and liberalized industrial policy have placed a heavy responsibility on engineering education and educators in India, which is causing distortions at Macro-level, to the spectrum of traditional technical manpower.

The coming of 21st century is now establishing new imperatives for institutions and managers of education. Success, not just survival, is the need today. In Indian context, in last millennium, just as the transition from an agrarian to an industrial economy transformed the lives of people, similarly the current transformation from an industrial to an information economy is transforming our lives. It is reflected in many spheres of our life.

With reference to engineering education in India, there have been:

- Changes in industry—*variety, volume and complexity;*
- Speed and flexibility of business—*lead time compression and market mix;*
- Quality awareness with value emphasis—*benchmarking of learning institutes;*
- Shorter product life cycle—*curriculum and pedagogy changes due to technological changes;*
- Global turbulence—*competition from foreign universities and institutions;*
- Obsolescence of previous experience—*strategy of past becoming irrelevant;*
- Socio-economic changes—*spending power of parents and easy finances;*
- Location redundancy—*technology enabled virtual universities and institutes;*

- Innovations and Leadership—*institutional and Individual;*
- Irrelevant past experience— *fundamental structural change in academic practices.*

The remarkable characteristic of new competition is that, there has been significant increase in local and global competition. No more competition limits itself to nations in world market but also between the firms from same country in the market. To face the new business challenges we need to increasingly depend upon adoption of better management practices.

Against this backdrop, two questions surface up.

1. Will Indian universities and engineering education institutions be able to survive and compete in terms of Value for money?
2. If so, how?

In this millennium, stability has disappeared. Gradual change has been replaced by rapid change. There is a whole new set of conditions in the environment in which educational institutions must operate. There is an entirely different thrust to the performance standards that every individual teacher and institution must now achieve.

Operating success will be determined not just by having the best curriculum in tune with technology in place, but also by having a workforce that can and will deliver them to the best of their ability to cope up with pressure of time, and quality of learning.

OUR ROLE IN CHANGING WORLD IN NEW MILLENNIUM

We need to recognize that there is a clear and critical link between nation development and a trained engineering workforce at all levels. From a traditional approach of unilateral teaching, research and scholarship, it has to adjust itself towards bilateral, multidimensional and proactive approach in development of future engineering manpower, which would eventually participate help in development function of industry and economy.

The role of engineering institutes and the people therein must shift from mere routine classroom instructions, to that of catering to the future needs of technological advances and cost effectiveness.

Value addition therefore becomes a paramount concern for all of us engaged in business of transformation of raw student—to an industry acceptable individual, capable of developing further.

An immediate and all out effort is needed in this direction, essentially through the people involved in the entire engineering education system. It is these same people who will be at the helm of affairs delivering the goods to their respective internal and external customers. After all the equipment and technology are the products of human mind and can be made productive and qualitative only through—the people!

Today's millennium has to be characterized by knowledge workers who will play a decisive role in determining competitiveness at all levels. More than the physical assets, engineering human capital of the nation will play a major role. There need therefore to bridge the knowledge gap.

The competitive advantage will thus go to:

- Those who can make best use of the information they have or can find;
- Those who can distribute information and knowledge most freely;
- Those who would be able to deliver the fruits of this knowledge to customers throughout the world.

We are working in a dynamic, competitive environment, wherein increasing global competition and shifting social expectations demand new responses. The total employee involvement concept has therefore become imperative. The focus has to be on *people building*, rather than *people using*, with major aim at making every worker a decision maker concerning his/her own work.

Suggested is a list of the skills and abilities, a Teacher/Trainer/Mentor should have, or he/she should develop in order to be effective in this changed environment:

- The ability to change the way he or she thinks and operates;
- The ability to be creative and learn and transfer knowledge;

- The ability to perform in a team setting;
- The ability to manage change and transition;
- Proficiency in developing global strategic skills and turning ideas into action;
- To operate with high degree of personal integrity and honesty.

CHANGE—WHAT IT MEANS TO INDIA?

India must recognize that the move to a free market and its attendant benefits are not without pain. Further, these changes represent a massive social and economic experiment with no parallels in history. Success in this endeavour will depend on the clarity of goals and the quality of new "ideas and concepts" that underlay the transition process.The globalization effort must start with a clear understanding of long-term goals-or the strategic intent. Do policy makers and the public share a vision of India's future?

Accomplishing the strategic intent of joining a select group of leaders in world education call for visionary leadership, political will and a shared national engineering education agenda. India's potential is not constrained by opportunity or resources but by imagination and will. This is the challenge of transformation in engineering education in India.

As much as the environment outside the organization has changed over the past twenty years, what is happening inside the organization may have changed even more. Management must now exercise its responsibility through a workforce it would not recognize from a generation earlier, using work designs and information technology that simply did not exist, and at a rate of change that could not previously have been conceived. This is the changing workplace. Technologists and engineers must be kept informed of the S & T achievements of the rest of the world through a highly developed technological and technological information system.

The key questions therefore are:

- How to break the barrier of mistrust between both Government bodies and institute Management?

- Will the management of institutes sincerely accept employees as partners and provide them with more autonomy and decision-making opportunity?
- Is participative way of working in Indian environment of "*chalta-hai*" and money-mindedness really feasible for technical education and manpower development?
- How to redesign the activities for Motivating teachers to involve themselves with management?

Advocates on Productivity and Quality have prescribed lot of models in Indian context against the backdrop of LPG era–mostly British and American. Yet the impact is little and the solution to the problem is still a distant dream. Going by current trends, we may not be in a position to equal the Quality and Productivity achieved by leading universities and institutions across the globe, in this decade—but our will to do so may curtail the time span.

Some Issues Related to Engineering Manpower in India

- Paradox—Surplus of Quantitative Manpower and Shortage of Qualitative Manpower;
- Mushroomed growth of Technical education Institutes;
- Surplus engineering graduates in particular branches;
- Ratio of job availability—Less jobs vs. more aspirants;
- Over-utilization of less experienced teachers;
- Under-utilization of potential of more experienced and qualified teachers;
- Improper HRD initiatives, with low emphasis on relevant training component;
- Mismatch of market requirement and offerings;
- "No-how" situation of students rather than required - "Know-how".

FEW REASONS FOR SHORTAGE AND SURPLUS OF TECHNOLOGICAL MANPOWER

India's unusually high definition of engineering manpower demand has increased the number of these people being trained over the years. Since science and technology enjoy top priority in India, it follows that most professional manpower shortages would occur in new technologies. Shortages of qualified manpower are also reported, especially in rural areas.

India continues to experience both surpluses and shortages of professional technological and engineering manpower in several fields of training. Disproportions occur due to:

- the changing demands of industry for technological specialists;
- improper use of available manpower;
- relying on forecasts and statistical staffing data, that may have inflated manpower needs;
- individual enterprise employment practices cause variations;
- pressures to hire more professional cadre than needed at an enterprise are strong;
- reluctance to fire personnel in these categories is high;
- reporting system aggregates large groups of related specialities under single heading.

Points to Ponder

- Statistics on the number of engineers employed in the Indian economy give an inflated impression of the amount of engineering activity going on in India. Such impressions result because we count all persons who have received an engineering degree as engineers, regardless of their employment.
- Employment of diploma/degree engineers outside their fields of specialization or as technicians in engineering positions. Thus, while definite specialist shortages exist in India, the main problem appears to be in the effective planning and use of the vast manpower pool, which, if corrected, would eliminate disproportions currently experienced.

- There is a common practice of organizing new departments, either directly or through re-organization of existing departments. Once a new department has been created, an experienced engineer or technological worker is then promoted to head the department, and new personnel are hired to staff it.
- One can hardly find justification for the fact that we continue to train them in quantities several times higher and that for equivalent volumes of production and introduction of new technology. Compared with developed nations, where fewer designers and researchers are put in place than we do! Is this not simply a waste of precious engineering labour on our part?
- An additional problem, which aggravates shortages of engineers because it leads to their misuse, is a deficit of business and industrial administrators and executives. India has not trained adequate numbers of economists and administrators for industry. Without the economists to participate in economic and planning functions, India has and, is being compelled to use engineers in administrative positions that require relatively less engineering education.
- Analysis of present in Technological manpower and educational policies indicates that, the current requirement is to turn from extensive (e.g., growth in the numbers of workers and increase in investments) to intensive factors (e.g., raising the productivity and improving the organisation of work involving research workers, professors, and students). It will be important for them to keep in mind both the qualitative and quantitative aspects of professional engineering manpower and put these factors in perspective with other appropriate indicators.

Training Component

Training is the link-pin and key element of any HRD initiatives including Quality/Productivity programmes. Of course, the training should be perpetual to bear the improvement of fruit in long term. For qualitative technical manpower, any investment made in training, especially in Quality Improvement, essentially involving Total Employee Involvement, is one of the soundest one. With change, we as trainers of "generation next" have to be ourselves conversant with changing technologies. This will only happen if we are putting in enough training component and certain man-hours.

There exists a wide gap between what is wanted and what we are doing. This needs to be changed if we are really concerned. Everyone is supposed to do things right, always, by way of his job description. These so called programmes would be effective and fruitful, if one and all of us consider improvement at the top of agenda—personally and organizationally. QIP, STTP, MDP and other programmes from relevant bodies at relevant times are being done from so many years. Yet their effectiveness is a question mark. Compared with rate of change of technology, if we see the gap between quantity and quality of training programmes provided to teachers, we have to seriously rethink our strategy and re-engineer the same urgently.

Programme Failures—Why?

- It is called Programme, often held as day or week;
- It is generally aimed and done for lower levels;
- It has an involuntary participation of employees;
- It only creates material remaining confined to file;
- It projects prerogative of few people image;
- It reflects that management wants fast outcome.

This needs to be changed if we are really concerned. These so called programmes would be unnecessary, if one and all considers Quality and Productivity at the top of agenda, personally and organisationally, and accepts it as natural way of doing things right, everywhere, every time. Everyone is supposed to do things right, always, by way of his job description.

SOME PRESCRIPTIONS FOR INDIAN ENGINEERING EDUCATION

- Think Global, Act local–balance to the local environment while integrating with global system;
- Segmentation of industry based Manpower requirement;
- Development of Common minimum programme for diploma, degree and PG;
- Unified syllabus and pedagogy within each segment. Adoption of credit systems;
- Review role of State in engineering education at degree level;
- Establishment of separate technological universities under AICTE umbrella;
- Cross subsidy model to fund government institutes starved of finances;
- Introduce multi entry and exit levels without barriers;
- Redefine work content and thereby teaching load for teachers;
- Strategically channelize from diploma to degree to PG in engineering;
- Plan in terms of courses, curriculum and educational products;
- Understand the global—local balance and constantly adjust it;
- Move from Isolation to Partnership–Identifying and developing key supporting alliances with others;
- Finding, training, and developing employees who are comfortable working in the global framework;
- Learning after Unlearning is the key.

CONCLUSION

Learning organizations are going through a revolutionary phase. It is now a broad outlook that has prompted these organizations to become more proactive than reactive. In doing so things have changed, but not so drastically as is anticipated. Somehow the old habits, methods, procedures, etc. are still not being shed so easily.

The challenge is, therefore, how to create an efficient system, which will liberate not only business and industry from rules and regulations and at the same time would also strengthen the hands of the Government to discharge its social obligations more effectively and efficiently.

The accelerated pace of the change, current and forthcoming—has put lot of concern on three vital areas:

- Performance excellence and Superiority;
- Attention on Value-addition; and
- Customer satisfaction.

—essentially focusing on Productivity, Cost-Profit relation, and Quality, respectively. All the above three areas can be dealt with, and upgraded through proper Human Resource Development (HRD) interventions. We need to address enhancement of quality of existing manpower, to guide and build coming generation, globally competitive and qualitative engineering workforce –*Certainly - Made in India!*

REFERENCES

1. Hess P., and Siciliano, J, *Management–Responsibility for Performance*, International ed., 1996, McGraw Hill, Inc., New York.
2. Schermerhorn, John R. Jr., *Management for Productivity*, 4th ed., John Wiley & Sons, Inc. New York, 1993.
3. Hunger, D. J. and Wheeler T. L., *Strategic Management*, 6th ed., Addison Wesley, Longman Inc, 1998.
4. Crossby, P.B., *Quality Without Tears*, McGraw Hill., New York, 1986.
5. Ramswamy V.S., & Namakumari S. *Strategic Planning - Text and Cases*, First ed, MacMillan India Ltd., New Delhi, 1999.
6. Agrawal,Raj., and Diwan, Parag, *Business Environment*, Excel Books, First ed, New Delhi, 2000.
7. Atmanand., 'Indian Managers for a Global Economy', *Paradigm*, Journal of IMT, Ghaziabad, Vol 1 #1, July 1997.

8. Neelamegham S., 'Managerial Challenges of New Millennium', *Journal of Management Research* FMS, University of Delhi, Vol. 1 #1, Sept-Dec, 2000.

9. Zahir, M.A., and Sachdeva, Y.P, 'Managing in 21st Century–Top Management Challenges', in Management in 21st Century, Ed., Bhagwati Prasad & Sugan Jain., Arihant Publishing House, Jaipur, 1995, pp. 23-36.

10. Gawhane, N. S., Productivity Improvement—Some Issues in Indian Context, National Seminar on Productivity Scenario and Safety in Indian Industry, *Vidarbha Productivity Council*, Jan 4-5,1997.

11. Natrajan, R., 'International and National Prespectives on Technical Education', Keynote Address at CII-AICTE Summit on Academe, Government and Industry—Working Together for Competitive Advantage, Chennai, January 28-29, 2002.

12. Earnest, Joshua., and Jain, K.K, 'Competency Based Technical Education(CBTE)- An Approach for Reform', *Indian Journal of Technical Education,* Vol 26, No.4, Oct-Dec 2003, pp. 17-22.

13. Chanda, Deepak., 'Challenges Ahead for Technical Manpower at National Level', *Indian Journal of Technical Education,* Vol. 27, No. 2, Apr-Jun 2004, pp. 119-120.

11

Planning of Technical Students Migration in Orissa

*Saroj Kumar Patel**

ABSTRACT

It is being observed that there is a growing interest among the students for the technical education due to better job prospects and opportunities. But there was no proportionate growth of technical education facilities in the state of Orissa. The students of Orissa used to migrate to other states for acquiring technical education. To reduce the students migration, few years back the government of Orissa has encouraged the private participation in technical education. In this chapter the growth profile of technical education facilities over the years and the details of students migration are presented. The migration data is analysed zonewise with reference to year of passing. The correlation coefficient between the number of institutes and outmigration is found out. The study is limited to engineering education both at degree and diploma level in the state of Orissa.

Key Words: Degree, Diploma, Engineering Education, Migration, Orissa.

* **NTMIS Nodal Centre for Orissa, National Institute of Technology Rourkela - 769008 (Orissa), Email: skpatel@nitrkl.ac.in**

INTRODUCTION

Technical manpower plays a significant role for the industrial development and economic growth of a country. Therefore, the facilities for technical education which produces technical manpower should grow proportionately with the growth of industries. Prior to independence, the facilities for technical education was inadequate and therefore the supply of technical manpower was low. After independence, keeping in view the anticipated growth of industrial development and diversification, the facilities for technical education have witnessed an enormous expansion. But the rate of growth has been different from state to state. This has led to the migration of students from one state to another in pursuit of technical education. In the recent past, to reduce the students migration the state government has encouraged the private participation in technical education leading to mushroom growth of technical institutions.

In this chapter the trend in growth of technical education facilities in the state of Orissa and that in the level of students migration for technical education to and from other states are studied. The correlation coefficient between the number of institutes and out-migration is found out. Here, the scope of study is limited to engineering education at degree and diploma level only.

GROWTH OF TECHNICAL EDUCATION FACILITIES

The state of Orissa was formed on 1st April, 1936 i.e., about a decade before the independence. Prior to independence, the facility for technical education in the state of Orissa was available only at diploma level. The first diploma level institution i.e., Bhubanananda Orissa School of Engineering, Cuttack was established in the year 1923. The first degree level institution i.e., University College of Engineering, Burla started in the year 1956. These institutions initially provided education in three basic disciplines of Civil, Mechanical and Electrical Engineering. When Regional Engineering Colleges were established all over India, one such college was established at Rourkela in 1961. Slowly, new technical institutions were added over the years. In the beginning, there were only government institutions. Table—11.1 presents the growth profile of engineering institutions of Orissa both at degree and diploma level since independence with a break up of government and private institutions. This is also graphically shown in Figures 11.1 and 11.2 for engineering degree and diploma institutions respectively.

Table—11.1 Growth of engineering institutions in Orissa

Year of Passing	Number of Engineering Institutions					
	Government		Private		Total	
	Degree	Diploma	Degree	Diploma	Degree	Diploma
1947		1				1
1952		1				1
1957		1				1
1962	1	4			1	4
1967	2	5			2	5
1972	3	6			3	6
1977	3	6			3	6
1982	3	7			3	7
1987	5	10		3	5	13
1992	5	11	1	4	6	15
1997	5	11	1	7	6	18
1998	6	12	1	8	7	20
1999	7	12	1	8	8	20
2000	7	13	3	10	10	23
2001	7	13	13	12	20	25
2002	6	13	13	12	19	25
2003	6	13	22	13	28	26
2004	6	13	22	13	28	26
2005	6	13	29	13	35	26
2006	7	13	29	14	36	27
2007	7	13	29	14	36	27
2008	7	13	34	14	41	27

Till 80's, the pace of expansion of engineering education facilities was very slow and limited to only government institutions as shown in Table 11.1. Till the year 1982 the students used to pass out from only 3 engineering colleges and 7 diploma schools. All these were government institutions. The number of institutions remained almost stagnated for a decade before that. In the next decade, the government encouraged private management for starting engineering institutions. The private institutions opened first at diploma level. During the next one decade i.e., till the year 1992 there was only 1 degree and 4 diploma level private institutions. During this decade 2 degree and 4 diploma institutions were also added by the Government. The degree engineers passed out from 3 private engineering colleges in the year 2000 whereas this figure rose significantly to 13 in the year 2001. The growth of private engineering colleges has taken place at a high rate in the subsequent years also. In the current year, admission has been taken in 34 private degree institutions who will pass out in the year 2008. Thus, the number of new institutions opened up in the current decade is maximum at degree level and it is in the private sector. At diploma level only four more new private institutions have started in the current decade. There has been no new government institution either at degree or diploma level producing technical manpower since the year 2000. Now the number of private institutions is about five times that of government institutions at degree level where as it is almost same at diploma level. This significant growth of engineering institutions has been possible mainly due to the private participation in engineering education.

MIGRATION OF STUDENTS

Introduction

Some of the students migrate to other states to pursue technical education due to many reasons like insufficient number of technical institutions, non-availability of seats in the preferred disciplines, nonavailability of required infrastructure, better reputation of technical institutions of other states, higher fee structure and expenses in home state, government policies, reservation of seats in NITs of other states, relaxation in minimum qualifying marks in private institutes under management quota etc.

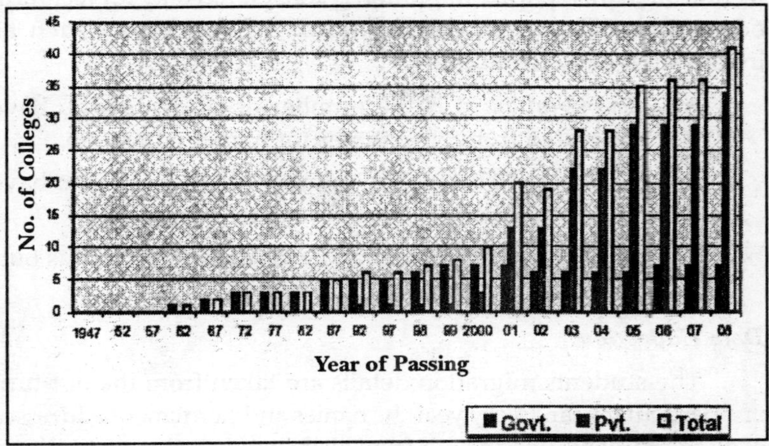

Fig. 11.1: Growth of engineering colleges in Orissa

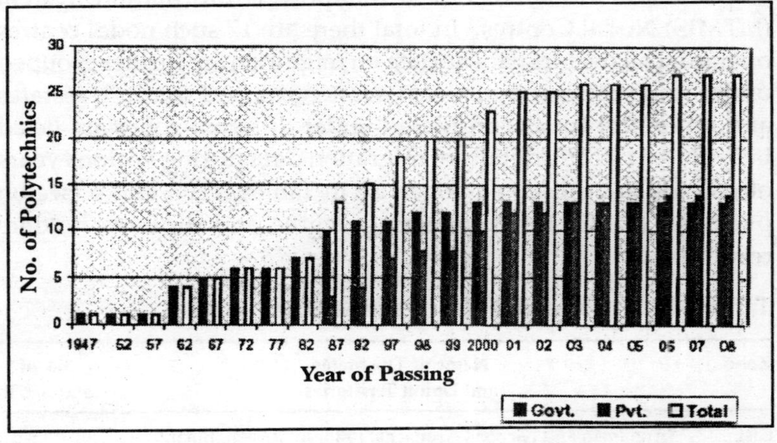

Fig. 11.2: Growth of polytechnics in Orissa

Types of Migration

Migration is defined as the number of students taking admission for higher education in states other than their home states. The higher education can be both technical and non-technical. In this chapter migration is considered only for technical education. The migration is mainly of two types such as inmigration and out-migration:

- *In-migration:* It is the number of students who have migrated from other states for higher education;
- *Out-migration:* It is the number of students who have migrated to other states for higher education;
- *Net-migration:* It is defined as in-migration minus out-migration.

Data Collection

The students migration details are taken from the out-turn of a particular year. Every year the names and permanent addresses of all the students passing out from all the engineering institutions, both degree and diploma, of a particular state are collected by the respective National Technical Manpower Information System (NTMIS) Nodal Centres.[1] In total there are 17 such nodal centres operating all over India. The data on migration are further grouped under four main zones i.e., east, west, north and south. The states and union territories considered under different zones are listed in Table—11.2. The details of migration data during various years of passing are presented zonewise in Tables/111.3 and 4 (see on page 144 & 145) for engineering degree and diploma holders respectively.

Table—11.2 Zonewise list of states/UTs

Zone	Name of The States and Union Territories	No. of States/UTs
East	Andaman and Nicober, Arunachal Pradesh, Assam, Bihar, Jharkhand, Manipur, Meghalaya, Mizoram, Nagaland, Orissa, Sikkim, Tripura, West Bengal	13
West	Chhattisgarh, Dadar and Nagar Haveli, Goa, Daman and Diu, Gujarat, Madhya Pradesh, Maharashtra	7
North	Chandigarh, Delhi, Haryana, Himachal Pradesh, Jammu and Kashmir, Punjab, Rajasthan, Uttaranchal, Uttar Pradesh	9
South	Andhra Pradesh, Karnataka, Kerala, Lakhadeep, Pondicherry, Tamil Nadu	6

Correlation Coefficient

The correlation coefficient r between two variables x and y is given as:

$$r = \frac{n\sum xy - \sum x \sum y}{\sqrt{\left\{n\left(\sum x^2\right) - \left(\sum x\right)^2\right\}\left\{n\sum y^2 - \left(\sum y\right)^2\right\}}}$$

where n is number of data sets.[2] Let x be the number of institutes from which the students pass out in a particular year and y be the number of students migrated to other states and pass out in the same year. r value is calculated separately for degree and diploma courses to find out the effect of number of institutes on out-migration.

RESULTS AND DISCUSSION

Migration for Degree Holders

Table—11.3 shows that for engineering degree holders the in-migration is always more than out-migration except for those who passed out in the years 1984 and 1985. From this it may be concluded that the state of Orissa has remained most of the time self-sufficient for engineering education at degree level. The in-migration is maximum for the batches 1995 and 1996 whereas the out-migration is maximum for the 2000 passed out batch. After 1996, the in-migration has remained more or less constant whereas the out-migration has steadily increased. This indicates that more and more students of Orissa are migrating to other states for engineering education at degree level. The trend of net migration has been up and down as shown in Figure 11.3. The trend is declining during 1996 and 2000. Looking at this trend with an objective of reducing out-migration and thereby increasing net-migration the Government of Orissa has encouraged private management in technical education. Therefore large number of new private engineering colleges have started in the recent years. The net-migration has again increased in the year 2001 which may be due to addition of 10 new private engineering colleges in that year. The migration data which will be collected from 2002 batch onwards would give a better picture on the effect of number of institutes on students migration.

Table—11.3 Zone-wise migration of engineering degree holders

Year of Passing	EAST			WEST			NORTH			SOUTH			TOTAL		
	IN	OUT	NET	IN	OUT	NET	IN	OUT	NET	IN	OUT	NET	IN	OUT	NET
1982	36	42	-6	14	7	7	18	18	0	19	16	3	87	83	4
1983	24	33	-9	16	4	12	22	10	12	28	26	2	90	73	17
1984	20	52	-32	9	7	2	16	21	-5	11	6	5	56	86	-30
1985	28	37	-9	10	5	5	26	20	6	13	21	-8	77	83	-6
1988	71	28	43	25	3	22	40	9	31	36	7	29	172	47	125
1993	61	25	36	19	5	14	43	12	31	34	5	29	157	47	110
1994	68	24	44	17	4	13	45	12	33	32	5	27	162	45	117
1995	71	28	43	25	5	20	58	11	47	57	7	50	211	51	160
1996	69	27	42	28	8	20	56	10	46	58	6	52	211	51	160
1997	58	41	17	23	17	6	62	19	43	37	26	11	180	103	77
1998	69	31	38	24	10	14	41	12	29	37	8	29	171	61	110
1999	70	28	42	20	22	-2	52	26	26	51	53	-2	193	129	64
2000	70	55	15	17	16	1	51	25	26	35	58	-23	173	154	19
2001	120	22	98	28	31	-3	69	31	38	58	55	3	275	139	136
TOTAL	**835**	**473**	**362**	**275**	**144**	**131**	**599**	**236**	**363**	**506**	**299**	**207**	**2215**	**1152**	**1063**

IN = In-migration, OUT = Out-migration, NET = Net-migration = IN – OUT

Table—11.4 Zonewise migration of engineering diploma holders

Year of Passing	EAST			WEST			NORTH			SOUTH			TOTAL		
	IN	OUT	NET	IN	OUT	NET	IN	OUT	NET	IN	OUT	NET	IN	OUT	NET
1982	6	0	6	0	0	0	1	0	1	1	2	-1	8	2	6
1983	14	4	10	0	1	-1	1	1	0	3	2	1	18	8	10
1984	5	4	1	0	0	0	2	2	0	0	2	-2	7	8	-1
1985	7	2	5	1	3	-2	2	6	-4	1	0	1	11	11	0
1988	28	2	26	4	0	4	11	0	11	1	1	0	44	3	41
1993	43	2	41	0	0	0	3	1	2	16	0	16	62	3	59
1994	12	2	10	0	1	-1	4	0	4	4	1	3	20	4	16
1995	18	2	16	3	1	2	2	1	1	3	2	1	26	6	20
1996	21	4	17	2	1	1	2		2	1	1	0	26	6	20
1997	13	5	8	0	1	-1	3	1	2	3	3	0	19	10	9
1998	16	13	3	1	7	-6	0	6	-6	2	6	-4	19	32	-13
1999	19	10	9	0	3	-3	1	3	-2	6	3	3	26	19	7
2000	20	12	8	0	3	-3	0	4	-4	3	8	-5	23	27	-4
2001	10	4	6	0	3	-3	2	0	2	2	25	-23	14	32	-18
TOTAL	**232**	**66**	**166**	**11**	**24**	**-13**	**34**	**25**	**9**	**46**	**56**	**-10**	**323**	**139**	**152**

IN = In-migration, OUT = Out-migration, NET = Net-migration = IN – OUT

As shown in Table—11.3 among the zones the total in-migration from the neighbouring states of East zone is maximum and whereas it is minimum from the West zone. Similarly the total out-migration is also maximum and minimum for the East and West zones respectively. This shows that the distance between the native place and the institution plays a major role in deciding the state for migration.

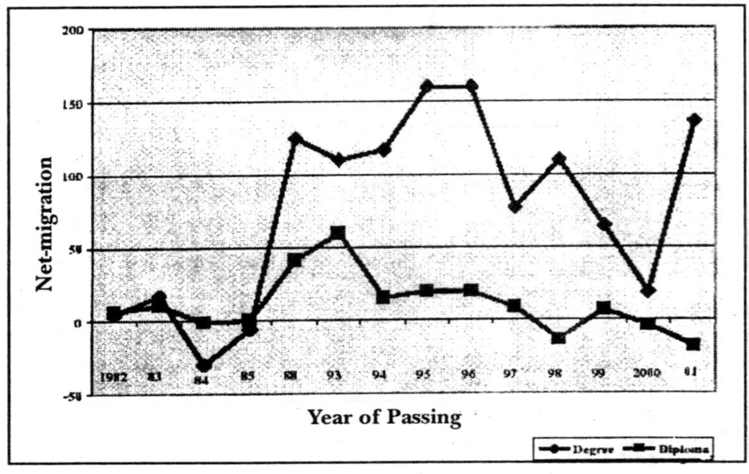

Fig. 11.3: Net-migration Trend

Correlation Coefficient for Degree Courses

The correlation coefficient r between the number of engineering degree colleges and students migrating to other state is found to be 0.6503 as illustrated in Table—11.5. This indicates that there is a positive relationship. The positive value of r shows that as the number of colleges increases, the out-migration also increases. Thus, in the recent years although new private colleges have started, the objective of reducing out-migration has not been fulfilled.

Table —11.5 Correlation coefficient for degree courses

Sl.	Year of Passing	No. of Colleges, x	Out-migration, y	x^2	y^2	xy
1.	1993	6	47	36	2209	282
2.	1994	6	45	36	2025	270
3.	1995	6	51	36	2601	306
4.	1996	6	51	36	2601	306
5.	1997	6	103	36	10609	618
6.	1998	7	61	49	3721	427
7.	1999	8	129	64	16641	1032
8.	2000	10	154	100	23716	1540
9.	2001	20	139	400	19321	2780
	TOTAL	75	780	793	83444	7561

$r = 0.6503$

Migration for Diploma Holders

Table 11.4 shows that the in-migration is maximum for the passed out batch of 1993 whereas the outmigration is maximum for the passed out batches of 1998 and 2001. Over the years the in-migration is steadily declining whereas the out-migration is showing upward trend. Consequently, the net-migration is declining. The net-migration is positive for engineering diploma holders till 1997 batch except for 1984 batch as illustrated in Figure 11.3. After the batch of 1997, it is remaining almost negative. From this it may be concluded that the state of Orissa has remained self-sufficient for engineering education at diploma level till the passed out batch of 1997. The educational facilities is now inadequate since 1998 batch as outmigration is more than the in-migration although number of polytechnics have increased from 20 to 25 during the period 1998-2001. In spite of this by the year 2008 the students will pass out from only 2 more polytechnics. Thus, the growth of diploma level institutions is not sufficient in view of the recent trend in student migration.

As shown in Table—11.4 the trend of migration with respect to zones is same as that observed in case of degree holders, i.e. both in- and out-migration are maximum and minimum for East and West zones respectively.

Correlation Coefficient for Diploma Courses

As illustrated in Table—11.6, the correlation coefficient *r* between the number of polytechnics and students migrating to other state is found to be 0.9193. This indicates that the relationship is very strong. Since *r* value is positive, as the number of polytechnics increases, the out-migration also increases. Even if new polytechnics have started, there is no reduction on out-migration.

Table—11.6 Correlation coefficient for diploma courses

Sl.	Year of Passing	No. of Polytechnics, x	Out-migration, y	x^2	y^2	xy
1.	1993	15	3	225	9	45
2.	1994	15	4	225	16	60
3.	1995	15	6	225	36	90
4.	1996	15	6	225	36	90
5.	1997	18	10	324	100	180
6.	1998	20	32	400	1024	640
7.	1999	20	19	400	361	380
8.	2000	23	27	529	729	621
9.	2001	25	32	625	1024	800
	TOTAL	**166**	**139**	**3178**	**3335**	**2906**

$r = 0.9193$

CONCLUSION

The following conclusion may be summarised after the analysis of growth profile of technical educational facilities and trend in students migration:

1. The growth of polytechnics in Orissa is at steady rate whereas that for engineering colleges was initially slow and then at faster rate in recent years due to private participation;
2. The growth of diploma level institutions is not sufficient in view of the recent trend in student migration whereas the recent growth in number of degree level institutions has made the state self-sufficient;

among the engineers. Rapid industrial growth and adoption of sophisticated technology by the appropriate type of technical manpower at all levels. This chapter presents national industrial growth, globalization, technical education system, future prospects of engineering education and accordingly technical manpower planning in India.

INTRODUCTION

These days a situation is observed where more and more technical graduates are going without jobs and at the same time more and more technical institutions are getting permission to start and the admission strength in the existing institution is also being increased.

This unplanned and unsustainable growth in Technical manpower output is definitely going to be a big burden to the government and probable danger to the society. If the circumstances force these unemployed professional graduates resort to high-tech anti-social activities due to frustration and disappointment. Hence it is imperative that the growth of number of technical institutions and selection of new discipline should be appropriately planned and sternly controlled to specific needs of the country.

STATUS OF INDIAN TECHNICAL SYSTEM

The rapid developments in the field of science and technology in the last three decades have radically transformed the socio-economic environment in the nations across the world. The unprecedented growth in the technologies and their applications has lead to tremendous increase in complexities in the industrial scenario and absolute knowledge by itself alone cannot provide for solutions to the problems of the technologically revolutionized era.

Moreover, the rapidly transforming and highly competitive global scenario characterized by radical technological advancements also calls for fostering of never and more efficient methods for solving problems of society despite serious handicaps of means and resources, the country has fostered a very large system of education in the last five decades and has created vast scientific and technological human resources capabilities.

Prior to independence the growth of institution of higher education in India was very slow with limited infrastructure and human resource capabilities. After independence, major efforts have been made to create wide base of infrastructure for higher education in general and technical education in particular including research laborites covering a board spectrum of disciplines and capabilities.

The technical education system has made significant progress in the last three decades through fostering of the state of the art research and post graduate programmes.

With regard to technical education institutions, there were only 38 institutions at degree level and 53 institutions at diploma level with an annual intake of about 2950 and 3650 students respectively at the time of independence. These have now grown to approximately 1058 technical institutes at degree level and 1231 institutes at diploma level in the year 2001 with annual intake of about 2,71,719 and 2,20,947 students respectively since early 1990's due to liberalization policies of the government, the Indian economy has witnessed widespread economic reforms leading to entry of many global players in the Indian market thereby exposing the Indian entrepreneurs to the global competition.

The opening up of Indian economy has created a vibrant industrial scene and the Indian industry is faced with unprecedented challenges from across the globe from which it was higher to protected in make of the still global competition faced by the world economy, the technical education system is faced with providing human resources capable of leading the nation's objectives of growth and sustainability by harnessing science and technology capabilities.

The radical progress of industrialization, rapid technological developments and adoption of sophisticated technology by industries in the country has resulted in a mismatch between the requirements of industries and product of technical education system. Moreover, there has been an unrestrained and exponential growth and expansion of technical education system in India and thus the quality of technical education in the country has suffered.

Thus the technical education system to remain competitive in the current rapidly changing global scenario, there is no choice but to improve the quality of technical education system, to develop the human resources capable of meeting the country's objective of sustained growth and self reliance in the fiercely competitive global environment.

FUTURE PROSPECTS OF ENGINEERING EDUCATION IN INDIA

An engineering institution can play an important role in developing certain qualities in students. If they themselves are outing as professional, students are bound to have entrepreneurial qualities. Since the Indian economy is opening up and offering fresh avenues to the engineers need for revising the present management of science and technology, which has become inevitable. It has become very necessary to inculcate entrepreneurial quality in students was to study for getting a job but now they will have to change such stereotype thinking, if they want to forge ahead in life. In India efforts have been made to build technical human resources that are capable of meeting future challenges. Here engineers have proved to be rather poor entrepreneurs.

Engineering education lacks creativity and training to meet the future challenges. To overcome this it is become necessary to introduce entrepreneurial avenues as an integral part of engineering education, this will be helpful to transform engineers from job seekers to job creators. Thus the objective of technical education is to inculcate the importance of entrepreneurship upon the engineering student himself and national development, objectives can be achieved through well-planned programmes, where more emphasis will be on individual development, so that the students are able to evaluate their competencies and capabilities in a realistic manner:

1. The curriculum should be set taking into consideration the requirements of entrepreneurship development in students;
2. Separate courses on entrepreneurship with implant training can be started in engineering education;

3. Teaching entrepreneurship should focus more learning and development rather than only teaching;

4. Apart from formal classroom teaching and group training, the individual counseling is also required to make really successful in engineering education;

5. Physical and emotional involvement of the students in workshop practice sense of achievement by allowing conversion of creative ides into tangible models, rewarding the better modals, sense of commitment by active involvement of teachers and work culture are the basic attributes of entrepreneurship. Their fundamentals are needed to be cultivated in technical institution;

6. The faculty needs to impart systematic and adequate training to teach entrepreneurship. This training may be imparted to undergo an intensive field practice so as to leave an indelible imprint his mind. They may be oriented as entrepreneurship and project appraisal in technical education environment;

7. Industry institute interaction needs to be strengthened on the job training planning industrial visits, industry oriented projects work and simulation exercises will add to practical knowledge of student/technocrat. Technical institutions to take the responsibility to integrate academic work with industrial experience in co-operation with industry.

Simultaneously industry should commit itself to work for this integration. Till today the industry has stayed out of the main stream of the education progress and assigned itself two roles as follows:

1. Critic of engineering education system;

2. Using the products whatever are present it.

It is a right time for industry to change over the new role of partnership in education and bridge the gap between teaching institute and industry. The theoretical experience of the institutions coupled with practical experience institutions coupled with practical experience of industry could produce a lot of interesting results and help to promote the right industrial culture capable of competing with the global standards.

It is specific to mention that realizing the need for bringing about proper interaction between the academics and industry. The success of the concept in the form of Silicon Valley providing opportunities for growth of computer industries in the united state has triggered establishment of similar setups in various developed countries around the world. In India, the emergence of new pool of technical entrepreneurs has the potential to become a force in accelerating the pace of industrialization.

The infusion of technology in the industry by them will go a long away creating a new technological culture in our country and make indigenous products competitive in the market.

CONCLUSION

1. In technical engineering education emphasis is to be given on a self-employment as career, in addition to development of technical capabilities.
2. Due to globalization and entry of multinationals in India the upcoming projects should be with new ideas and aim of constant upgradation in product/service, as per global standards for its sustainability in the competition with this philosophy. There is wide scope for technocrat in entrepreneurial field.
3. The language of an engineer cum entrepreneur is to be thought and developed around five alphabets *TCQMP*

T	—	Time consciousness
C	—	Cost consciousness
Q	—	Quality consciousness
M	—	Money consciousness
P	—	Profit consciousness

In today's society it is the technology that drives the economy, since engineers creates the stuff they are the real masters of the society. Engineers cum entrepreneurs should not forget that technology to be adopted in new ventures should be omnipotent, omnipresent and Omni euphoric for its sustainability.

REFERENCES

1. R.Bhaskaran,"*Technical Education and Global Competition*", The Indian Journal of Technical Education Vol. 19, No. 3.
2. Kumar, Anil and Praveen Kumar, *Prospects of Engineering Education and Employment in India,* The Indian Journal of Technical Education, Vol. 26, No. 1.
3. Chaturvedi, Pradeep, *Engineering and Technical Education in India,* 1st ed., Concept Publishing Company, New Delhi, 2003.
4. Palit, S.K., *The Development of Engineering and Technical Education in India,* Global Journal of Engineering Education, Vol. 2, No. 5.

13

Technical Education in Kerala
Issues and Concerns

*S. Sunitha**
*Malathy Duraisamy***

ABSTRACT

Technical education system has a very significant role in the process of economic and technological development of a nation. It helps in producing high quality manpower needed for the key sectors of the economy. Technical education in India is a matter of great concern to policy makers and stakeholders. India has the second largest pool of scientific and technical manpower in the world. But there exist interstate disparities in technical education. Moreover education is predominantly a state subject. Hence it would be valuable to examine the issues in technical education in the state level. This chapter makes an attempt to address some issues in technical education in Kerala, which has the distinction of being the most literate state in the country. The impressive Human Development Index of Kerala as comparable to developed countries like US has attracted interest across the globe. The state has outstripped the rest of the nation in several socio-economic indices like health, education, women's status etc. and often treated as the Kerala

* **Research Scholar, Department of Humanities and Social Sciences, Indian Institute of Technology, Madras, Chennai-600036, TN, India, Email: ssunitanair@yahoo.com**

** **Professor in Economics, Department of Humanities and Social Sciences, Indian Institute of Technology, Madras, Chennai-600036, TN, India, Email: mdurai@iitm.ac.in**

model for the rest of the states in India and also for the other developing countries. Available evidence indicates that the state has comparative advantage in terms of strategic location, worldwide connectivity, rich resources and large pool of skilled manpower. However there seems to be a sluggish growth in the state's industrial sector due to low quality of higher education, weak infrastructure etc. This chapter examines the structure and growth of higher technical education in Kerala and also tries to explore the issues such as the role of private and the government sectors in providing technical education. This chapter also considers the state's funding to technical education as well as a comparison of select quality indices across the educational institutes that provide engineering degree. Secondary data from various sources are used for the purpose.

Key Words: Technical Education, Kerala, Private, Government, Budgetary resources, Quality.

INTRODUCTION

The national stock of human capital and its rate of increase are critical to a country's level and rate of economic development, primarily because human capital is the most important determinant of a country's ability to produce and adopt technological innovations. Mounting evidence shows that technical and vocational education are vital to accelerated growth and that work force education is a significant determinant of productivity. This chapter discusses the role of technical education in the state of Kerala.

Indian Higher Education

India has one of the largest systems of higher education in the world with over 260 universities, 10000 colleges and 7.5 million students and teachers or knowledge workers (Neelakanth.A.Kalyani)[12]. Technical education forms one of the major components of the tertiary education system in India. India has the second largest pool of scientific and technical manpower in the world. But there is widespread disparity in the strength of technical manpower across the nation. A study of technical education in Kerala would be a valuable exercise considering that the state has several achievements to its credit. It is the most literate state in the country. The literacy rate of the state in the year 2001 is 91 per cent. It is also the first state to fulfill the constitutional mandate of providing universal, free, primary education to all the children up to the age of fourteen years. However Kerala's performance in the field of higher education especially in technical education is far behind several other states. The spectacle of thousands of candidates from Kerala seeking admission to Engineering and other professional courses in neighbouring states every year has become a regular phenomenon. It is indeed a desperate and costly hunt for higher technical professional education. (Kerala Calling, January 2004)[5]

ISSUES IN THE PRESENT STUDY

This chapter addresses the issues like the trend and growth of technical education and the relative role of government and the private sector in providing technical education. *Section 1* discusses the growth of engineering colleges categorized by type of management, over a period of time and intake of students into these institutions. Using the available data, the growth of polytechnics that impart diploma in engineering is also examined in *Section 2*. An exploration into the state's budgetary allocation to technical education is presented in *Section 3*. In *Section 4* we have tried to compare the select quality indicators across the engineering colleges in Kerala.

1. Growth of Engineering Colleges in Kerala

The growth of technical education in Kerala is studied here in terms of the indicators like the number and growth of institutions that impart degree and diploma in engineering over a period of time and student intake into these institutions. The data on these aspects are gathered from the Handbook of Professional Education (HOPE)[6] and the Careers Professional Excellence 2004[14]. The state of Kerala had only one institution imparting technical education in 1939. The number of engineering colleges remained more or less stagnant till 1980. A sudden surge in the number of institutions can be seen after 2000, when the establishment of self-financing institutions was sanctioned in the state. In the years 2001 and 2002, 13 and 27 private non-aided self-financing colleges sprang up in Kerala. At present there are 76 engineering colleges out of which 12 are government or government aided that come under the control of Directorate of Technical Education (DOTE), 45 private non-aided self-financing colleges and 19 colleges that come under some cooperative management control (such as the IHRD, CAPE, LBS, KSRTC). The three managements are mainly distinguished on the basis of the fees structure. Government colleges are characterized by low fee structure as against the private self-financing colleges those charge higher fees in spite of huge capitation fees. The third category of others those work under cooperative management charge comparatively lesser fees than the private self-financing institutes. The engineering education in the state has entered a very challenging phase since the year 2000.

It would be interesting to look at the engineering institutions by management in order to study the emerging role of private sector in technical education. Unaided self-financing engineering colleges in the private sector have entered the scene in a big way in the state. The number of engineering colleges and their growth over a period of time are represented in the figures 13.1: and 13.2: respectively.

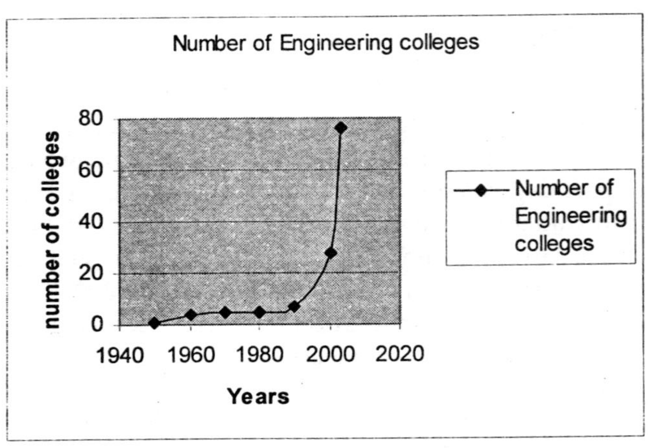

Fig. 13.1

Source: **Handbook of professional education (HOPE)[6]**

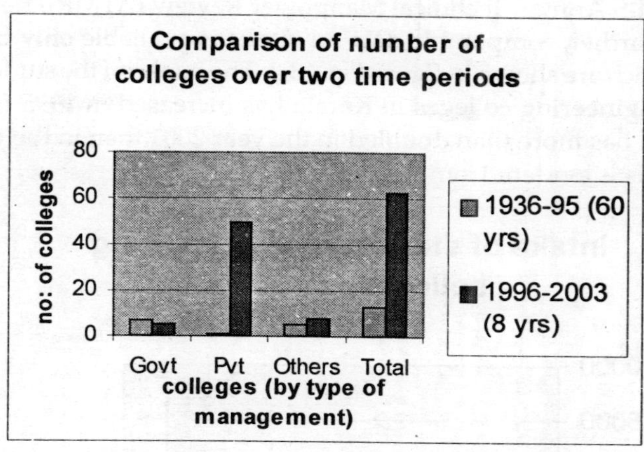

Fig. 13.2

***Source:* Careers professional excellence 2004[14]**

The Fig.13.1 shows that the number of engineering colleges in Kerala has steeply increased from the year 1996. In the Fig. 13.2 we have shown the comparison between the increase in number of engineering colleges by type of management over two time periods namely from 1936-1995 (i.e. over a 60-year time period) and from the time period 1996-2003 (i.e. over 8-year period). The figure shows that the time period 1996-2003 shows a large influx of new engineering colleges in the state and out of these; new colleges which fall under the category of private unaided self-financing colleges. This shows that unaided self-financing private sector has a major role in the state's technical education in the recent years.

Another indicator of the growth of technical education in the state is the intake of students into these institutions. As the data on the intake by the type of management-wise is not available, intake into all the engineering degree institutions is taken into account.

The data on the intake of students into these engineering colleges in Kerala from the time period 1991 to 2001 are taken from the NTMIS Annual Technical Manpower Review (ATMR), Kerala 2003[11]. Further, comparable data on intake is available only from 1991, which are shown in figure Fig. 13.3: The intake of the students in the engineering colleges in Kerala has increased in 1995 from 1991 and has more than doubled in the year 2001 than in the year 1995. This is evident from the Fig. 13.3.

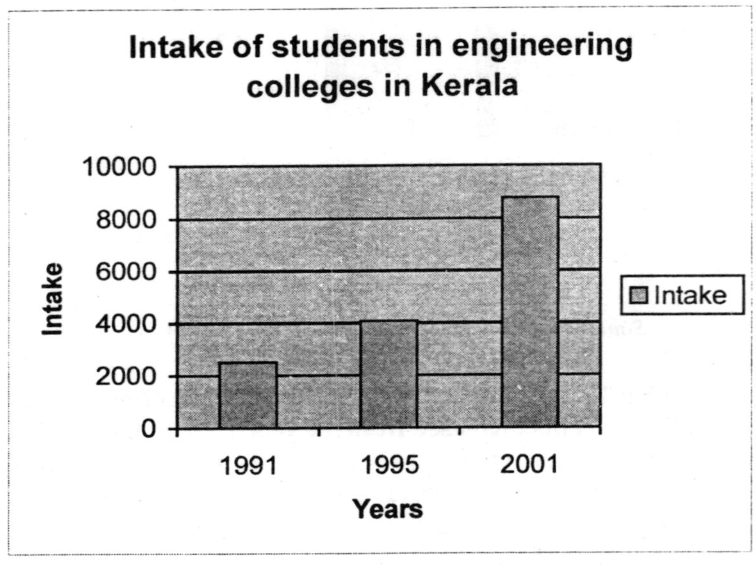

Fig. 13.3

Source: **Annual Technical Manpower Review (ATMR), Kerala 2003[11]**

The average annual growth rate of intake of students into the engineering colleges for the 1991-95 is 15.6 per cent and 1995-2001 is 19.2 per cent. That is the growth rate of intake of students into these institutions is showing an increasing trend. The above analysis shows that there has been a phenomenal growth of engineering colleges and student intake especially after 1995.

2. Growth of Polytechnics in Kerala

Let us now have a look at the data on polytechnic institutions, an important element of technical education that provide diploma in engineering. The study depends on the data from the Annual

Technical Manpower Review (ATMR) Kerala, 2003[11], a database prepared by the National Technical Manpower Information System (NTMIS).

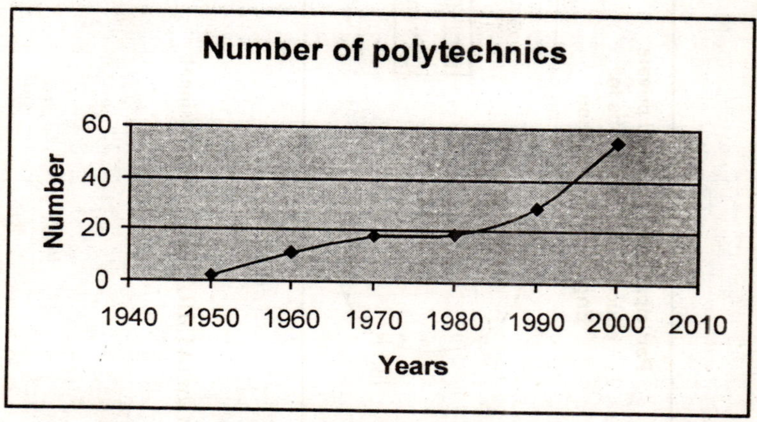

Fig. 13.4

Source: **Annual Technical Manpower Review (ATMR), Kerala 2003[11]**

It can be seen from the Fig. 13.4 that the number of polytechnic institutes from the time period 1950-2000 has increased steadily. The comparison between the participation of the government and the private sectors in technical education is shown in the figures Fig. 13.5: and 13.6 respectively.

Out of 56 polytechnics in the state in the year 2001, 49 are government institutions; and remaining 7 are self-financing institutes. But in the case of engineering colleges, out of the 76 colleges in the year 2003, only 12 are government and the rest 54 are self-financing unaided private colleges.

Thus the private self-financing sector has a dominant role in engineering degree colleges while the share of government is more in the case of diploma institutions. We will now proceed to examine the state's expenditure on technical education.

3. Budgetary Resources for Technical Education

The expansion and growth of the educational sector depends crucially, on the input of financial resources into the system. The

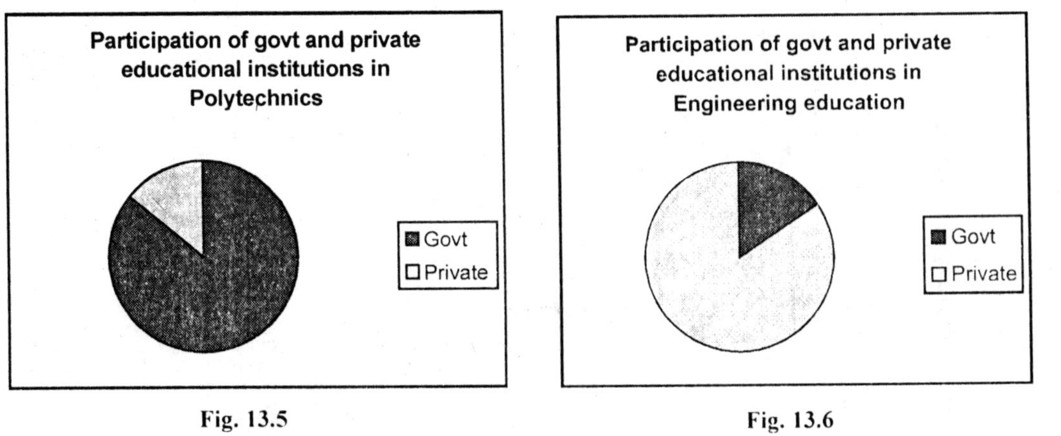

Fig. 13.5

Fig. 13.6

Source: Annual Technical Manpower Review (ATMR)[11], careers professional

sources of finance for education is not to be restricted to government alone, but households, corporation and other NGOs etc participate in investing in education. But the role of government still remains more important. Education is a quasi-public good with substantial spillover benefits. Hence state's support appears warranted. Here, we have tried to compare state's budgetary allocation to technical education in Kerala with other South Indian states. The data is available only up to the year 1993-1994. Based on the data on budgetary resource allocation for technical education we examine the trends in public spending during the time and the share of technical education funding to total education budget and state's SDP. The data are shown in the Table—13.1 (see on page 166).

From the table it is clear that Kerala spends more than 4 per cent of its educational budget on technical education in the year 1993-1994. During the period 1980-81 to 1993-94, the state has received above 4 per cent throughout the period. Kerala tops the other states in this respect followed by Tamilnadu 3 per cent, and Andhra Pradesh and Karnataka respectively. The table shows that during the period 1980 to1994, public expenditure on technical education to the total expenditure on education has increased in Kerala.

As a percentage of State's Domestic Product (SDP), Kerala state is spending 0.25 per cent of SDP on technical education in 1993-94. This is again way above the ratio of technical education expenditure to SDP in other states. The table shows that Kerala's expenditure on technical education has been consistently increasing whereas it has been falling in all the rest of the South Indian states where technical education is far developed.

The state spends 4.32 per cent of total education expenditure on technical education and 0.25 per cent of SDP share reflects on technical education. Across the other south Indian states, Kerala leads in the share of technical education funding to the total education spending in the period throughout the period.

Unfortunately available data on budgetary allocation to technical education is shown only up to the period of 1994, whereas phenomenal increase in the number of technical education institutions has taken place only after 1996. However a more recent evaluation of the state's funding on technical education is required.

Table—13.1 Public expenditure on technical education in relation to total education expenditure and SDP by States, 1980-81 to 1993-94

States	1980-81			1990-91			1993-94			
	Technical Education Expenditure (in Rs. Lakhs)	% of Total Education Expenditure	% of SDP	Technical Education Expenditure (in Rs. Lakhs)	% of Total Education Expenditure	% of SDP	Technical Education Expenditure (in Rs. Lakhs)	% of Total Education Expenditure	% of SDP	Growth Rate (1980-84)
Kerala	890	4.22	0.23	3106 (1342)	4.08	0.26	4888 (1584)	4.32	0.25	13.09 (4.43)
Karnataka	535	3.16	0.1	2226 (987)	2.85	0.11	3579 (1190)	2.54	0.11	14.62 (6.15)
Andhra Pradesh	698	3.08	0.09	2805 (106)	2.84	0.09	4507 (1222)	2.71	0.09	14.35 (4.31)
Tamilnadu	896	3.81	0.12	4302 (1931)	3.41	0.16	5585 (1771)	3.15	0.12	14.08 (5.24)

Notes: Figures in parentheses denote expenditure at constant (1980-1981) prices

Source: Duraisamy M., 2000[8]

It is important to note that the increase in demand for technical education as suggested by the student intake figure seems to be catered to more by the private self-financing engineering degree colleges in the state in the recent years. The responsibility of providing technical education seems to have shifted from the government to the private sector. The private self-financing as is well known is causing a heavy burden of expenditure on the households. This is a matter of concern. A noteworthy finding is the state has maintained its expenditure on technical education throughout the period 1980-1994. The recent trends need to be examined.

The research questions here are to find out whether the increased government spending in technical education has been effectively utilized. Also enough concern should be given to decide whether public funding should be raised more, or the costs of education should be borne by the private beneficiaries of education. It is very important to discuss about whether Government colleges in the state or do the unaided self-financing ones in the private sector should be given the major role in imparting technical education. This can be thought about only if the present performance of these private institutions in comparison with that of the government colleges are considered. This can be viewed by looking at the select quality indicators of technical education institutions in the state.

4. *Quality of Engineering Education in Kerala*

The quality aspects across the engineering colleges in the year 2003 have been studied based on the estimates taken from the, Handbook of Professional Education for Engineering College Selection(HOPE[6], Kerala. The various parameters to capture the quality of education are the *faculty adequacy ratio, faculty student ratio, doctorate percentage* of the faculty, *computer to student ratio* and *library book ratios* and the recreational *facilities* of the institution. *Faculty adequacy ratio* is defined as number of faculty per branch per batch of students in the college. *Faculty student ratio* is the number of faculty per student expressed as a percentage. *Doctorate percentage* is the percentage of the teaching staff that has doctorate degrees. *Computer to student ratio* indicates the ratio of the number of computers in the college to the number of students. *Recreational*

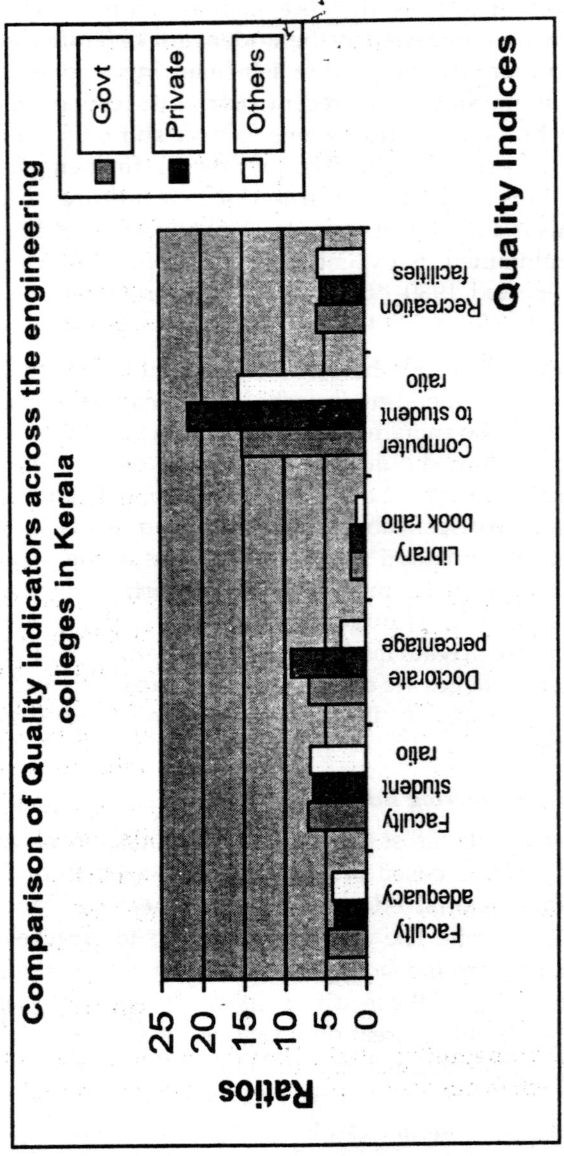

Fig. 13.7

Source: Handbook of Professional Education(HOPE) 2004[6]

facilities was given points on a ten-point scale based on the sports facilities, auditoriums and extra-curricular activities of the students (NSS, IEEE, ISTE, Student clubs, Cultural festivals). They estimated ratios for various parameters.

Comparison of quality indicates across the colleges categorised by management type in shown in the figure 13.7 on page 168).

Government colleges lead in the faculty adequacy ratio, faculty student ratio and library book ratio, recreational facilities. Of these, apart from the availability and accessibility of computers to students, government colleges rank first in all the other variables followed by self-financing unaided private colleges and then by other colleges, which are under cooperative management. This shows that private self-financing colleges are dominant strength-wise, but they are weak quality-wise.

CONCLUSION

Technical manpower is an indicator of the strength of an economy. The findings of the study are that out of the colleges that provide engineering degree which are run by the three types of management namely government, private and others, government colleges perform well whereas private are predominantly strong strength-wise. There has been a steep increase in the number of engineering colleges in the private sector after 1996. The study shows the predominant role of self-financing colleges under the private management play a major share in providing engineering degree, but in the case of Polytechnics, government plays a major share in providing education. The intake into the engineering institutions have more than doubled from 1995 to 2001.The increased demand for technical education is reflected in the increased intake into the engineering degree course. Owing to the budgetary resource crunch, government could not cater to this increased demand, therefore self-financing colleges in the private sector took up the active role in providing technical education. Hence the burden of costs of technical education has been shifted to the private beneficiaries of education. Due to lack of sufficient data, quality performance of polytechnics could not be analyzed. Based on the data on budgetary allocation for technical education up to the period of 1980 to 1994, Kerala's share of budget allocation to technical education out of the educational budget as a whole is quite satisfactory when compared with the other South Indian states where technical education is more developed. A noteworthy finding is the state has maintained its expenditure on technical education throughout the period 1980-1994. However we analyzed the budgetary data only up to the period of 1993-1994, whereas the spurt in the establishment of self financing technical educational institutions have come up after the time period of 1996. Hence the budgetary allocation to technical education in the post 1996 period is to be studied and analyzed.

REFERENCES

1. Amartya Sen, Inaugural Address at National Conference on "*Education in Kerala's Development Towards a New Agenda*" Organized by Institute of Social Sciences on 26-28 December 2000 at Thiruvananthapuram.
2. Ghatol A. A., Naik B N, Joshi S V, "Vision for Technical Education in the Country—An Opinion Survey", *Journal of Engineering Education* Oct 2003/Jan 2004.
3. Gupchup Vijay N, Future of Technical Education in India: Concerns and Challenges, *The Journal of Engineering Education*, Oct 2003/Jan 2004
4. Institute of Applied Manpower Research, *Technical Manpower Profile 1995 India and the States*, IAMR, New Delhi.
5. Kerala Calling, January 2004 (*Kerala Educational Scenario Strengths and Weaknesses*).
6. Krishna Kumar V L and Krishnaswamy A, "*HOPE" (Handbook of Professional Education) 2003 for Engineering College Selection, Kerala*, The Mathrubhumi Thozhilvartha Publications.
7. Kulandaiswamy V C, Present Scenario of Engineering Education in India with Special Reference to Private Sector Participation, *The Journal of Engineering Education*, Jan 1996.
8. Duraisamy M., Financing Technical Education in India, *Journal of Education Planning and Administration*, Vol XIV No 1, Jan 2000, pp 23-43.
9. MHRD, Budgetary Allocation of Resources.
10. National Technical Manpower Information System, *NTMIS Bulletin*, Vol VIII No. 4, Jan/Mar 2003
11. National Technical Manpower Information System, *Annual Technical Manpower Review (ATMR)*, Kerala 2003.

12. Neelkanth A Kalyani, Industry and Expectations from Engineering Education, *The Journal of Engineering Education*, Oct 2003/Jan 2004.

13. Palit, Sajit K, Development of Engineering and Technical Education in India.

14. The New Indian Express, *Careers Professional Excellence,* 2004.

15. Uma S, *MS Thesis* on the Study of Growth, Financing and Cost of Technical Education in Tamilnadu, July 1999.

14

Technical Manpower in Engineering Institutions in India

Present Scenario and Future Needs

*Santhanam Needhidasan**

*V.Jaiganesh***

ABSTRACT

Development of a nation depends on technology or technical education, which is considered as a tool for solving the problems of the society and its upliftment mainly relies on qualified Technical Manpower. We know that there has been tremendous growth in technical education since independence. This fast leap has resulted in many anomalies and problems and the important one is the shortage of qualified technical manpower. Technical Manpower plays a vital role in this fast changing scientific and technological era to meet the global standards. Both the quantity and quality demands of human resources are the primary considerations in an engineering institution. Teacher is the prime facilitator in the teaching-learning process. Apart from teaching the teacher has to play a multifaceted role but lacks in almost all the areas except teaching and this has to be improved much. Rapid technological changes especially in the field of communication and computer science

* **Faculty of Civil Engineering, SRM Easwari Engineering College, Chennai– 600 089. Tamil Nadu. Email:sneedhidasan@rediffmail.com**

** **Faculty of Production Engineering, St. Peter's Engineering College, Chennai– 600 054. Tamil Nadu.**

have to be made essential for teachers irrespective of their disciplines to update their knowledge. This chapter discusses the systematic provision of technical manpower according to the actual requirements for the development of technical education. The need of the hour is collective thinking and determined action to redeem this shortage. This chapter also deals with the future needs to develop more technical manpower in engineering institutions to meet and sustain the global challenges.

Key Words: AICTE, IT, Multifaceted, NBA, Shortage, Self-financing, Technical Manpower.

INTRODUCTION

"India has remained a developing country for more than half a century. What will you do to make it a Developed India?" is the question repeatedly put forth by the President of India, Dr. A.P.J. Abdul Kalam. Education has always been recognized, though with varying degrees of conviction, as a vital element for individual self-fulfillment and development of society. Development of a nation depends on technology or technical education, which is considered as a tool for solving the problems of the society and its upliftment mainly relies on qualified Technical Manpower. A recent study by the World Bank across 192 countries revealed that 64 per cent growth was due to human and social capital. Nations, which have developed mastery in the production of knowledge, its dissemination, its conversion into wealth and social good, have been catapulted as world leaders today. Therefore technical knowledge is the instrument for development and transforming the life of people and improving their prosperity and happiness, standard and quality of life. The generation of improved technical manpower has been accepted as a sound strategy for survival of poor nations in the present age of global competition. Since early eighties, due to rapid industrialization and economic growth, growth of technical education in India has been faster than anywhere else in the world and India now has the second largest number of engineering students in the world. Prior to 1980's almost the entire technical education activity was carried out by institutions managed and maintained by the Government and some others which received grant-aid from the Governments, both Central and State. Later in the 1980's entry of more private sector entrepreneurs in the system promoted self-financing institutions and provided an alternative for the expansion of the system. On one hand it was a welcome development but on the other hand it resulted in many quandaries.

HISTORICAL REVIEW OF TECHNICAL EDUCATION IN INDIA

Since Independence technical education has grown into a well established system offering opportunities for education and training in a wide variety of trades and disciplines at certificate, diploma, degree, post-graduate and doctoral levels in institutions located throughout the country. In the year 1947-48, the country had 38 degree level technical institutions with intake capacity of 2500 and intake for post-graduates was only 70. There was rapid expansion of the system in the next two decades. By 1967-68, the degree level institutions had increased to 137 with intake capacity of 25,000. In the next 10 years (1977), the intake capacity increased only marginally to admit 30,000 students for degree courses, and 6000 for post-graduate courses. The system capacity increased very rapidly in the next 20 years, with the major role played by the private sector. The system by 1997 had 547 degree institutions with admission capacity of about 1,31,000 and admissions to post-graduate courses increased to 16,900. In year 2000, the total size of the system had increased to 838 engineering degree institutions with admission capacity of 232,000 students and post-graduate education was offered in 246 institutions with admission capacity of 21,460. In 2002 there were about 1195 institutions in all where 3,48,350 were admitted in under graduate and 23,910 were admitted at post-graduate level. Approximately, two-third's or nearly 70 per cent of these institutions are in private self-financing sector. This rapid growth has resulted in many problems and paved ways for severe criticism of the technical education in the recent days.

RECENT DEVELOPMENTS IN TECHNICAL EDUCATION

Leading higher education institutions of engineering in India are the seven Indian Institutes of Technology (IIT's) located in Delhi, Mumbai, Kharagpur, Guwahati, Chennai, Kanpur and Roorkee, which are National level institutions set up and functioning under an Act of Parliament. The IIT's and Indian Institute of Science, Bangalore are rated as the best in the country as far as research and teaching are concerned.

Central Universities are those which have been established by individual Acts of Parliament and function under the control of Central Government. These Universities can admit students from all over the country and offer engineering programmes through their engineering departments and confer degrees.

National Institutes of Technology (NIT's), the erstwhile Regional Engineering Colleges located in 17 States in the country have been given the status of 'Deemed to be University' and are now empowered to confer their own degrees at three levels for the engineering programmes conducted by them.

State Level Universities are set up through Acts of State Legislature of different states in India and offer engineering programmes either through their constituent colleges or through affiliated engineering colleges. They conduct examinations and are empowered to confer degrees at Bachelor's, Master's and Doctoral levels. Some of the affiliated colleges are run by State Governments or aided through grant-in aid system; a large number of them however, are self-financing Institutions. In some states, there are Universities of unitary type which have engineering departments but do not affiliate any colleges, whereas some other states have established Separate Technological Universities, some being of unitary nature while others are of affiliating type. Major expansion in the technical education system in recent years has taken place in the self-financing group of colleges. All the above mentioned technical institutions are held responsible for producing qualified manpower, but still there is a huge gap between availability and actual requirement.

ROLE OF ALL INDIA COUNCIL OF TECHNICAL EDUCATION

The AICTE, an apex organization given the responsibility of planning and coordinating the quality improvement in technical education was instituted in 1987. The AICTE is responsible for the accreditation of both state and private engineering colleges. AICTE monitors the growth of technical education in order to plan quantitative growth and proper maintenance of norms and standards and to produce required amount of manpower to compete with global standards. Vested with the statutory authority to protect and improve the standards of technical education, AICTE set up National Board of Accreditation (NBA). The NBA was established for the ensuring quality in technical education. The goal of NBA is to develop a quality conscious system of Technical Education where excellence, relevance to market needs and participation by all stakeholders is assured. AICTE has initiated many programmes to increase the technical manpower to overcome the shortage viz., Quality Improvement Programme (QIP), Faculty Development Programme (FDP), Early Faculty Induction Programme (EFIP) and recently introduced National Doctoral Programme (NDP), but still this does not meet the actual requirements.

TECHNICAL MANPOWER—PRESENT SCENARIO

The twenty first century has witnessed a phenomenal explosion of knowledge and application of communication cum information technologies, accelerating the access to knowledge and skills thereby affecting occupations. The demand for commitment-driven teachers in an information society is no exception. Today, technical persons with high and improved quality are of paramount importance for any nation. India accounts for third largest science and technology manpower in the world. The fact, however, is that the ratio of skilled to unskilled personnel in India is very low compared to the developed world and the research culture has also deteriorated. With the emergence of knowledge as capital resource, education in a number of disciplines has become an economic viability and a marketable commodity. Educational opportunities as well as instruction materials now have commercial value and consequently private enterprise has entered education in a significant way. It is a universal phenomenon and India is also a witness to substantial participation of private enterprise. This is to be welcomed and encouraged but, at the same time, this system has to meet the present demand. Therefore we need to promote innovation in every field of activity to bring out qualified manpower. The main reasons for the decline in technical manpower in India are:

- Abnormal growth of self-financing Engineering Colleges;
- Minimum entry standards;
- Non-uniform distribution of colleges and allocation of seats;
- Commercialization;
- Shortage of Qualified teachers;
- Lack of Continuous updating of knowledge;
- Lack of Innovation;
- Lack of Encouragement to faculty members;
- Negligence in Human Resource Development.

Self-financing Engineering Colleges

Today nearly 1045 private institutions with an intake capacity of 312682 are prevailing. Older private institutions are largely aided by government. Since 1980's we have been witnessing the tremendous growth in self-financed technical institutions shown in Table—14.1, which produces 82.67 per cent of the total engineers in the country. This uncontrolled mushrooming needs to be largely addressed. Private engineering colleges have the greatest variation in the level of development, infrastructure facilities and standard of education. Though some of the private institutions have exhibited tremendous growth and also earned national and international recognition, a majority of them are way behind. Teachers are paid less, i.e. just 50 per cent of scales prescribed by AICTE. Lecturers are hired not recruited even at Rs. 3000/- and 5000/- per month by some institutions. Many of them are terminated before the vacation starts and fresh stock hired when the session begins, just to save vacation salary and annual increments. The freshers are headed by a few retired professors who also may not last long. As an outcome of this, institutions cannot get good and committed teachers to develop the students as well as them.

Table—14.1 Growth of engineering institutions and sanctioned intake B/W 1950-2003

Year	Engineering and Technology	
	No of Institutions	Intake
1950	50	3700
1960	110	16000
1970	145	18200
1980	158	28500
1990	337	66600
2000	776	226000
2003	1208	399000

Minimum Entry Standards

With rapid expansion of under developed self-financing institutions and steep hike in fees combined with slump in employment opportunities these institutions are not able to get enough students to admit. Therefore the entry standards are drastically lowered from a minimum of 60 per cent to 50 per cent, and even 45 per cent in Physics, Chemistry and Mathematics at the qualifying examinations. Such low entry standards compounded with poor quality of teaching and training are producing a vast majority of ill equipped engineering graduates which leads to declination of technical manpower.

Non Uniform Distribution of Colleges and Seats

The main criticism about technical education in recent days is non uniform distribution of engineering colleges in various states. This scattered distribution has to be streamlined first, and equal weightage has to be given to all regions to improve the shortage of technical manpower. Region-wise scattered distribution of AICTE approved engineering institutions (up to 1999) are shown in Table—14.2. On verifying the percentage analysis of the AICTE approved institutions in Figure 14.1, the Southern and Western regions take major percentage, while the Eastern and Central regions are lagging behind. If this trend is encouraged by AICTE and other approving bodies, it will lead to disproportionate production of the technocrats in the country and also this trend will pave voids in employment scenario having surplus of technocrats in one region and deficit in other regions. Apart from this, allocation of seats for certain courses exceed the demand, while for other courses the allocation is far less than the demand. This has to be rectified in a proper manner to streamline quality so as to get balanced technical manpower in all fields of engineering. The intake is gradually increasing year after year, and this unprecedented growth of AICTE sanctioned intake in engineering institutions between 1990 and 2003 is shown in Figure 14.2. The AICTE and other approving bodies have to play a major role by adopting stringent norms and standards to check this unavoidable inflow, if we really bother about the need for quality manpower.

Table—14.2 Region-wise distribution of AICTE approved engineering colleges and total intake capacity (1999)

Region	Engineering and Technology Institutions
Central	67
Eastern	34
Northern	75
North Western	89
Southern	259
South Western	95
Western	157
Total	**776**

Commercialization

Most of the private institutions are run as money laundering business-enterprises with the obvious motive of profiteering. The motto is "more number of students more money". When the number of seats in a college reaches maximum, the same entrepreneur opens more colleges, under the garb of a separate society if possible but at the same place. The new colleges will have partial infrastructure and students get the same instruction

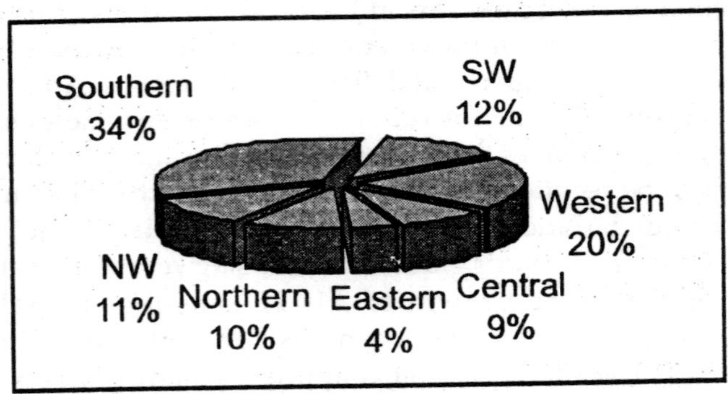

Fig. 14.1: Percentage analysis of AICTE approved engineering institutions (1999)

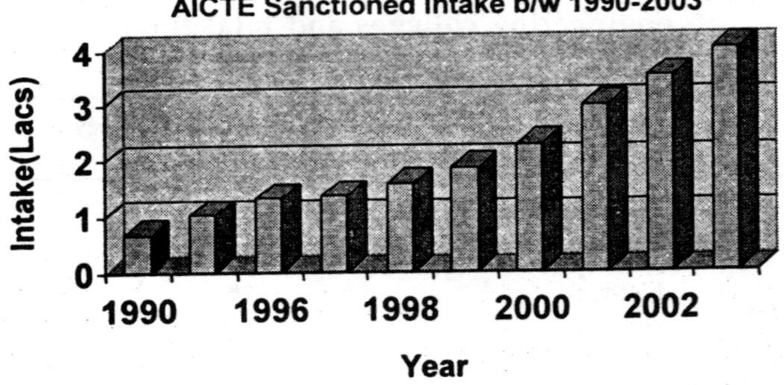

Fig. 14.2: Growth of sanctioned intake in engineering institutions between 1990 and 2003

and training given at the old college of the same management. The concerned functionaries' right from the state governments, through universities and AICTE, to Government of India are politically pressurized or brought in to give approvals for deficient colleges and programmes. AICTE inspection committee is duly briefed. If the committee disapproves the college re-inspection is promptly arranged by a compromising committee to recommend approval and this trend has to be changed if we need qualified manpower.

Shortage of Qualified Faculty

Shortage of qualified technical teachers is the major problem in declination of technical manpower. If college pays very meager salary of Rs.3000/- per month and gives purely temporary and short term appointments, how could a good technical force be produced? Institutions are not adopting AICTE pay scales. It is observed that AICTE norms of Professor-Reader-Lecturer ratio 1:2:4 and Teacher – Student ratio 1:15 are not maintained properly leading to inadequacy of senior faculty members and shortage of lecturers. Assistance from supporting staff is not enough for conducting experimental work. The faculty member has to spend most of his time in teaching, conducting practicals and evaluating the students and is left with meager time to undertake any research and development activity. Regional-wise faculty requirement for 2005 is shown in Table—14.3 and percentage of region wise requirement of Ph.D's is shown in Figure 14.3. Discipline-wise Ph.D qualified teachers available in year 2000 and required in year 2005 are also shown in Table—14.4.

Table—14.3 Requirement of faculty (region wise) in 2005

	Requirement of Faculty	
Region	**Ph.D**	**Total**
Central	2207	5888
Eastern	1183	3106
Northern	2319	6138
North Western	3054	8076
Southern	13783	36757
South Western	5691	15179
Western	5574	14867
Total	**33811**	**90011**

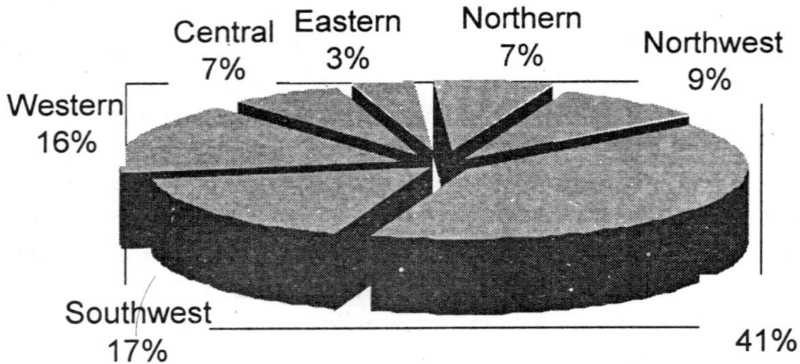

Fig. 14.3: Region-wise Ph.D requirements in 2005

Lack of Continuous Updating of Knowledge

Teacher is the prime facilitator in the teaching-learning process. Apart form teaching, the teacher has to play a multifaceted role like leader, administrator, counsellor, mentor etc., but lacks in almost all the above mentioned spheres, except teaching and this has to be improved. Information technology, as we know is gripping all the phases of human life and knowledge about these rapid technological changes, especially in the fields of communication and computer science, has to be made mandatory for teachers, irrespective of their disciplines to update their knowledge.

Lack of Innovation

Innovation requires autonomy and strong internal institutional mechanisms to develop the quality. In view of the lack of innovation in technical education, the industries have become godowns of outdated technologies, outdated products and processes. Institutions have become warehouses of outdated and old curriculum. The industry and society at large can be crippled if the situation continues. It is the apt time to revitalize and revamp the situation. In western countries on the other hand, students are taught essentially by discoverers. Their teachings flow from what they have discovered. Every student and faculty in a college is a partner in the process of discovery, innovation and its implementation. Improvement is very much essential in this area for achieving qualified technocrats.

Negligence in Human Resources Development

Excellent students, outstanding and dedicated faculty, good infrastructure and a faultless system are the essential components of a premier educational set up. Quality engineers will be in ever increasing demand in the world. For improving their role and performance in the new scenario, they should receive training under expert guidance in the following areas of human resources development viz, Quality in education, Teamwork, Leadership role, Communication skills including listening etc., which will make them a full-fledged technical force, to reckon with.

Table—14.4 Discipline wise teachers available during 2000 and required in 2005

Discipline	Ph.D Qualified Teachers Available in 2000	Ph.D qualified Teachers required in 2005
Civil	1245	1410
Mechanical	1152	4290
Electrical	0780	5140
Electronics	0402	8570
Production	0202	0643
Chemical	0352	0727
Computer	0351	8570
IT	–	6860
Instrumentation	0101	0860
Others	0915	2930

Lack of Encouragement of Faculty Members

Faculty members of un-aided; self-financing engineering colleges should be encouraged by providing incentives for their technical excellence. Special allowances can be provided for participating in national and international seminars/conferences. Tour allowances may also be considered. More opportunities have to be given to them for doing research and development activities so as to improve and enhance their own ability which will help the society at large. Fee concession for pursuing part-time research may also be considered.

SUGGESTIONS FOR FUTURE IMPROVEMENTS

The following suggestions are made to enhance technical manpower in engineering institutions:

- Mushrooming of Technical institutions at the present speed need an immediate check by AICTE and concerned DTE to get well equipped technical manpower;
- Entry system into the technical education field should be more stringent;
- The institutes have to recruit the appreciable number of faculty members per discipline as per AICTE norms;
- The faculty members of the institutions have to be paid uniform pay scales and perks prescribed by AICTE;
- The technical education should not be under the influence of the shortsighted whims and fancies of politicians. It should go on and on, uninterrupted regardless of, which Political party comes to power. Academicians should be allowed to think and act freely for human welfare;
- Bringing policies and practices from developed countries and adapting them to suit our situations is the crying need of the time;
- It is a well known fact that despite innumerable seminars over the years which have discussed the issue in the hope of building meaningful strategies for promoting Industry-Institution Interaction, the interaction remains in a sorry state of affairs. Both sides speak of the need for it, but neither has made any beneficial effort. Industry will have to compete globally if it wishes to survive. In this environment, industry would be forced to seek out the intellectual resource capital from the institutions. New modalities of interaction would have to be added. The relationship would be seen as symbiotic by both industry and institution;

- Faculty members working in self-financing engineering institutions have to be encouraged by giving allowances /concessions for attending national seminars etc.;
- Tour allowance may be given for faculty members working in self-financing institutions.

CONCLUSION

It was felt that the present engineering curricula in general are heavily biased towards imparting skill and knowledge. The factors that determine the ultimate success in realizing the vision of engineering education are quality input of students, outstanding faculty and good human resource development practices. Since teachers and instructors play the key role in influencing learning, recruitment of good quality teachers and instructors, their induction into the field of teaching and continuous updating of their knowledge and skills should be given emphasis in the system of management of technical institutions to produce more quality technical manpower. There has been a growing demand for raising the standards of service rendered by our institutions to produce qualified technical manpower. The dream of quality assurances in engineering institutions will be a reality only when adequate qualified teachers with utmost devotion to elevate the knowledge, skill and attitude of the learning community are available in the technical education system. Technical manpower of the highest caliber is what India needs to generate today.

REFERENCES

1. Patil.A.S, Engineering and Technical Education in India – Current Issues and Trends, *Proc.1st Asia Pacific forum on Engineering and Technical Education*, Monash University, Australia, 1997.
2. Patil.S.K, The Development of Engineering and Technical Education in India, *Global Journal of Engineering and Education*, Vol. 2, No. 3, Monash University, Australia, 1998.
3. Shrivastava, J.P, National Issues of Technical Education and Suggested Solutions, *The Indian Journal of Technical Education*, Vol 26, No. 1, 2003.
4. Anil Kumar and Praveen Kumar, Prospects of Engineering Education and Employment in India, *The Indian Journal of Technical Education*, Vol. 26, No. 1, 2003.

5. Hariharan, R, Globalisation of Technical Education and WTO, The *Indian Journal of Technical Education*, Vol 26, No. 3, 2003.

6. Needhidasan. S and Jaiganesh. V, Quality of Technical Education—An Overview, *Proc. of National Seminar on Technical Manpower Development and Utilization*, NIT, Rourkela, 2004.

7. Needhidasan. S and Jaiganesh. V, Current Development in Technical Education, *Proc. of National Seminar on Technical Manpower Development and Utilization*, NIT, Rourkela, 2004.

8. *University News*, 42(16), April 2004.

9. Saroj Rangnekar and Krishnamachar, P, Higher Technical Education – Present Status, *The Journal of Engineering Education*, Vol. XVII, No. 2 & 3, 2004.

15

Technical Manpower Planning and Development

*P. Palani**

ABSTRACT

The Technical and management education has made substantial contribution to the process of industrial development in the country. It has produced high quality skilled, technical and managerial manpower needed at different levels in the country. The Ninth plan period witnessed a phenomenal increase in the number of institutions on technical education mainly through private initiatives. These encompass courses/ programmes in Engineering, Technology, Management, Architecture, Town Planning, Pharmacy etc.

The key issues in technical and management education during the Tenth Plan would be for continuing the focus on intake capacity, quality, faculty development, optimization of resources through networking, development of information technology education, improving the quality in research, modernization development of curriculam, developing new and emerging technology areas and strategic planning and management of technical education system.

Appropriate Technical Manpower planning is both essential and desirable for development in the right directions. Due to the forward economic momentum, the job market is ever in a constant state of flux.

* **Tamil Nadu Nodal Centre, Department of Economics and Statistics, Chennai- 600 006, Email: des@md2.vsnl.net.in**

This shifting pattern of priorities among occupations is inevitable in the present day context of induction of new technologies, globalization and the changing economic scenario.

INTRODUCTION

The economic prosperity of a country is largely dependent on the general level of education that it provides to its masses. This dependence is even greater on Industrial development without which the vast physical expansion the country has witnessed in the past decades since independence in the field of industry would not have occurred. Technical education is one of the key sectors catering to the scientific and technological manpower needs of the country for its developmental and productive activities.

Technical education is to be designed in such a way that it encompasses all the recent developments in the field so that the engineers/technocrats produced are of a world class. The productivity can be enhanced with the improved knowledge of the engineering personnel on different fields and exploitation of vast resources available in a most advantageous manner. Tamil Nadu has been in the forefront in providing facilities for technical education in the country. This chapter discusses the growth of technical manpower in Tamil Nadu over the decades not only in terms of numerical strength of institutions, intake, out-turn but also the utilization of Engineers and Technicians.

CURRENT DEVELOPMENT IN TECHNICAL EDUCATION IN TAMIL NADU

The past decades saw many significant developments in the field of Engineering/Technical Education. The State of Tamil Nadu had only 3 Engineering Colleges and 8 Polytechnics imparting engineering degree and diploma courses prior to independence. After independence till 1981, there was a gradual increase in both the Engineering Colleges and Polytechnics. By 1981, the number of Institutions in the State was 13 Engineering Colleges and 40 Polytechnics. But the growth of Technical Institutions in Tamil Nadu was catastrophic after the introduction of self-financing models, a new concept in technical education in the State. Number of Engineering Colleges and Polytechnics were started to meet the growing demand from technical education aspirants in the State. The process of expansion of facilities for engineering education which started during the eighties in small measure and continued till 2001-2002, reached its pinnacle in the later years.

The Engineering Colleges in Tamil Nadu are affiliated to Anna University with a few exceptions like the Indian Institute of Technology, Chennai and National Institute of Technology (REC), Tiruchirapalli. There are also two other universities viz. Annamalai University and Bharathidasan University offering engineering courses, apart from nine Deemed Universities.

The growth of Technical Institutions in Tamil Nadu from 1946 to 2003 are presented in Table—15.1 and Table—15.2 below.

Table—15.1 Growth of technical institutions in Tamil Nadu

Sl. No.	Year	Engineering Colleges	Polytechnics
1.	1946	3	8
2.	1951	5	8
3.	1956	8	12
4.	1961	11	25
5.	1966	13	33
6.	1971	13	33
7.	1976	13	34
8.	1981	13	40
9.	1986	38	123
10.	1991	42	132
11.	1996	85	155
12.	1997	89	162
13.	1998	121	199
14.	1999	123	200
15.	2000	156	210
16.	2001	229	210
17.	2002	235	210
18.	2003	238	210

Table—15.2 No. of deemed universities and university faculties offering engineering education

No. of Deemed Universities	University Departments
9	2

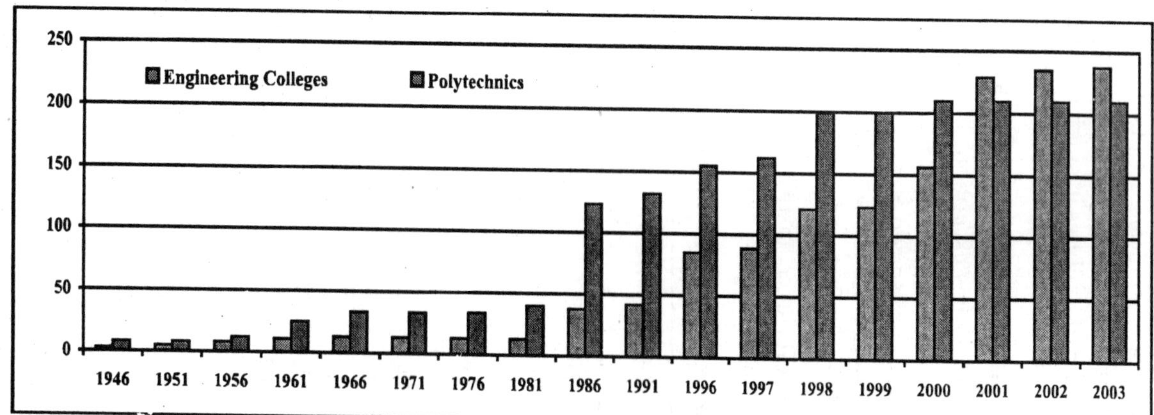

Fig. 15.1: Growth of technical education facilities

GROWTH IN INTAKE

The year-wise growth in intake in both Engineering Colleges and Polytechnics in the State from 1991 to 2003 are given below (Table—15.3).

Table—15.3 Sanctioned intake and actual intake (1991-2003)

Year	Engineering Colleges		Polytechnics	
	Sanctioned Intake	Actual Intake	Sanctioned Intake	Actual Intake
1991	8800	8695	28760	20060
1996	21220	20605	33640	31052
1999	36600	34795	40400	32888
2000	50544	48991	43060	41156
2001	65450	53805	47410	36609
2002	70180	62634	47410	37877
2003	78800	62840	47410	42785

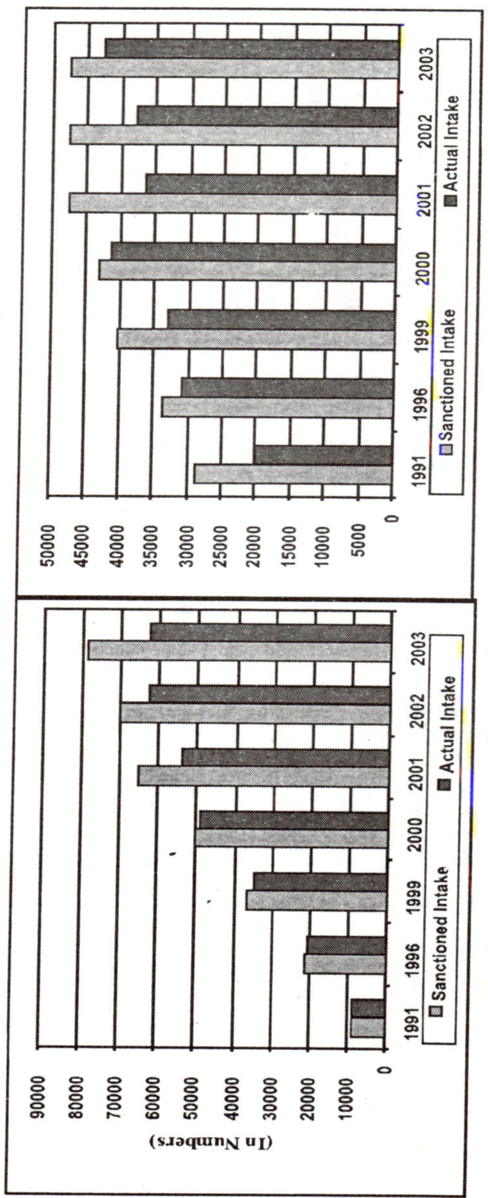

Fig. 15.2: Sanctioned intake and actual intake (1991-2003)

Table 15.3 presents data on the sanctioned intake and actual intake at the degree and diploma level during the period 1991-2003. It can be seen that the actual intake in the year 1991 was 8695 at the degree level and 20060 at Diploma level. A substantial increase has been observed in the subsequent years and the actual intake was 62840 at Degree level and 42785 at Diploma level in the year 2003.

The growth of Technical education connotes not merely to an increase in the number of institutions and its intake, but also the range of subjects offered for study over the years both in Engineering Colleges and Polytechnics in conformity with industrial development and due to the emergence of special and new technical disciplines needed for specific industry.

The number of different disciplines offered for study under degree and diploma courses are presented in Table—15.4.

Table—15.4 Branches of study offered in engineering colleges, and polytechnic (1991-2003)

Year	Degree	Diploma
1991	24	33
1996	32	48
1999	48	55
2000	48	55
2001	55	57
2002	56	57
2003	56	57

The undergraduate and diploma courses in Engineering and Technology are offered on a variety of subjects with the object of developing a specialised skill in the fields. It can be seen from the above Table, that 56 disciplines at Degree level and 57 different disciplines in Diploma level were offered during 2003.

GROWTH IN OUT-TURN

In tune with the steady increase in the facilities created for engineering education both at Degree and Diploma level in terms of number of Institutions and the capacity for admission, there has been a corresponding increase in the out-turn in the state (Table—15.5).

Table—15.5 Growth of out-turn (1991-2003)

Year	Degree	Diploma
1991	5920	10105
1996	7441	14902
1999	13395	20763
2000	15524	21430
2001	16670	23169
2002	20550	24253
2003	28107	27764

In the year 1991, the number of students who passed out from engineering institutions was 5920. Due to the increase in number of institutions, the out-turn started increasing and has touched the figure of 28107 in the year 2003.

Corresponding to the growth in the number of institutions and their intake at diploma level in the State, the out-turn also increased significantly. In the year 1991, the out-turn at diploma level in the State was about 10105, which increased to 27764 in the year 2003.(Table 15.5).

PARTICIPATION OF PRIVATE SECTOR IN TECHNICAL EDUCATION

The role of private sector participation is predominant in the growth of Technical Education in Tamil Nadu. The Ninth plan period saw a phenomenal increase in the number of Institutions in the technical and management education sector in the state with All India Council for Technical Education granting approval for new institutions mainly through private initiatives. Table—15.6 presented below shows the number of institutions under different categories both at degree and diploma level.

Table—15.6 Growth of technical educational institutions by type

Type	Engineering Colleges						Polytechnics					
	1981	1986	1991	1996	2001	2003	1981	1986	1991	1996	2001	2003
Government Institutions (Including Anna University)	11	11	11	11	11	11	19	21	21	21	21	21
Aided Institutions	3	3	3	3	3	3	28	33	35	35	35	35
Private Institutions	–	25	29	72	213	224	–	69	76	99	154	154
Deemed University	–	–	–	–	–	3	9					
Total	**14**	**39**	**43**	**86**	**230**	**247**	**47**	**123**	**132**	**155**	**210**	**210**

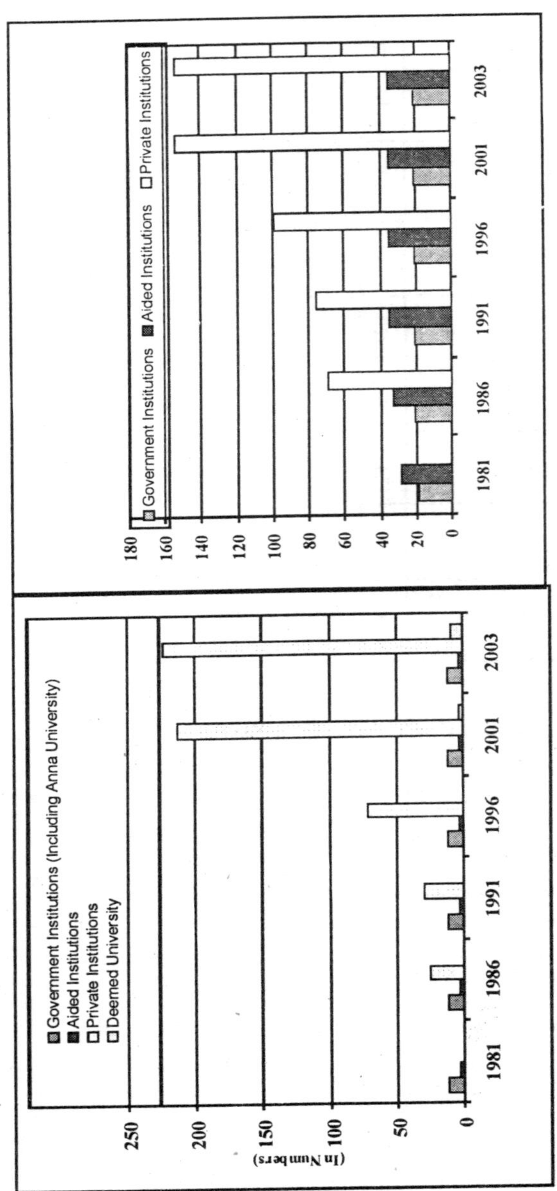

Fig. 15.3: Growth of Technical educational institutions by type

It can be seen from the Table above, that majority of the degree and diploma institutions are under the private category. After the introduction of the concept of self-financing institutions in the sphere of professional/technical education by the Government of Tamil Nadu, there was enthusiasm in the private sector to start new engineering colleges and polytechnics.

It is seen that 95 per cent of the Engineering Colleges and 73 per cent of the Polytechnics are under the private management.

Employment Scenario

The employment status of almost all categories of educated manpower is generally employee or wage earner and engineering manpower is no exception to this general pattern. The Labour market situation for engineering graduates and diploma holders in Tamil Nadu has been analysed based on the data collected through the Student Follow up Survey under National Technical Manpower Information System. The data thus collected from Engineering graduates and diploma holders have been analysed level-wise and discipline-wise.

The analysis has been done based on the Graduate Follow up Survey 1996, 1997, 1998, 1999 and 2000 passed out degree and diploma holders in order to know how the situation has changed over a period of time.

Pattern of Absorption

Degree Holders

Percentage of absorption of degree holders within two years after obtaining degree for certain categories of engineers in the State of Tamil Nadu is presented in the Table—15.7.

It could be seen that fairly good opportunities of employment existed in the earlier years as more than 50 per cent of the graduates of 1996, 1997 and 1998 batch got absorbed within two years of obtaining their degrees. The situation has changed, as there has been a decline in the absorption of degree holders in the subsequent years.

Table—15.7 Percentage absorption of engineering degree holders in certain disciplines

Sl. No.	Discipline	Percentage Absorption within two years of				
		1996 Batch	1997 Batch	1998 Batch	1999 Batch	2000 Batch
1.	Chemical Engineering	100.0	66.5	62.7	46.9	22.3
2.	Civil Engineering	52.3	56.0	49.5	62.0	37.7
3.	Computer Science & Technology	63.0	59.7	66.3	63.0	35.0
4.	Electrical & Electronics	66.1	51.3	55.3	44.5	26.9
5.	Electronics & Communication	56.6	54.3	51.4	49.5	32.7
6.	Electronics & Instrumentation	46.4	52.2	100.0	81.4	39.5
7.	Information Technology	–	–	–	–	40.0
8.	Mechanical Engineering	56.0	54.4	50.7	51.0	29.1

The employment prospects of degree holders in Chemical Engineering, Civil Engineering, Computer Science and Technology, Electrical and Electronics, Electronics and Communication, Electronics and Instrumentation, Information Technology and Mechanical Engineering appears to be unsatisfactory as the absorptions varied between 20 to 40 percent only, for the passed out degree holders of 2000 Batch (Table—15.7).

Diploma Holders

In the case of diploma holders, the percentage of absorption is not encouraging in almost all the disciplines. It could be observed that there has been a decline in the percentage of diploma holders getting absorbed within two years of obtaining their diploma as seen in the Table—15.8 presented below. It clearly indicates not only an unfavourable labour market situation for diploma holders in the State but also the mismatch between demand and supply of diploma holders in the labour market.

Percentage absorption of diploma holders within two years after obtaining diploma for certain disciplines in the State of Tamil Nadu are presented in Table 15.8.

Table—15.8 Percentage absorption of diploma holders for certain disciplines

		Percentage Absorption Within Two Years				
Sl. No.	**Discipline**	**1996 Batch**	**1997 Batch**	**1998 Batch**	**1999 Batch**	**2000 Batch**
1.	Civil	40.9	43.7	47.0	58.7	12.3
2.	Chemical	57.2	93.6	41.5	37.6	10.2
3.	Computer Science	36.3	44.4	44.2	35.7	9.3
4.	Electrical & Electronics	35.9	35.6	31.4	33.0	9.9
5.	Electronics & Communication	47.0	30.8	29.6	40.2	12.9
6.	Electronics & Instrumentation	41.2	36.7	42.6	44.9	–
7.	Mechanical Engineering	42.4	56.2	46.0	35.5	10.5
8.	Electronics	36.9	57.3	50.0	16.3	14.3
9.	Commercial Practice	26.1	29.1	30.6	20.0	9.7

The employment situation among Degree and Diploma holders are not so good as the absorption was hovering around 50 per cent in the case of degree holders and 40 per cent inrespect of diploma holders as seen in Table—15.9.

Table—15.9 Percentage absorption (1996-2000 Batch)

Category	Percentage of Absorption within Two years of				
	1996 Batch	1997 Batch	1998 Batch	1999 Batch	2000 Batch
Degree	52.7	57.5	48.7	51.51	31.3
Diploma	40.81	41.17	36.6	41.1	11.7

QUALITY OF TECHNICAL EDUCATION

Global competition combined with information technology revolution have lead to a shift in Engineering practice. It demands newer technology, skills in communication, ability to create, lead and work effectively as a member of team. The emerging engineering graduates have to be prepared with the change in demand. The major issues are quality and relevance in the context of changing scenario: viz.

1. The engineering curriculum should be more responsive to the needs of industries and must be flexible enough to accommodate technological changes happening every now and then;
2. To provide qualitative education, thrust and focus should be on proper co-ordination between institutions and industries;
3. More areas of specialization at the master degree level and maximum possible elective subjects at the under graduate level;
4. Industries should come forward to adopt institutions to guide students in order to have better exposure to the needs of industries and emerging technologies.

FUTURE PERSPECTIVES IN TECHNICAL EDUCATION

The phenomenal growth in Technical Institutions in the State over the years has to be analysed and the issue of further growth should be carefully looked into and well planned.

Another major issue is improvement of infrastructure, conducive academic atmosphere and more importantly good faculty.

16

Technical Manpower

How It Means to Us Now?

P. Murali Krishna[*]

M. Sudhir Reddy[**]

ABSTRACT

India has grown tremendously beyond our imagination. Today it stands not only in improving its internal environs but also simultaneously creating vibrations in the western economies with its superb human resources. So the power of our internal human strength and values have got an opportunity to expose themselves in elevating Indian manpower across the world. Global corporations have continuously acknowledged the Indian brainpower. The prevailing backlash against outsourcing (BPO) in USA may work well for the election season in the US but the growing popularity of Indian human resources among global companies shows that the world is after India. These companies are moving further in their efforts in roping in on Indians for their business needs. It is not restricted to call centres along. The trends are very visible in (i) Finance; (ii) Research; (iii) Technology; (iv) Software; (v) Engineering etc. Credit Suisse First Boston already taken decision to transfer its 100 core jobs in financial analysis to Indian towns. Nokia will soon set up a CDMA R&D

---

* **Associate Professor, Sri Krishnadevaraya Institute of Management, S K University, Anantapur (AP).**

** **Project Officer, NTMIS Nodal Centre,, JNT University, Hyderabad, (AP).**

unit in India. The Unisys Company is contemplating to invest $180 million in a software and BPO business. Logica is looking for 400 engineers in India in 2004 and above 500 in 2005. Like this there are several incidents to prove India's brain worthiness.

This chapter attempts to concentrate thought-provoking discussion on the present status of manpower in India, the environment and the organisations. It also touches upon the human competency factor, distinguishes between knowledge work and routine work, and with this what is to be done to overcome the human resource planning and management situation in this country.

WHAT IS AILING WITH US NOW?

It has been a tricklish issue for the Indian management and the academia as to what happens to Indian human resources with all the above accomplishment in, may it be, meeting challenges or facing global players in performance. It is to remind us now to a management sequel that the employee's performance is based on his potentials, barring other things. Hence, the organisations must identify a junk of techies with high potentials for technology intensive jobs. We have another major area of concern for the success of today's organisations – the Strategic Management. This new dimension to effective management has brought finest results in improving organisations all over the world today.

On the other side, the vibrant environment that created breakthrough in our lifestyles, thinking, our programmes and practices. Today the world has been tremendously interlinked to make it a small hub. This has a lot of impact on the working of organisations and profiles of personnel working for them. While the organisations across the globe have been catching the changes in time, many organisations in India, some how, are lagging behind in responding to adopt these changes through competence enhancement and world class performance improvement. It is in this context that the necessary brainstorming on the ways and means to be adopted is becoming imperative. Let us look into the aspect of what needs to be done urgently.

THE ENVIRONMENT

First of all one should be convinced that in India there is no dearth for employment opportunities. One side the enterprises are offering VRS to their employees and on the other side, the doors are wide open to young corporate soldiers with higher degree of commitment calibre, capacities and capabilities. The organisations' moves in shifting jobs to India do support this observation. There are number of examples to quote in support of this observation since the recent past. On the one side the government with its liberalisation and open market policies created an opportunity for enterprises to invest with confidence. On the other side, the human resources also realised the importance of competence enhancement to compete with world class work practices. In summation we prefer to say that the present day Indian organisational environment has improved manifold to compete with western environment. We may see in near future a phenomenon of Indian talent shifting backwards to India.

THE ORGANISATION

The organisations on their part in a global competitive environment are observed to be putting in maximum efforts in their performance to catch world class trends. Some domestic organisations have even raised to the level of *trendsetters* to the world. This is possible for an organisation with continuous improvement of its human resources. This has been an established fact. Organisations are continuously and constantly changing themselves by enhancing their competence in raising to the standards demanded. Some time back there was a dilemma on the status of human resource in the changing patterns of economic system and globalisation. The actual status of human resource in the total organisation structure depends on whether a unit is small or large. Lot many routine services are being outsourced to India. Thus shrinking the actual size of human resources in the organisations today. In the dynamic changing environment the organisations and human resources are forced to learn that change involves challenges. Thus it is essential that human resources learn to look at change with new eyes, recognise the future, master new forms of intelligence and harness energy to achieve organisations' goals.

THE HUMAN RESOURCE COMPETENCE FACTOR

It is since the recent past we have been carving for higher competence with quality in people. In fact we are now convinced that the enhanced human competence plays most important role in leading organisations to excellence. There are number of studies that identified what comprises higher level competence. Of course, one should realise that the components or factors of competence depend on several organisational, individual, environmental and personal factors. Joseph J (1987) discussed at length about the specific competence needs among Indian enterprises as given in *Exhibit 1*.

EXHIBIT—16.1

SPECIFIC COMPETENCE NEEDS AMONG INDIAN ENTERPRISES

- *Ability to understand the job specifications.*
- *Create processes to achieve the specifications and maintain the adherence to them.*
- *Expand volumes to achieve the advantage of economies of scale develop tools to conform to quality requirements.*
- *Install and operationalise special purpose machines or equipment needed to meet quality.*
- *Control over cost and driving down cost to provide for cushion, as the price would not be within their control.*
- *Strive for external certification of internal processes and systems to assure quality like ISO– 9000.*

Source: Joseph J., Indian Institute of Management, Ahmedabad, 1987.

THE PROFILE OF TECHNICAL WORK

Having employed high paid technical personnel any organisation is certainly be interested to get the best from them. There are two key elements of technical knowledge. Namely (i) Knowing what to do and (ii) the discipline to do it. They are required to be aware of the latest advances in their fields and apply the knowledge in their work. Otherwise they become incompetent. Engineers and the technical professionals face the dilemma

EXHIBIT—16.2

KNOWLEDGE WORK VS. ROUTINE WORK

	Knowledge Work		Routine Work	
From the perspective of →	Employees	Employer	Employees	Employer
Close Supervision	Disliked	Not needed; low supervision saves money	Expected	Needed
Individual Input Such as Judgement, Creativity	Demanded as part of the job	Needed and encouraged for competitive advantage	Not expected; not prepared	Not wanted; can create problems in highly standardised production processes
Developing the Scope and Process of the Job	Want to be involved	Required to participate	Not expected	No involvement wanted or desirable
Autonomy	Expected and demanded	Granted with focus on output rather than input	Desired but not expected	Controlled and limited
Flexibility	Expected and demanded	Granted	Desired but not expected	Controlled and limited
Networking for Learning	Integrated into the job	Encouraged and expected	None	Not needed
Core Processes of the Job	Experimentation and thinking	Learning; creativity	Physical/routine	Physical or routine procedures
Career Identity	Individual and knowledge based	Knowledge based	Employer based	Employer based

Source: Anil Verma, Rotman School of Management, University of Toronto.

between continuing as a specialist and getting into managerial positions. While they seek the satisfaction of accomplishment and the consequent recognition, they realise that rewards in conventional organisation are linked to positions and that they must get the right assignment in order to make progress. This one fact explains why so many of them move into management to have more control over their careers. *Exhibit 2* distinguishes knowledge work from routine work, which gives expectations of the employer and the knowledge employee.

THE NEED OF THE HOUR

Having discussed the above for clear understanding of the present environment that warrants new breed of human resource planning techniques and models we need to concentrate on certain specific issues.

Human resource planning is *a chain of events that are designed to ensure the provision of adequate and sufficiently skilled people.* Contemporary human resource planning is *a strategy for procurement, development, allocation and utilisation of an enterprise's human resources*. Every organisation whether technology based or not has to perform certain specific steps in human resource planning. They are (i) Analyse and define the system in which it works. This is in other words we may call as *'Environmental Scanning'*. (ii) The organisation has to determine in advance the time horizon of its plan since this will affect the system. (iii) The thread-bearing step in the process of human resource planning is the forecasting of the demand and supply of manpower, for a period for which the plan is outlined. There is numbers and methods of forecasting available today that suit to specific and special requirements of the organisations. (iv) The cost implications of the manpower plan are to be compatible with the company's finances. (v) The final action plans must be prepared within the scope of manpower requirements, productivity and manpower costs. These action plans could cover the subjects such as (a) Recruitment; (b) Redundancy; (c) Training; (d) Improvements in productivity and (e) Improvement in practices of retaining employees.

The Channel Tunnel

The channel tunnel project is without doubt a unique showcase of technology, but it also represents a fantastic laboratory of human resources. The tunnel was built by people, and not by machines. Nearly 13,000 Engineers and Technicians worked together on both sides of the tunnel. The popular press in Britain called them "The Tunnel Tigers".

Source: Sadler Tony, "Human Resources Management: Developing a Strategic Approach", Kogan page, London, 1995.

HUMAN RESOURCE PLANNING AS VALUE ADDITION FUNCTION

For employers the value of the HR function lies in the bottomline. Greater productivity, higher quality, better customer service, positive employee relations and lower costs are among hundreds of factors that typically contribute to higher profits. Innovative and effective HR practices often directly improve such factors. Historically, businesses would account for HR functions as an expense and learning as a depreciable asset. Today when we are talking about value addition from every process and function, HR is viewed as an investment that can lead to future exponential gains, which was not the case earlier. What underpins the success of organisations is their ability to add value to the inputs they use. Adding value in this sense is the central purpose of business activity. A commercial organisation which adds no value – whose output is worth no more than the value of its inputs in alternative uses – has no long-term rationale for its existence. Many surveys have revealed that the management perceives that the value addition by the HR function in their organisation will increase in the future.

REFERENCES

1. Joseph J., Indian Institute of Management, Ahmedabad, 1987.
2. Anil Verma, Rotman School of Management, University of Toronto.
3. Sadler Tony, "Human Resources Management: Developing a Strategic Approach", Kogan page, London, 1995.

17

Gibbs Phenomenon, Technology Development and Technical Education in India

*Shubhada Gadre**

ABSTRACT

When a finite discontinuity (i.e. a step change) is fitted by using finite number of terms, it results in overshoot near the edge of discontinuity, as well as oscillations reminiscent of the Gibbs effect.

The present rate of technology progress is so fast that it is like a Step Change. Infinite resources are necessary for efficiently facing such a fast change. This chapter attempts to analyze the present status of technical education in India, in the light of Gibbs effect.

Key Words: Gibbs effect, Technical education, Technical person-power.

INTRODUCTION

The last two-three decades have witnessed the rapid advances in digital computer technology and software development. The evolution in VLSI (Very Large Scale Integrated Circuits) and signal processing technology have been fueling this growth. Further advent of Information Technology has broken down all the barriers between different application areas. All these

* **V.J. Technological Institution, Matunga, Mumbai- 400 019, Email: shubhadagadre@hotmail.com**

synchronized developments have brought almost a Step Change in Technology growth. This chapter first elaborates this situation.

The progress in Communication technology has removed the barrier of physical distances. Combined with this the global village concept has brought many job opportunities to our doorstep with added possibility of becoming job creators. This situation demands high quality expertise.

Technical education in India has to accept this challenge in order to compete with other nations and reserve India's place in the world of technology. It is a question of a survival too.

In order to bring fast changes in technical growth, technical education system needs to be strengthened. It is necessary to perform a thorough analysis of present system with open, unbiased mind. This involves examining the resources in hand and setting the appropriate goals. This chapter attempts to perform such indepth analysis. What changes, modifications, extensions are needed in the present system for best performance is the next aim of This chapter.

According to Gibbs phenomenon, a step change is a finite discontinuity. It demands infinite terms to realize such discontinuity. If fitted by finite terms, an oscillatory behaviour is observed. This chapter further analyzes the Gibbs phenomenon[1] and the interpretation of oscillatory behaviour in context of technical education. On the basis of this analysis this chapter concludes by giving the guidelines for deciding whether it is necessary to get rid of old model of Technical education system and to redesign the new one.

STEP CHANGE IN TECHNOLOGY DEVELOPMENT

Technology development is a continuing process ever since the existence of human species. Ages have passed since the existence of the universe. The human race has progressed from the status of just a "living organism' to today's most progressive human being. This could only happen due to technology development which started with the invention of a wheel. Since then the human race has marched a long way on a time axis simultaneously making progress in technology.

However, starting from the beginning of the world to more than half of the previous century, this progress was very slow, increasing gradually. History has witnessed technology progressing in different parts of the world at different times and in different walks of life. However a very fast rate of growth, almost like a step change never had been experienced because these developments were non- synchronized and therefore could not be complementary.

This was the case until very recent past. The last two-three decades however have witnessed the rapid advances in digital computer technology and software development. The evolution in VLSI (Very Large Scale Integrated Circuits) and signal processing technology have been fueling this growth. Further advent of Information Technology has broken down all the barriers between different application areas. The progress in Communication technology has brought the world so near that physical distance has not remained a barrier. The tools like internet, mobile communication and video conferencing make a physical presence of a person-power at a site of operation unnecessary.

All these synchronized developments happened in less than a half century. If one compares the rate of technology development in past and in present, it is almost a step change. Half a century is like a zero time compared to crores of years in past thus making the growth rate infinite. We are all witnessing a miracle.

Taking the advantage of the situation worldwide industry now gets the work done by wherever cheap labour is available. The global village approach is coming to existence in real sense. Many opportunities knock our doors today if we have desire to take them. All types of jobs, right from call-centers, IT applications to software development, IC chip designing etc. are at our doorstep.

PRESENT TECHNICAL EDUCATION SYSTEM

Technical Education Model

Technical education may be expressed by a simple equation,

$$y(n) = P[\,x(n)\,] \tag{1}$$

where $x(n)$ = System input at instant 'n' = student joining the Institute

$y(n)$ = System output at instant 'n' = Engineer ready for industry

$P[\, x(n) \,]$ = Processing on the input

Execution of this equation has three parts:

First is about the input x(n). This involves control over the entry point i.e. admission process. The main process P is the technical education imparted to a student converting him/her into a full-fledged engineer $y(n)$. This processing depends on software (governing all aspects of the technical education) and hardware (infrastructure and funding). Though both are indispensable, the distinction between the two institutes depends on their governance (software).

Next task is quality control of output $y(n)$ which involves evaluation (examination) process.

The technical education system is a decision making system which includes

(i) deciding about who is going to execute eq. (1).- this concerns about giving permission for starting technical institutes/branches, deciding intake etc. It mostly involves setting the rules for hardware aspects of the system promising at least minimum threshold of quality.

(ii) deciding how to execute eq. (1). This contains all three parts mentioned above.

All India Council of Technical Education (AICTE) is the highest body who is involved in taking decisions about the aspect (i). This is the body who should decide the goals/objectives about the technical education, track the worldwide technology progress time to time, and accordingly monitor the direction of the technical education in the entire country. This involves vision and determination.

In general, in India, there are three types of technical institutes: Govt. aided, Private and Autonomous. In case of the first two types the three operations in the execution of eq. (1) are more or less decentralized. Whereas autonomous body is responsible for conducting entire process.

Decentralized Operation

(i) Technical education department of the state decides the norms of the entry point (admission process) and actually performs this process partially or fully for Govt/Govt-aided and private institutes respectively.

(ii) The quality control of the product $y(n)$ is entirely left to the respective universities which demands the execution of student evaluation process mainly by conducting examinations.

(iii) The main processing of imparting technical education is entirely controlled by the management trusts of the respective institute as they are the financial providers. Though AICTE, Government and universities provide the guidelines in different aspects, actual execution is entirely in the domain of institutes.

For a good quality Technical education, it is necessary that all of these bodies should work in harmony. However in reality the conflicting objectives of these bodies cause pollution in education quality. In that case the final authority should not only involve itself in decision making but also in implementation. Decision and implementation by separate bodies result in chaos.

IDEAL TECHNICAL EDUCATION SYSTEM

Here are some of the points which need to be considered by respective governing bodies, for accepting the challenge of step change in technological developments:

- *Goal:* On National level, this factor carries very high weightage because it decides the fate of the nation in the field of technology. The technology is developing with a very fast rate so tracking and corresponding changes must be with the same pace. At local level, this factor decides whether the Institute should act as a coaching class, ITI or like IIT;
- *Admission process and fee structure:* Giving opportunity to deserving candidates should be the aim of this process. The plan of execution of admission process

should be made very carefully taking into consideration all possibilities. A carefully prepared plan eliminates further complications like courtcases, changes in the plans etc. This expedites and completes the admission process in time;

The other important decision here is a fee-structure when it is considered as a main channel of financial resource. This view-point restricts the entry on the basis of financial conditions. *It is essential for policymakers to establish justice and give opportunity to the deserving students without discriminating on any basis;*

Infrastructure: There are rules about the minimum infrastructure like laboratories, central computing facility, internet, library, hostels, canteen, playground etc. etc. All these facilities require funding. In the case of private institutions, these rules are therefore looked upon nuisance instead of essentialities. In the case of Govt.-aided/Govt. institutions, the funding provided is barely sufficient for routine expenses;

The provision for human resources is the most important factor in the education. This factor is always been neglected in all types of the institutions. In Govt. institutes filling of the faculty positions is looked upon as a financial burden. Naturally the trend is not to fill all the posts. Non-aided institutes also suffer as they do not get the senior faculty. The rigid rules about qualifications create many problems. When the entire world is braking the walls between different disciplines, in our country, entry in any branch need basic degree in that field. Knowing the vast difference between the changes in the examination gradation in last 30 years, the same rules about first class etc. is made applicable to the teachers who have graduated long, long ago. Credit for the experience is out of question because entry itself is prohibited. This restriction is the root of many vacant higher positions.

- *Evaluation system:* Being a main quality control device, the evaluation system should be full-proof and of high standard. The system is very sensitive to unhealthy factors in the society and gets very easily corrupted. The quality also gets deteriorated with a high burden experiencing a trade-off between time and quality;
- *Curriculum development:* This factor should match the vision of the nation and must have a sensitive tracking of global scenario. Contribution from Industry may give these efforts a practical orientation;
- *Training of person-power:* The teaching faculty and support systems should be trained time to time in order to cope up the changes in technology;
- *Industry-Institute Interaction:* Industry can interact in various capacities. Curriculum development, personnel training, evaluation system are the few areas. Apart from these, industry also can sponsor the laboratories and create facilities;
- There are many other factors which should be considered while planning and execution phase of the technical education system. A working document[2] is created by Technical Education Quality Improvement Project (TEQIP) of Government of India. Student welfare, faculty development, research and development activities, services to community and economy and many more such factors are responsible for a good quality education. The list is not exhaustive as there are infinite considerations.

GIBBS EFFECT AND TECHNICAL EDUCATION

As mentioned above there are infinite factors to be considered. In practice there are many constraints imposed by many factors like funding scarcity, time restrictions, non-availability of important factors, human weaknesses like selfishness, laziness, irresponsible behaviour, lack of vision etc. The number of factors actually used in the implementation are thus get restricted. According to Gibbs phenomenon, when finite terms are used instead of infinite requirement, the oscillatory behaviour is observed, while dealing with step changes.

The world had witnessed one of the examples of the Gibbs effect in the last decade of the previous century. With the advent of Information Technology many new IT companies started and collapsed due to finite resources and preparation. The whole economy of the entire world experienced rise and fall. This oscillatory behaviour is still continuing. If the challenge of steep rise in technological progress is accepted with bare minimum finite resources, the educational quality would definitely experience ripple in its quality.

CONCLUSION

This chapter attempts to perform an un-biased analysis of technical education in India, step change in technological growth and a probable Gibbs effect.

It discusses the issues related to the technical education system explaining the responsibilities of the various governing bodies. The attention is demanded on the fact that these bodies instead of working in harmony, stand in front of each other in contradictory modes. This happens because each one of these bodies has their set objectives and constraints. Sometimes these objectives are conflicting, causing deterioration in education quality.

For example, there are many issues like tuition fees, donation policy, admission procedure, staff salaries and qualifications, the infrastructural and other requirements etc., where the Government policies and views may not match with those of the private trusts. AICTE decides whether the new colleges, expansion in the intake capacity and/or disciplines are permitted or not. The tasks like student' evaluation (examination system), declaring results in time and awarding degrees are governed by the universities. When every year number of colleges, branches increases, the respective universities get loaded with additional burden. The universities then try to push some part of the work to the institutes.

This chapter further discusses the major factors which need consideration, for high quality technical education. It further explains that the number of such factors are infinite and usually a compromise is made by considering only few of them, thus attempting to cope up the step change in Technology by finite, limited resources. This situation calls for the Gibbs phenomenon resulting in oscillatory behaviour.

This situation demands a change in the old educational model into a new one which is less restrictive, full of a promise for high quality education.

REFERENCES

1. Mitra S. K., *Digital Signal Processing: a computer-based Approach* McGraw *Hill International Editions, Singapore,1998*.
2. National Project Implementation Unit: *Working Documents for States and Institutions,* Technical Education Quality Improvement Project of Government of India, Noida, 2002.

18

Technology Induced Manpower Downsizing VRS-2000

An Experience in Public Sector Banks

*K.Narayan**
*A.H. Sequeira***

ABSTRACT

Manpower adjustment is considered as an effective strategy for increasing the productive efficiency of the firm when sizable labour force becomes redundant due to restructuring or mechanization of an enterprise. The 90s saw Indian Banking sector being transformed with policy shifts from manual to technology-based operations on one hand and social to profit oriented business on the other. Having recruited large manpower with a poor vision on future changes and needs, most of the Banks were saddled with more weight than they could carry when they entered the 21st Century. Hence downsizing became inevitable and VRS was the immediate option for the Banks.

The article deals with the conceptual framework of downsizing and VRS, the benefits and loopholes in the scheme introduced by Banks, the threats and opportunities posed to the employees etc. The article also

* **Former Senior Banker and Presently a Research Fellow at (NITK), Surathkal. Email: narayan@nitk.ac.in**

** **Head, Humanities, Department, National Institute of Technology, Suratkal.**

dwells on post VRS scenario, survivor syndrome and a few case lets. In conclusion the article suggests an improvised model for effective implementation of the scheme.

Key Words: Downsizing, Ex-gratia , Public Sector Undertaking (PSU)Banks, Restructuring, Voluntary Retirement Scheme (VRS), VRS Optees.

INTRODUCTION

Changed Scenario

The ushering in of the new economic policy in India around the 90s created different kinds of quantitative and qualitative needs of the existing as well as future manpower. The assumption of 1980s that "Bigger is better" changed to "lean is mean" in 90s. Accordingly, companies started introducing Voluntary Retirement Schemes (VRS) or "Golden Handshakes" as the basic component of labour adjustment strategies both in public and private sectors.

In India, VRS have been introduced in a few cases for quite sometime earlier but the number of companies offering VRS has risen steadily from 100(1996-97) to 366 (2001-2002) as per a study reported in Economic Times dated April 7,2003. In Western countries downsizing was a quite familiar organizational process. In United States itself since the mid 1980s, 85 per cent of the fortune 1000 companies have engaged in some downsizing activities.[1]

The Concepts of Downsizing, VRS etc.

The word downsizing might not have found place in older dictionaries but today the term has come to have almost a generic meaning of overall reduction in the size of a firm's workforce. Freeman and Cameroon[1] defined downsizing as "a set of activities, undertaken on the part of the management of an organization, designed to improve organizational efficiency, productivity, and/ or competitiveness. As per W.R.Tracey,[2]"downsizing is a management strategy for streamlining an organization, making it more efficient and cost effective by eliminating unnecessary and duplicator functions and people. It may also stem from an unexpected market downturn, competition or a hostile takeover." A wide range of activities such as rightsizing, resizing, restructuring, delayering and re-engineering have been addressed under the general rubric of downsizing.[3] Voluntary Retirement schemes have been acclaimed as one of the popular downsizing methods of late.[4]

The word "Retirement" implies leaving active productive activity or withdrawing from employment.[5] In the context of industrial relations it implies termination of employer-employee relationship at the conclusion of pre-agreed terms/ conditions on attaining the age of superannuation.[4] Thus voluntary retirement relates to a situation when a worker, for one reason or other, resigns from his job and thereby terminates the employer-employee relationship prior to the maturity of terms and conditions of employment. It is a premature termination of employment. Generally, standing orders or service rules of the organizations provide for such options.

"Voluntary Retirement Scheme" as the name suggests is a specially devised scheme for early retirement, which is optional for employees, to attract them in more numbers to seek early separation. Therefore the scheme contains additional payments than a normal early retirement. Cash compensation for job loss is usually one of the most important components of assistance strategies for redundant workers.[6] While the employers might have proposed and initiated such schemes, on paper it is an option chosen by the employee to voluntarily terminate the employer-employee relationship, thus side stepping the rigours of section 25 *(o)* and 25 *(n)* of the Industrial Dispute Act 1947. It is this process by which manpower reduction takes place without getting entangled in the rigmaroles of the ID Act 1947. The scheme is generally kept open for a limited time span for employees to exercise their option.

VRS is a "legally" more hassle free way to downsize than retrenchment, which makes it more attractive to the management. By offering an attractive package of benefits, VRS enables the firm to rationalize labour strength, reduce average age profile and attain cost effectiveness to go well into strides again. Particularly in times of sluggish business and economic crisis, VRS is found to help recovery and stimulate growth. The Chairman of a large non-banking company noted that the success of the VRS in his company had given him an "opportunity to restructure the business all over the country to make it highly competitive in the finance industry" *(Financial Express, Calcutta Aug 31, 2000).*

The Rationale of Downsizing

Economic theory dictates that for organisations to thrive we need a judicious combination of the four factors of production, viz. capital, entrepreneurship, labour and land. All of these operate in tandem and in the context of the larger economic system. It is on the basis of this philosophy that manpower adjustment by way of downsizing is considered an effective strategy for increasing the productive efficiency of the firm specially when a sizeable labour force becomes redundant due to restructuring or mechanization of an enterprise.

According to the World Bank Economic Review (WBER)[7]" Public Sector downsizing is not the final goal of economic policy, but economic reforms may require mass lay offs. Severe labour redundancies characterize transition economies where the shift for plan to market requires millions of workers to be relocated out of the public sector. A voluntary approach to reduction in public sector employment is increasingly popular among developing country governments, multilateral organizations and donor countries. The voluntary approach offers severance pay to encourage the redundant workers to quit thus overcoming their resistance to downsizing, restructuring and privatization. " Further, the advantage of downsizing as advocated by World Bank are that it reduces public sector expenditure, reallocates the workforce and reduces long term liabilities in the form of old age pensions.

Ethical Issues in Downsizing

The routes for downsizing like layoff, retrenchment and dismissals are painful and inhuman acts to cover up the inefficiencies and misdeeds of the Management. Even Voluntary separation schemes are sometimes not 'voluntary'. Studies have shown that while those who have been laid down never recover emotionally, those who are retained also lose motivation and become skeptic. Downsized employees do not generally get new jobs at their old salaries. Sometimes companies end up in employing newer inexperienced persons in place of older experienced loyal employees paying higher salaries.

TECHNOLOGY AND MANPOWER REDUNDANCY

Technology in Banking

Today banking is one sector in India, which has been undergoing paradoxical transformation due to the all-pervasive breath taking influence of Information Technology, Electronic Data Processing and growing telecommunication network. Due to the initiatives on Liberalization, Globalization and Privatization introduced in India to integrate Indian Economy with Global Economy, the winds of change are blowing in Indian Banking horizon faster than ever.

Technology Adoption

By 1993, technology adoption had become an essential priority and not an optional exercise for Indian Banks. The PSU Banks then were controlling more than 90 per cent of Indian Banking Business. Hence unless PSU Banks get mechanized, Indian Banking would get isolated from their counterparts in the world where the Banks have already been riding high tech. Nevertheless, the PSU Banks faced the following three major challenges in technology adoption for a smooth transition from Traditional Banking to Technology Banking.

(a) The employees were reluctant to accept and adopt the change as switching over to technology involved additional learning, displacement and disruption of a set routine. The unions became skeptic and feared that machines would replace men and also that with the Management depending less on working hands, the unions would be powerless. So the resistance from employees side was visible everywhere.

(b) The computers were not only new to the employees but also to the officers and Executives who were ignorant of the use and utility of these machines. From the operators to the power centers, there was a great vacuum of knowledge. Officers with technical background within the organizations were very few, and hence everybody had to depend on outside help.

(c) The Banks had already recruited heavily during their social Banking era as a result of which establishment cost was one of the major expenditure in the Balance sheets. Having on the one hand mounting overhead charges and on the other a need for heavy outlay on technology, the Banks were to tread in a very cautious path to make further investments.

To address those challenges Banks first signed an agreement with the unions on 23.10.1993 for partial computerisation and then slowly increased the pressure towards total computerization. The fears of the unions became true, i.e. as and when the process of computerization was on, the voice of the unions became feeble and the resistance slowly waned away. Extensive training was given to officers and employees for operational usage of computers whereas the software for Banking was either hired from or developed by leading software companies like Infosys (Finacle),I-Flex(flexicube) etc. Thus initiating the process with Automatic Ledger Posting Machines (ALPM), the computerization has now reached to a stage of establishing network of ATMs and interbranch/interbank connectivity.

Government Initiative

Meanwhile, the Government also extended helping hand by arranging World Bank Aid for technology infusion and allocating budgetary support of 21000 crores as recapitalisation to clean up the Balance sheets. A committee headed by Dr.Rangarajan was formed to advise computerization in public sector Banks. Thus the Banking in India entered the new millennium with a new outlook and optimism on technology adoption. The years in the new millennium have seen further in roads in technology up-gradation in Banks. Automatic Teller Machines, Credit Cards, Debit Cards, Electronic Money Transfer, Networking of the branches and E-Banking are some of the milestone in this direction.

A Peep into the Future

With Wireless Application Protocol (WAP) technology adventing the world, internet Banking being popularized already, RBI moving towards establishing Real Time Gross Settlement System, there are strong signals that urban Banking in India is set to go High-tech very soon. 'Clicks' will replace 'bricks' i.e. pushing buttons would suffice customer needs than entering into Bank Premises. Banking transactions may take place on palmtops and mobiles. Technology is to play a major role in customer delight.

VRS IN PUBLIC SECTOR BANKS

Metamorphosis of HRM in Indian Public Sector Banks

The Indian Banking scenario was dominated by a number of Private sector small/medium sized Banks prior to 1969 (except the State Bank of India) when 14 major Banks were nationalized. With another bout of nationalization of 6 more Banks in 1980, more than 90 per cent of Banking was brought under the Public Sector. During the next two decades from 1969 to 1989, the concept of Banking changed from Class Banking to Mass Banking. Branches were opened in every nook and corner of the country and the Banks grew in size at a rapid pace. This shift towards Social Banking not only led to phenomenal increase in the customer base but also resulted in mass scale recruitment of employees at clerical and officer levels. The recruitment drive in almost all the banks was so immense as to doubt whether the future changes were envisioned or the people at the helm foresaw the long-term effect on profitability. Meanwhile the unions also became strong and militant and they successfully bargained for improved wages and facilities. Even today the salary and service conditions of Bank Employees in Public Sector is governed by Bipartite Settlements with Unions.

However the entire scenario changed in 1991 when Narasimham committee on Banking reforms made significant recommendations on working of the Banks. The prudential norms for income recognition, concept of Non Performing Assets (NPA), and capital adequacy norms were some of the international practices adopted by the Banks in India as per the committee recommendations. Consequently Banks had to classify a huge chunk of their credit portfolio as NPA, as a result Balance sheets of most of the public sector Banks slipped in to Red. The recruitments in Banks were almost totally stopped. A new conceptual change was seen in the Bankers by reversing their focus from Social Banking to self-sustainability through profit. Meanwhile the tacit monopoly enjoyed by the PSU Banks came to an end with the advent of competition from the tech-savvy new generation banks.

Need for VRS in Banks

With competition from foreign and private banks, the public sector banks in this country felt the need for consolidation and level playing. It is belatedly realized that productivity of the staff has come to have a significant bearing on the Banks overall performance. Being a service industry, the staff efficiency becomes an important factor for assessing the bank's performance. The profit per employee as an average of all the PSBs in lakhs in 1999-2000 was 0.65, for the private banks 1.46 and for the foreign banks it was 5.61.[8] This low profitability in PSBs was attributed to excess manpower built up over the years. As estimated by Finance ministry in Nov 1999, on the basis of business per employee (BPE) of 100 lakhs , there were 59338 surplus employees in 12 nationalized banks while based on BPE of 125 lakhs the number shot up to 1,77,405. It was realized that the setback of eroded profitability and productivity could be rectified only by rationalizing the huge manpower accretion inherited as a past legacy. To redeem the banks from the recurring burden of surplus manpower the Government advised one time measure of Voluntary Retirement Scheme.

The Planning and Designing of the Scheme

Government in the middle of the year 2000 cleared a uniform Voluntary Retirement Scheme (VRS) for the Banking Sector giving a seven months timeframe to implement the same. Indian Banks Association framed the scheme and circulated among the public sector banks for adoption. The scheme was open till 31-3-2001. No concession was made to weak banks. The scheme was envisaged to assist banks to optimize use of human resource and achieve a balanced age and skill profile in tune with their business strategies. A text of the scheme and guidelines as approved by the Government is appended.

As per the scheme all permanent employees with 15 years of service or 40 years of age are eligible for availing VRS. The ex-gratia was pegged at two months salary for each completed year of service or the salary for the remaining months of service left whichever is lower. The right for rejection of VRS was vested with the Bank .

Implementation of the Scheme

Out of 8,63,117 employees in 26 public sector Banks as on 31-3-2000, about 1,26,814 employees applied for the scheme and 100810(11.7%)were granted VRS.[9] Those who faced charges/ disciplinary action were not granted VRS The response to VRS was high in case of officers (27.1%) in comparison to clerical (11.4%)and subordinate staff (6.8%). SBI group allowed VRS to only those who completed 55 years and restricted the outflow to 12.1per cent officers and 8.9 per cent clerks. In case of Nationalized Banks 22 per cent officers and 13.3 per cent of clerks were relieved under the scheme. Thus the banking sector resorted to VRS in a big way in the year 2000.

The Benefits

As per Indian Banks Association, the scheme was aimed at increasing productivity levels, controlling operational costs and reducing average age profile. Mr. N.S. Nayak, General Manager, Bank of India says, "with computerized systems having been installed, we realized we were carrying excess flab that was adversely affecting our bottom line. Therefore we decided to implement VRS." Mr. R.M. Nayak, General Manager, credit and international banking, Bank of Maharashtra says, "Not only has our bank now become more customer friendly after implementing VRS, it is also more profit oriented largely because the average age of our employees has fallen to 49 from about 55 a few years ago." Similarly for Bank of India, the average age has come down to 49 from about 54 a few years ago (domain-b.com, 16th May, 2001).

Some authors argue in favour of VRS as a profitable proposition. They say that VRS is not a financial burden, "but it is an immensely profitable investment...Golden handshakes typically amount to around 1.5 to 2.5 years of pay plus the fringe benefits...If a company pays Rs. 500 crores in VRS, it saves Rs. 200 crores annually in its wage bill, meaning it is getting a whopping return of 40 per cent in its outlay. No other outlay can yield such a high return (Aiyer, 1995, p. 1359). They suggest that companies short on cash should therefore float bonds for VRS offering attractive rates of 18 per cent (now the rates have plunged far lower) since they get an internal rate as attractive as 40 per cent. This will still leave them with a surplus of 22 per cent, which can be put in bond reduction on redemption reserves. Within five years the reserve will be large enough to redeem the bonds. So VRS will pay for itself in a very short time (Times of India, Sept. 12, 1993).

Loopholes and Pitfalls

The VRS was aimed at shedding inefficiency but in many cases it has ended up losing good performers and skilled people. The target was to reduce redundancy in clerical level due to manual work shifting to mechanized, but the figures indicate that VRS optees in officers cadre were (27%)more than double of clerical staff.(11%). Further, those who faced disciplinary actions were retained there by carrying the disgruntled staff, instead of shedding them at the right opportunity. In view of the exodus of young officers, the average age of employees of nationalized Banks have come down by only 1.3 years from 43.7 years to 42.4 years.

Post VRS Syndrome and Challenges

Informal discussions with employees have revealed that they have a feeling that the whole work culture has changed post VRS. They feel that the unions have become weak, management has become impersonal and job security is linked to 'perform or perish theory'. However, they look up at the future career with higher salary, and faster promotion. There is a sizable workforce waiting for another opportunity probably with a pension offer. Hence, post VRS, the Banks have an increased responsibility in their HRM to motivate and reassure the employees .The lacunae created by the exit of skilled employees are to be filled in by promoting and training the existing employees and also by making selective recruitments. Achieving organizational excellence is the work of HR.[10] The challenge of downsizing is not merely to reduce staff but to achieve some greater goal, usually defined as some improvement of organization productivity.[11]

A Review of the Decision of VRS Optees

About a lakh of trained and skilled employees have been drawn away from the banking system. Though they have received a fair amount of compensation, they are all attuned to a monthly budget of recurring income. They have to hold on to the lump sum till it is exhausted in the spiral of inflation. Only a few have planned their finance well and many have already started feeling the pinch and their life style has to be restricted. Those who were above 55 and those who had opted for pension are financially happy but a common regret observed in many of them is loss of brand image and social status. A very small number of the VRS optees only could either get better opportunities in job markets or flourish in their own business started after VRS. A few cases observed in the preliminary survey are briefly discussed below (Names changed)

CASE 1: Jayanth was an officer in scale 2 in bank X. He is a B.Sc. graduate, joined as clerk and got his promotions belatedly. He did not have the ambition/hope to become Top Executive. Aged 47years, he was already disturbed on his transfers to Culcutta earlier. He looked VRS as an opportunity to settle in native place. Calculating the interest at 11-12 per cent on hisVRS benefits plus proportionate pension, he assumed a monthly income of almost same as salary drawn earlier. But after three years now he regrets a lot. Less income due to interest rate slide, investment on house and growing cost of children education have unnerved him. More than anything he finds difficulty in social gatherings to explain his position.

CASE 2: Harish was an attender in the Zonal office of the Bank, aged 53 years. Lured by the VRS money he took VRS . Big money changed his life style, bought a new house, bike for son and jewellery for wife and daughter. Within two years his money is almost spent and now he is reportedly seeking short term debts from friends. Plans for mortgaging house bought three years back.

CASE 3: Ravi was an extra ordinarily brilliant guy in his school and colleges. Entered the bank by chance , got good promotions early and also was a good performer. However due to the sluggish growth in Bank, his further promotion was delayed for 12 years. Three years before the VRS he was promoted to Senior Management. He says that he had to take the hard options because of the faulty HR policies of the Bank. Now employed in Private sector and having made wise and safe investments of the VRS money, he earns almost twice the net salary in the Bank. Still he says that the emotional attachment with the Bank where he served for more than two decades pricks him.

CASE 4: A pathetic case where Sriram invested Rs 8 lakhs in a Finance Company of repute and got a job in his native place. The NBFC collapsed within a year and Sriram lost both his job and money. Having family responsibilities, He is totally broken down.

CASE 5: Bhat at 56 was a Senior Manager living alone in a distant place away from his family. VRS came as a boon to him, he left the job to join his family. He says that he could perform the marriage of his daughter and also could visit USA to spend some time with his son a software engineer. To keep himself busy he is taking active part in community and social organizations.

SUGGESTIONS AND CONCLUSION

Based on the feedback, preliminary survey and discussions made the following improvised model for VRS in public sector banks is suggested.

Modified VRS Scheme

1. The scheme will be open to all the employees who have completed 30 years of service and aged above 55 years;
2. Those who have not opted for pension may opt now. Pension to all will start from the age of 60 years;
3. Those who have opted for Contributory Provident Fund may draw their balance and management contribution immediately or retain the same to earn interest and draw in installments before attaining the age of 60 years;
4. All other terminal benefits will be settled immediately;

5. The ex-gratia will be equal to the basic pay plus DA multiplied by the remaining number of months of service;
6. Employees facing disciplinary action will be relieved after the completion of the proceedings and imposing of penalty if any;
7. Management reserves the right to accept the VRS and to fix relieving date;
8. The scheme will be open till the Bank notifies the closure. Cases will be considered on priority and merits.

Scope for Further Research

There is a need to collect empirical data on the present prospects and perceptions of the employees who opted for VRS and also to verify whether the Banks have been successful in achieving their goals by implementing the scheme. What strategies could be evolved to motivate and reassure the employees who are swayed by the technological invasion is a question for HR managers. A feedback from Management and employees on modification of existing scheme would be of great value.

ANNEXURE

SALIENT FEATURES VOLUNTARY RETIREMENT SCHEME–2000

Eligibility	All permanent employees with 15 years of service or 40 years of age as on 30th November, 2000. Following categories of employees are not eligible under this Scheme: 1. Specialist officers/employees who have executed service bonds and have not completed it. 2. Employees/officers serving abroad under special arrangements/ bonds. The Board of Directors may however waive the above conditions, subject to fulfillment of the bond/other requirement. 3. Employees against whom Disciplinary Proceedings are contemplated/pending or are under suspension. 4. Employees appointed on contract basis. 5. Any other category of employees specified by the Board.

Amount of Ex-gratia	1.	60 days' (2 months') salary (Basic Pay plus stagnation increments plus special pay plus dearness relief) for each completed year of service or salary for the number of months of service left, whichever is less.
	2.	For the purpose of calculating ex-gratia, fraction of service of six months and above will be reckoned as one year.
	3.	Income tax shall be deducted at source in respect of ex-gratia exceeding Rs. 5.00 lakhs or such other ceilings as may be prescribed under the Income Tax Act.
Other Benefits	1.	Gratuity as per Gratuity Act/Service Gratuity, as the case may be.
	2.	Pension (including commuted value of pension) as per Syndicate Bank Employees' Pension Regulations 1995 Bank's contribution towards PF as per rules.
	3.	Leave encashment as per rules.

REFERENCES

1. Cameroon. K , Strategies for successful Organizational Downsizing , *Human Resource Management*,1994, 33(2), pp. 183-188.
2. William R.Tracey: The Human Resource Glossary. CRC Press, N.Y Second Edn,(1998) pp. 149,155.
3. Legaski.Ted.W, Downsizing, Downscoping and Restructuring, *Research in Organizational Change and Development*, Vol 11, (1998) pp. 253-270 JAI Press.
4. P. Ray & Kaustav Dey ,VRS and Its Effect on Productivity, *IJIR 39*, July 2003.
5. Suri A.K & Poonam, Analysis of Reasons for Voluntary Retirement, *Delhi Business Review*, Vol. No. 1, Jan-June 2003, p. 93.
6. Martin Rama, Efficient Public Sector Downsizing, *World Bank Publication*, 2002, www.worldbank.org/publications/workpapers.
7. John .H & Manisha Singh, Public Sector Retrenchment *World Bank Economic Review* Vol. 13 No.1 Jan. 1999.
8 Thingalaya.N.K, VRS—A Golden Handshake, *Industrial Economist* 15-29, Sept. 2000.
9. Sahoo & Peireira, Post VRS Challenges, *IBA Bulletin*, April 2000.
10. Ulrich Dave K, A New Mandate for Human Resource, *Harvard Business Review*, Jan-Feb 1998.
11. Jones V.D, Management of Public Sector Workforce Reduction, *N.Y Sharpe*, Inc. 1998.

19

An Approach to Assess the Quality of Technical Institutions

*K B Mishra**
*A.Jain***

ABSTRACT

Liberalization, globalisation and privatization has resulted demand for technical manpower in last few years, giving rise to the increase in technical degree holder. This uncontrolled growth could not lead quality along with. Now it felt that quality should be assured with quantity to achieve benefit of liberalizations and globalization. Data shows only 2.5 per cent institutes/5 per cent programmes are covered by existing accreditations process.This drastically low figure pushed us to study number of systems available to scale quality. Be targeted our stack holder, interacted with them and leave to design questioner to get quality indicator. After that these quality indicators are put back to stack holder for their consideration to get weight age. In form of questioner and design the simple quality scale, tested it for results to insure compatibility as other systems have. This Quality Model can be easily understood and adaptable in order to asses the performance of any institute and the quality of technical manpower coming out from it.

* **Madhav Institute of Technology and Science, Gwalior-474005, Phone: 0751-5049313, Fax: 0751-2364684, E Mail: kbdar2003@yahoo.co.in**

** **Madhav Institute of Technology and Science, Gwalior-474005, Phone: 0751-5049313, Fax: 0751-2364684.**

The parameters for quality assurance have been compared with the existing one i.e. National Board of Accreditation(NBA) and the model has practically applied to a institute and than results are compared with NBA.Some suggestions are also given in this chapter to improve the existing policy of present NBA.

Key Words: Stakeholders, Quality indicators, Quality Model.

INTRODUCTION

During past many years there has been constant cropping up of technical education institutes. But as quantity always can not promise of quality, same is the case here. The ever growing of institutes has lessened the level of quality up to a great extent. Which has come up as great effect on students, parents, faculty and top of every thing industry?

Globalisation of words has put an end to boundaries. India being a democratic country every person has the right to choose carrier of his/her choice. More or less technical institutes have scored highest in this seen.

As per as deployment of country is concerned in this age of through cut competition and struggle for survival, a high quality human resource is required.

To maintain the level of quality all technical institutes has to apply quality assurance system. Issues which are relevant factors for quality are teaching learning process, need base curriculum , effective industry institute interaction, better faculty and development institution improvement in institute management, strengthening the learning process by predicting betterment of library and computer facility, more focus on student services, application oriented practical and resources, various model and quality assurance system play eminent role.

After the bench marketing studies carried out in the technical education sector. The ranks given to institutions not only depend on teaching and research but over the entire range of knowledge mission. (Sheffield 1998)

For approaching this wide range of quality indicators discussion has been carried out with stack holders of technical education. On the basis of prolonged discussion questionnaire has been prepared for stack holder and on the basis of feed back received from them and literary survey. Varied categories for quality as well as indicators which source quality have been listed out. These qualities indicators hold back to the stack holders to give most necessary, necessary, not required ratings according to contributions toward quality. After the analysis of the result, a model is prepared for quality assurance.

NEED FOR THE QUALITY OF TECHNICAL INSTITUTIONS

Honorable president of our country Dr. Abdul Kalam has highlighted that future of country lies with the technological developments, thus role of technically trained manpower is becoming increasingly important and will be one of the pre determinants of all futures development and growth.

National policy of education was developed in 1986, recognized be significant contribution made by technical education into India economical development.

Several issues have been identify which require immediate attention to maintained the pace in this policy i.e. obsolescence of machinery and equipment, updating and up-gradation of curriculum, in-ability to attract good teachers(30% short fall on the average), industry institute interaction, Lack of work ethics in the majority of institution, industrial investment in R&D, quality assurance in technical education.

Technical education in engineering and technology especially at undergraduate level has expanded exponentially after 1981.

Some important facts are:

1. The increase in intake of degree level was 17 per cent in 1961 which have gone to 221 per cent in 1991-01.
2. While basic engineering education i.e. diploma level the intake is increased 84 per cent from 1971-81 further decline to 60 per cent in 1991-01.
3. The student at degree and diploma level is recorded as 3.59 lacs and 2.35 lacs respectively.

Various quality assurance mechanism and models are working world wide as a result acceptance of quality assurance system is increased publicly.

The demand for perpetual improvement of all types of technical education (Government and Private) will raised from all stack holders and they have to come up to the level of students with more transparency in approaches and decisions.

Presently the quality assurance body exist in our country, they are: NBA (National Board of Accreditation) by AICTE and NACC(National Assessment and Accreditation Council). Setup by UGC in1994 for higher education institutes.

No. of colleges and their intake capacity shown in the given table.

Year-wise	Diploma No. of Colleges	Approval Intake	Degree No. of Colleges	Intake Approved
1947	53	3676	44	2500
1950	46	4200	50	3700
1960	1935	26500	114	16000
1970	309	43500	139	18200
1980	332	49200	158	28500
1990	879	122000	387	66600
2000	1224	188300	838	232229
2002	1203	233296	1057	295706

This accreditation process provides guidelines for assessment of quality of existing programmes as well as a continuous process of improvement is stimulated.

Accreditation process is useful for both institute as well as stack holders. This is useful for rectifying the strength and weakness of the programme. This helps the institution in identifying of the gray areas where immediate action is required to upgrade the quality of education.

Accreditation indicates the stack holders that the academic aim and objectives of the institutions are known to the honesty passed and effectively achieved.

Since establishment of NBA, in past 14 years only 1019 programmes have been accredited, where as1071 applied for accreditation .While AICTE has the target of accreditation to all the engineering programmes by the end of 2005.

In our opinion technical Institutes has major advantage and proving to be more beneficial if they adopt quality assurance i.e. (self evaluation accreditation , academic audit etc.) But process of accreditation is complex and not easy to understand . Now what is the basis of awarding marks to different categories internally? What is the datum line to get marks for particular indicator? All this is not known to anyone.

To solve these problems I developed a quality assurance model which is easy to understand and if followed by any institution .They can easily identify their strength and weak areas as well as the gray areas on which they need to more attention.

The programme quality has to found out satisfactory with this model. After the self evolution, if institutes applied for accreditation , it is sure that the institute will get accredited.

PRESENT SCENARIO

The reason for fast growing of technical education providing institution is that this is highly appreciated professional education in India society. Due to government policies entrepreneurs came forward to promote undergraduate education .Since it was found rewarding on commercial ground.

This profit making approach is creating more quality assurance problem. On one hand intake capacity of institution has increased as far as fascination for the Engg. Which concerned, on the other hand because of the ban on recruitment of faculty (Govt. and Semi Govt. Institutions) , no faculty is appointed anywhere during the past seven or eight years, only part time and contract based teachers in order to carry the responsibility. So half of the time they channel their energies towards the directions of final settlement. Promotion has been banned for regular faculty, which may turn out as frustration. In the absence of qualified, experienced and regular teachers, the quality of the newly opened institutions became half baked which further added to the decline of quality.

This rapid admission policy of institution respective of the Engg. Aptitude can be counted once again as down fall in the quality. For example it can be coated that in the Madhya Pradesh one student who got supplementary in XII unfortunately got admission in Engineering. As technical institutions are need based, it hardly effects national Mechanism .The policy of good reason of curriculum is hardly being implemented strictly. Industrialist and subject expert are hardly bothered about the setting up of board for curriculum reason. The working environment of technical institution is pathetic and lacks moral. Every next person is busy in finding fault in others. No sprit self improvement rather "Tuition at home "and sheer negligence towards teaching has become very commonly seen scene of technical institution.

Director of technical education of M.P. has signed MOU with CII and other organizations but effective utilization of resources of both partners is still waiting to the started.

QUALITY ASSURANCE

What is Quality?

Quality is a relative term and it is generally used with reference to the end use of the products. For example, a gear used in sugarcane juice extraction machine or grass cutter may not required the general parameter of quality like surface finish, accuracy, noiseless operation etc.

The definition it changes in context of time frame and economical growth.

The Old View

"The product and services that are provided exactly to specification"

According to quality gurus the quality is:

1. conformance to requirement (Crosby 1979);
2. fitness for use is quality (Juran 1986);
3. quality means getting every one to do what they have agreed to do and do it right the first time and the every time (Cross by 1992);

4. quality is what the customer say it is.(A.V. Feign Bawm) so the journey which starts from confirmation of specification is reached to delight the customer.

The New View

"Product and services that totally satisfy our customer need expectation in every respect on a continuous basis."

PROPOSED MODEL

First Step

After the problem identification the first thing is to be done is to find stack holders and enlist them. The stank holders are:

1. student
2. teacher
3. parents
4. employees
5. industry
6. society

After enlisting stack holders to define the quality of technical education, I personally met stack holders and tried to get views about quality and issued relevant to quality. I have also gone through the existing accreditation mechanism of NBA, NACC and different journals of ISTE to get more information regarding quality of technical education.

After this literature survey and analysis, I have prepared four questionnaire for student(at present), passed out students, industrial people, teacher. The sample size for each type of questionnaire is 50.

Second Step

After the literature survey and feed back received in the form of questionnaire deep study and analysis carried out. Quality parameters are defined and end enlisted. Since these parameters has variety in nature as well as its contributions towards quality is different. It is grouped under 13 sub categories on the basis of similarities in nature.

According to new concept the quality parameters responsible for the quality in technical education system can be broadly categorise in three major categories:

1. Hardware
2. Software
3. Humanware

These major categories further divided into sub categories:

Hardware

1. Management efficiency
2. Lab/workshop/equipments
3. Library
4. Computer centre
5. R&D

Software

1. Mission goals and organisation
2. Teaching learning process
3. Supporting process

Humanware

1. Feedback of image of college
2. Faculty/faculty development
3. Student placement/output performance
4. Supporting staff
5. Industry institute interaction

Third Step

To award marks for these 3 broad categories and 13 sub categories, a committee constituted of 10 faculty members 2 industrial people 3 pass out and 5 present students. Under the leadership of my project guide and head of the department of our programmes, I m taking an opportunity to present the facts collected through literary survey as well as existing quality assurance systems regarding the marks and contributions toward quality. After the deep discussion and evaluation the marks are awarded to respective category and sub categories.

In my opinion based on experience as a faculty as well as literature survey and approval of committee, the marks for these major categories are:

1. Hardware : Infra structure 25%
2. Software : Process and systems 35%
3. Humanware : Human being uses the in fractures and maintained the process 40%

The marks for these sub categories are:

Hardware

1. management efficiency 120
2. lab/workshop/equipments 30
3. library 60
4. computer centre 30
5. R&D 20

Software

1. mission goals and organisation 70
2. teaching learning process 220
3. supporting process 50

Human ware

1. feedback of image of college 30
2. faculty/faculty development 150
3. supporting staff 50
4. student placement/output performance 100
5. industry institute interaction 70

Fourth Step

After the marks awarded to categories and sub categories, distribution of marks to each quality parameter in the sub category is the next target i.e. formulation of the problem and solution in the mathematical form.

After a long discussion and search a formula derive for the same. For getting feedback about the weightage to these parameters based on the need and power of perception of stack holder. These quality indicators hold back to the stack holders under these heads:

1. most necessary
2. necessary
3. not required

After collecting ratings for these parameters from the stack holders, inputs analyze for proper allocation of weightage tin the form of marks to respective parameters.

No. allocated to ratings are:

1.	most necessary	1.5
2.	necessary	1
3.	not required	0

The formula derived for allocation of marks to parameters

Marks =marks/no. received by indivisual parameter * no/ marks given to this sub categories/Sum of the no./marks received by this individual category.

For example:

No received by parameter no 1 = 54

Total No received by this Subcategory = 447

Total No given to this subcategory = 30

Marks =5 4 * 30/447

= 3.624

Figures are rounded off to reduce complexities in calculations.

Counseling of all stakeholders is done before involving them in evalution process for deciding quality parameters. To get the realistic feedback:

Fifth Step

After the literature survey and study of different accreditation process, it is found that the weightage for subcategories are fixed but the quality parameter for this subcategories and its reference line is not declared.In our opinion that is the main reason due to which the only 1071 programmes were applied for accreditation while the target of AICTE is to completing the process by the end of 2005.

In order to reduce the difficulties and hesitation to adopt the quality assurance process with more transparency we decided reference line for these individual parameters.

Validation of Proposed Model

The process of validation is still going on and we are trying to compare the results of our model to that of NBA. We have chosen our department for this purpose and the validation will be complete by the end of August'04.

CONCLUSION

1. Our model is quiet transparent and easily understandable by each stake holders.
2. This model can be used by newly established technical institutions as a reference before they actually encountered with NBA accreditation process.
3. Institute strength and weakness can be easily identified by our model and necessary action should be taken to strengthen those areas.

REFERENCES

1. *Manual for NBA Accreditation*, AICTE New Delhi.
2. Prof Prem Vrat, Quality Assurance in Technical Education: Recent Trend and Challege Ahead, *ISTE Journal of Technical Education* Vol. 26. No. 2, April-June 2003.

3. Prof R S Sirohi, Prof P C Sinha, Technical Education Programme and Quality Assurane Process, *ISTE Journal of Technical Education* Vol. 26. No 2, April-June 2003.

4. *Quality Model for Technical Education, M.Tech Thesis*, Submitted by Ajay Jain, Department of Mechanical Engineering, Madhav Institute of Technology and Science,Gwalior (M.P).

20

Forecast on Needed Growth of Technical Education in India

*Dr. J.P. Shrivastava**

ABSTRACT

Analytical method is developed to estimate the intake capacities in degree level engineering institutions of the states by using parameters like population, enrolment in XII class, state domestic product and employment opportunities. Three groups of states have been identified. In one group increase in intake must be avoided, in second be moderately increased and in third group it should be increased considerably to minimize the regional imbalance.

INTRODUCTION

Facilities for technical education in the states need to be related with parameters like Population, Net State Domestic Product, Enrolment in XII class in science stream, Employment, and new emerging technologies. The facilities developed during the last 10 to 15 years did not account for these parameters but are based on policies focused on infrastructure norms and standards, controlled by statutory bodies. Entrepreneurs found these policies financially highly rewarding and Indian society got ample access to socially acceptable technical education. In the absence of demand and supply mechanism, imbalanced growth took place. Three major issues cropped in:

* **Former Director S.G.S.I.T.S., Indore Tel. 2433305.**

1. Geographical and discipline-wise imbalance;
2. Facilities for degree education outnumbered the diploma level;
3. Shortage of senior faculty.

Realizing the acute shortage of teachers and falling educational standard especially in the areas of Computers, Electronics, and Information Technology, entrepreneurs started looking for ties with foreign universities of any standard. The foreign education service providers took it as a boon and developed 'twinning programmes'. The basic issues of evolving demand/ supply policies for graduates and diploma holders by the sates and developing qualified teachers by the entrepreneurs is brushed aside. Regulations for entry and operations of foreign institutions in India is a must. However, more important issue is to assure the good quality of teachers at home. Removing shortage of teachers needs second stage of privatization process in which entrepreneur shall establish education technology centres like Technical Teachers Training Institutions and secondly enhancing facilities for PhD and ME in National Institutions of repute which is discussed elsewhere.[1] An analytical method is developed to estimate the intake capacity in various states and is presented here.[2]

PARAMETERS FOR BALANCED GROWTH

The data for various parameters stated above are obtained from different sources[3,4] for the years 1996 to 2000 and then by extrapolation up to 2005. Sixteen states having higher values of parameters are clubbed together that have 98 per cent of total intake capacity and therefore practically represent the whole country. The values of these parameters are given in[2] that are used in the text to follow.

METHODOLOGY FOR BALANCED GROWTH INTAKE CAPACITY

Examining the nature of Carl Pearson coefficient of correlation between intake capacity and parameters as well as 'statistics' generated in Simple Regression, it is observed that enrolment in XII class is the single best parameter to estimate the intake capacity. In order to consider the effect of other parameters,

Multiple Regression is carried out and the model that gave the best 'statistics' is chosen which consists of three parameters i.e. population, enrollment in XII class and employment. The regressed intake capacity is obtained and named as Balanced Growth Intake Capacity for the year 2000. The regressed intake capacity of 2000 is increased by 5 per cent for each state. Taking these values of intake capacity and balanced growth parameters for the year 2001, again Multiple Regression is carried out with several combinations of parameters to obtain the best 'statistics' and hence, balanced growth intake capacity in 2001. This time the best model is obtained from four parameters, viz. population, enrolment in XII class, employment and net state domestic product. Similar procedure was carried out with 7.5, 10, 15, 20, and 25 per cent increase in the regressed intake capacity for the year 2000 and balanced growth intake capacities for 2001 were obtained. Using the parameters for 2002 to 2005 in succession and following the above procedure for each year the balanced growth intake capacities are obtained for the years 2003, 2004 and 2005 for various growth percentages, where as for 2006 to 2008 it is extrapolated. The 25 per cent growth over intake capacity in 2000 is chosen to arrive at the intake capacity sanctioned in 2002 i.e. the year up to which sanctioned intake capacity is known. Later from 2003 to 2008 , 5 to 15 per cent growth is considered to be adequate.

CRITICAL REVIEW OF SANCTIONED AND BALANCED GROWTH INTAKE CAPACITY

Graphs for sanctioned and balanced growth intake capacity with 5 to 15 per cent growth are prepared for sixteen states. It is noticed that two groups of states have much higher/lower intake capacity than the balanced one and third group has more or less equal values. Thus, three groups of states are identified and one from each group is discussed below.

States in Which Intake Capacity has Reached to Saturation

In Andhra Pradesh sanctioned intake is much more than balanced intake capacity. Thick solid line in Fig. 20.1 shows sanctioned intake and dotted line thereafter indicates that intake capacity should remain constant. Thin line gives balanced intake capacity up to 2003 and thereafter dotted lines show the balanced

In Thousand

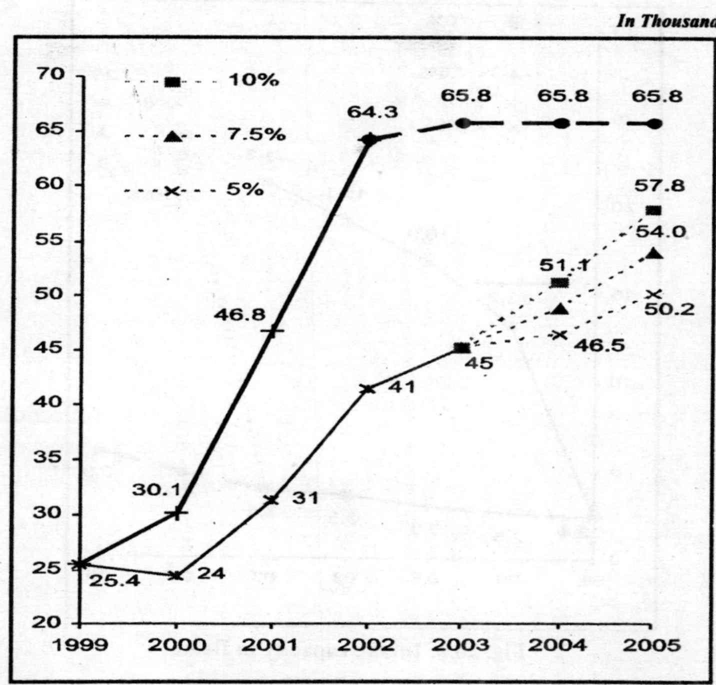

Fig. 20.1: Intake capacity in Andhra Pradesh

intake capacity for various growth percentages. Since the actual intake capacity is much more than balanced one it indicates saturation. Haryana, Kerala and Tamil Nadu are also saturated states.

States in Which More Intake Capacity is Needed

Fig. 20.2 shows that actual intake capacity in Delhi is much less than balanced one since 1999 to 2002. At this stage it is not possible to follow the path of thin dotted line and therefore intake capacity should be increased judiciously in future as shown by the thick dotted line. Similar is the case with Assam, West Bengal, Maharashtra and M. P.

In Thousand

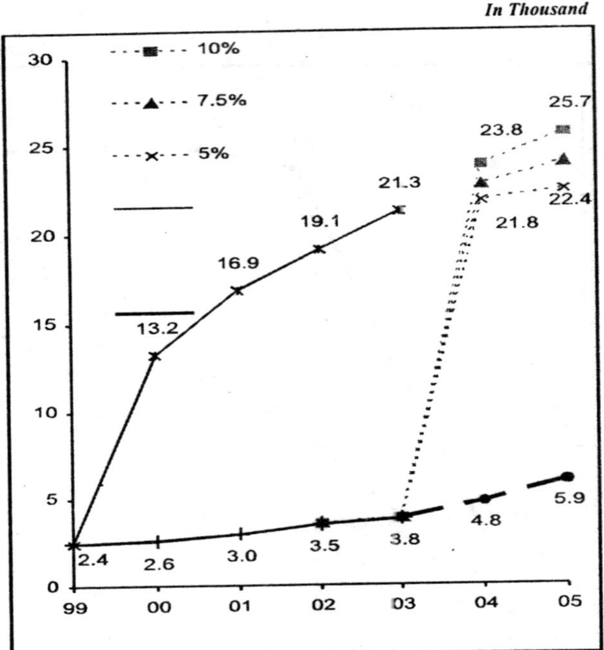

Fig. 20.2: Intake capacity in Delhi

States in Which Moderate Increase is Desirable

Fig. 20.3 shows the cases of Karnataka where sanctioned and balance intake capacity are more or less equal. Same is the situation in Punjab, Uttar Pradesh, Gujrat, Bihar, Orrisa and Rajasthan. In these states moderate increase in intake is desirable.

Remarks

The critical review indicates that growth rate in saturated states must be restricted. Only marginal changes in intake discipline are to be considered. The increase in intake capacity in remaining two groups may differ from state to state in the same year because the earlier growth was too slow, and now may not sustain very high growth rate. A judicious judgment has to be made by states to increase the intake capacity. These issues are important because absorption and unemployment of fresh graduates are closely linked with outturn of graduates.

In Thousand

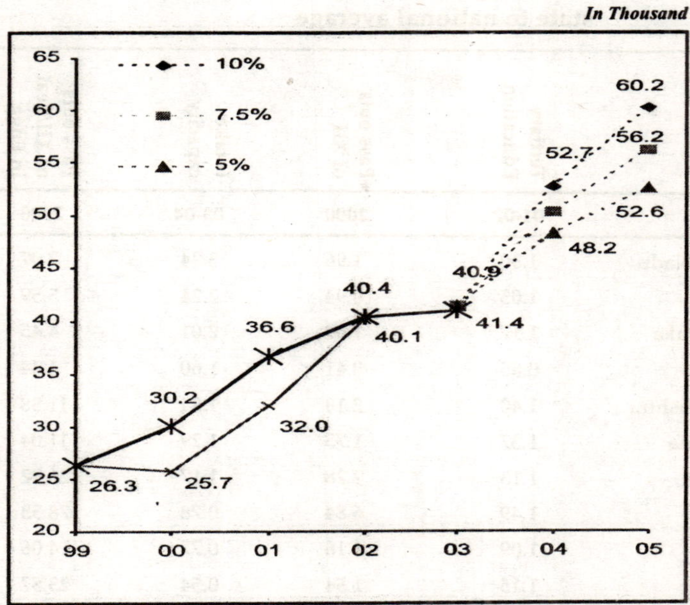

Fig. 20.3: Intake capacity in Karnataka

SECOND APPROACH FOR BALANCED GROWTH

In another independent study, the ratio of tertiary enrolment per million population of the state to national average is obtained. Similar ratios for net state domestic product passouts of XII class and intake capacity are also calculated and given in Table—20.1. From this table it can be seen that in one of the saturated state the intake capacity per million populations is three and half times the national average where as passout of XII class per million populations to the corresponding national average is only 2.

Table—20.1 Ratio of parameters per million population of the state to national average

State	Tertiary Education	Pass outs of XII	Intake capacity	Pass outs of XII/Seat in Engg.
	01-02	2000	03-04	2000
Tamil Nadu	1.30	1.96	3.34	7.07
A.P.	1.05	0.94	2.24	5.59
Karnataka	1.17	1.09	2.01	4.45
Kerala	0.85	0.41	1.60	4.44
Maharashtra	1.40	2.18	1.34	11.38
Haryana	1.37	1.75	1.29	11.04
Punjab	1.13	2.28	1.17	26.92
Delhi	1.49	6.84	0.78	78.53
Orissa	1.09	1.16	0.77	14.06
Gujarat	1.15	1.54	0.54	23.82
Rajasthan	0.72	1.37	0.50	33.66
M.P+	0.84	1.35	0.50	24.52
West Bengal	1.03	1.10	0.43	28.76
U.P+	0.77	1.43	0.36	34.21
Bihar +	0.75	0.25	0.09	18.74
Assam	0.97	0.92	0.07	86.15
India	1.07	1.66	1.06	10.44

Further, the situation is worst in some states where the intake is very high and availability of XII pass-out per seat is very low (4 to 7) compared to other states (>15). In order to bring the regional balance and equity in access to the technical education, the growth in intake capacity need to be restricted in saturated states and judiciously increased in deficit states. It is also true that all the states cannot have the same national average. However; AICTE may set the limits which may be above or below the national average so that no state goes beyond or falls below such limits. Indicative upper limit could be 1.5 times the national average and in deficit states lower limit may be 0.75. States in which, intake capacity per million populations to the national average is very high or low are not likely to come close to the national average very soon. Special attention is required in these states both by the states as well as AICTE.

Table—20.1(A) Indicative intake capacity in India

Year	Intake Capacity
2004-05	421000
2005-06	437000
2006-07	454000
2007-08	474000
2008-09	495000
2009-10	517000

Several aspects stated above have been included in both the analytical studies to arrive at indicative intake capacity at national and state level given in Table—20.1(A) and Table—20.1(B) which will be helpful in minimizing the present regional imbalance and also planning of technical education in the country.

Table—20.1(B) State-wise indicative intake capacity at beginning of academic session

In Thousand

State	04-05	05-06	06-07	07-08	08-09
1	2	3	4	5	6
A. P.	67	67	68	69	69
Assam	1	1	1	1	1
Bihar	4	4	4	5	5
Delhi	4	5	6	7	8
Gujarat	12	14	16	18	21
Haryana	10	10	11	11	11
Karnataka	41	42	42	43	43
Kerala	20	20	21	21	21

(Contd...)

1	2	3	4	5	6
M. P.	17	18	19	19	20
Maharashtra	50	52	55	58	61
Orissa	12	13	14	16	17
Punjab	11	11	11	11	11
Rajasthan	11	12	13	13	14
Tamil Nadu	80	80	81	81	82
U.P	27	30	33	36	40
W.B.	15	18	20	23	27
Sub-Total	383	397	413	431	450
Others 10 %	38	40	41	43	45
India*	421	437	454	474	495

SOME IMPORTANT OBSERVATIONS

National Technical Manpower Information System (NTMIS) publishes Annual Technical Manpower Review for each state. Based on NTMIS data some important information has been compiled to assess the intake capacities, which are:

1. Around 10 per cent of sanctioned intake capacity remains unfilled, at national level;
2. The ratio of outturn to intake capacity at national level is 0.734. It varies from state to state from 0.65 to 0.82;
3. 10 per cent graduates of the total outturn enroll for higher studies in India and abroad;
4. 5 per cent graduates get jobs outside India or not interested in job;
5. 2 per cent graduates go as apprenticeship training.
6. 63 per cent of total sanctioned intake capacity is available for labour market in the country;
7. 50 per cent of degree holders available in labour market get first employment within a year;
8. It takes 3 to 4 years to get first employment for complete absorption of the batch passed out in a particular year.

CONCLUSION

The intake capacity at degree level is estimated by evolving analytical methods in which population, enrolment in XII class, net state domestic product and employment in each state are considered. Intake capacity in the year 2000 is taken as base. Balanced growth intake capacity for major sixteen states is obtained with various growth percentages. It is observed that intake capacities in Andhra Pradesh, Haryana, Kerala, and Tamil Nadu have already reached to saturation level in 2002 and thus there is no scope of its increase until 2005. Substantial increase in intake capacity is required in Assam, Delhi, West Bengal, Maharashtra and Madhya Pradesh. The intake capacity in Karnataka, Punjab, Uttar Pradesh, Gujarat, Bihar and Rajasthan is close to the requirement and therefore normal increase is to be maintained. Estimated intake capacity in India would reach close to 5 lacs in 2009. In this chapter a mechanism has been put forward to regulate the intake capacity in various states of the country, however further work is required for discipline wise growth in each state.

REFERENCES

1. Shrivastava, J.P. Demand and Supply of Engineering PhD Personnel in India by 2010. *Report Submitted to AICTE*, 5th September 2000.
2. Shrivastava, J.P. Forecast on Needed Growth and Development of Technical Education in India. *Report Submitted to AICTE*, August 2003.
3. *Selected Educational Statistics* 2000-01, MHRD New Delhi.
4. IAMR, Manpower Profile India *Year Book 2001*. New Delhi.

21

Window-Model

A Solution to Gibbs Effect in Technology Growth and Technical Education in India

Shubhada Gadre[*]

ABSTRACT

A step change resulting in oscillatory behaviour is an indication of Gibbs effect. This further causes the loss of energy in the side-lobes (unwanted pockets). A technological solution to this problem is to use tapered window model instead of a rectangular.

During the last three decades technology is growing with a very fast rate bringing almost a Step Change. The last decade has witnessed a global transformation in most of the fields of technology. The entire world experienced an overshoot in terms of industry growth and job opportunities, followed by a downfall due to growth prediction errors. These observations match the consequences of the Gibbs effect.

Analogous to windowing in technological world, it is necessary to design the window models for technical education function, with tapered (finite) slopes instead of infinite slope. This in turn sets unequal weights as per priority.

This chapter discusses the concept of such window models, defining their features and bringing self-designing aspect.

* **V.J. Technological Institution, Matunga, Mumbai– 400 019, Email: shubhadagadre@hotmail.com**

Key Words: Gibbs effect, Technical education, Technical person-power.

INTRODUCTION

The Opportunities

The Technological developments are bringing a revolution in the world. The progress in Communication technology has brought the world so near that physical distance has not remained a barrier. The tools like internet, mobile communication, and video conferencing make a physical presence of a person-power at a site of operation unnecessary. Taking the advantage of the situation worldwide industry now gets the work done by wherever cheap labour is available. The global village approach is coming to existence in real sense. Many opportunities knock our doors today if we have desire to take them. All types of jobs, right from call-centers, IT applications to software development, IC chip designing etc. are waiting at our doorstep.

This situation has brought two types of opportunities to us. The first one is definitely bringing many job opportunities to our country but we cannot be dictating the terms. These jobs may be high paid for Indian conditions and need expertise only in respective fields. These may be available to us until we prove to be cheaper in labour cost, to those offering us jobs, compared to others in queue.

However, if we have insight obtained from thorough knowledge, foresight gained after field experience, courage of taking challenges and unified approach of looking at different application areas, and then we may very well be in a position of dictating the terms. This of course could not come to us as a free package. It will take some more years of genuine efforts and dedication.

Need for the Solution

Both types of challenges demand a high quality expertise in technical fields. Creating such expertise is a responsibility of Technological Institutions. It has been already established[1] that the quality education in itself demands infinite quality factors in all types of resources including financial and faculty expertise. When finite terms (resources) are used to fit into infinite slope (finite discontinuity) then Gibbs phenomenon is observed, which gives oscillatory response.

At this juncture, any type of degradation in the quality of technical education would result is disaster. All job opportunities which are available now would no longer wait for us if once we lose the reputation. It is therefore necessary to search for a solution, suitable for Indian circumstances.

Technology has provided a way for restricting the consequences of Gibbs phenomenon. This chapter first discusses this technological solution. It further attempts to apply it to the problem of quality degradation of technical education and energy loss in unwanted pockets, due to the limited (finite) resources.

WINDOWING: THE BEST FIT-MODEL FOR THE GIBBS EFFECT

The Reason for the Gibbs Effect

When the finite number of terms is considered in the place of infinite terms, it is like truncating the data suddenly. This involves multiplying the data function by a rectangular window.[2] This may be shown as:

$x(n)$ = infinite length data function

$w_R(n)$ = Rectangular window function = 1 for $0 \leq n \leq N$, otherwise zero. .... (1)

$y(n)$ = truncated data function

= $x(n) \cdot w_R(n)$ .... (2)

The Fourier Transform $Y(\omega)$ of $y(n)$ is therefore given by the equation

$Y(\omega)$ = $X(\omega) \cdot W_R(\omega)$ .... (3)

where '. denotes convolution operation.

$W_R(\omega)$ is a Fourier Transform of a rectangular window function and it is a Sinc function. Convolution between $x(n)$ and a Sinc function results in a ripple which is known as a Gibbs phenomenon.

Solution for Gibbs Effect

The ripple due to the rectangular window is very high because its Fourier Transform is a Sinc function. It is simple to show that if the Fourier Transform of a window function is like an impulse, the ripple is eliminated. This suggests the use of window functions which have respective Fourier Transforms like an impulse. Many such window functions like Hann, Hamming, and Blackman etc. have been in use and they reduce the ripple effectively.[3]

$W_H(n)$ = Hann window function = $[\,0.5 + 0.5 \cos\{(2n)/(2M+1)\}]$ .... (4)

Where total window length = $2M + 1$, $-M \leq n \leq M$

The above equation shows that this function has different values at different instances. Similar to this all window functions are basically weighting functions, where variable predetermined weight values are generated. Rectangular window has equal weights throughout the length thus differing from the other window functions in this respect.

The performances of these windows are compared on the basis of width of the main lobe (which shows how far it is from ideal window function) and ripple in the side lobe (energy loss in unwanted regions). There is always a trade off between these two features. A self adjusting window named Kaiser window automatically performs this trade off.

WINDOW MODEL FOR TECHNICAL EDUCATION

The concept of using window function may be tried for the technical education system. According to the windowing technique unequal weights should be set for the different features. In turn, this demands a list of priority of the factors (resources) needed in the technical education system as per their importance.

Thus for a good quality education, following priority list may prove to be appropriate. Digits in parenthesis indicate the weight based on priority.

- Tracking the global technological progress–the vision (100);
- Teaching faculty in adequate number (99);
- Funding by Government (98);
- Admission process (97);
- Curriculum development (96);
- All laboratories as per curriculum(95);
- Library (94);
- Research facilities (93);
- Internet facility (93);
- Continuous evaluation system(92);
- Faculty development(91);
- Industry-Institute Interaction (90);
- High staff/student ratio (89);
- Training and placement (88);
- Lab development in hi-tech fields (87);
- .
- .
- .
-

The list could be extended to any extent. This priority list gives the guideline where no compromise is possible to the features with less or more compromise possible.

TRIANGULAR/RECTAGULAR MULTI-LAYER MODEL FOR TECHNICAL EDUCATION

Models with Unequal Bases

The present technical education system gives equal importance to all the branches/fields that are identified so far. These include the core disciplines like electrical, mechanical, civil, electronics, computers, information technology, chemical, instrumentation, electronics and telecommunications, biomedical etc. Though each of the field is progressing due to the computerization, the progress in all the fields is not with equal pace. In recent years, fields like information technology, communication, signal image/speech processing and VLSI are advancing with faster rate than the other fields. The opportunities in these fields are increasing while those in the general areas are almost constant. It is therefore necessary to promote these fields giving these areas higher priority and more resources for the development. Once this policy is accepted, then it would easy to estimate the number of graduates in different disciplines every year. Accordingly less required courses should be discouraged for expansion whereas the active field may be given further scope. This would result unequal base length in different branches.

Rectangular Models

As mentioned earlier, jobs demanding various levels of skills are available. It is appropriate to have more training opportunities for less skilled levels. Such programmes may be of less duration, thus solving the problem of many ordinary youth which are presently jobless. The educational opportunities should be planned with linear relationship with the demand i.e. more demand, more opportunities. However, it must be noted that high-skill jobs are also available in large numbers. It is therefore necessary to use rectangular models for the areas where both low skill and high-skill jobs are available in the same field. With such arrangement sufficient opportunities may be created. The hi-tech skill along with the experience at global level, may give confidence to our engineers to turn into job-providers.

Triangular Models

The usual triangular model is sufficient for the traditional areas as there is a less opportunity for high-skill jobs. Such policy would create mixed (triangular + rectangular) models with unequal length. It is like using unequal weighting factor. This will take care of fewer graduates in the field demanding less person-power whereas more number of graduates in prospering fields.

India is a developing country. More than 50 per cent of the Indian population is still illiterate. The revolution in the Hi-Tech world therefore has no correlation to their lives. It is an injustice to the illiterate/lagging class of this country to deny the fruits of technological revolution. Nevertheless it is also difficult to wait until the uneducated class becomes educated. The technical education system in India needs to choose for imparting technical education to this class also. It is necessary to think upon such non-traditional ways of teaching learning where basic education may not be a pre-condition.

CONCLUSION

A technological solution for the Gibbs effect is to use tapered window instead of a rectangular one. This chapter tries to apply the concept of windowing in technological world, to the problem of Technical education, establishing a need for designing the window functions with tapered (finite, pre-determined) slopes instead of infinite slope. This in turn sets unequal weights as per priority.

The chapter further suggested triangular and rectangular models for the area with less and more developments respectively.

REFERENCES

1. Gadre S.C., Gibbs phenomenon, Technology Development and Technical Education in India, *Proceedings of the National Seminar on Technical Manpower Planning in India—Issues and Concerns,* to be printed, 2004.

2. Ambardar A., *Analog and Digital Signal Processing,* Second Edition, International Thomson Publishing Co., Mexico, 1999.

3. Mitra S. K., *Digital Signal Processing A Computer-based Approach* McGrawHill International Editions, Singapore, 1998.

22

MET's Thrust of Building IT Manpower

*Prasad Kulkarni**

ABSTRACT

When we dream of "India Tomorrow" (IT) we imagine that right from the farmer collecting his money of his crops or milk supplied to dairy or sugarcane supplied to a factory from ATM's to the child collecting his monthly Train or Bus Pass from Automatic machine installed out side the Bus stand or Train station. All industries, services, work places, banks will be IT enabled with the state of the art communication support. All this leading to effective time and cost cutting in the existing operations and towards the great amount of the transparency in transactions.

Now to achieve the above objectives we need to train our existing manpower with IT education. We need to impart different IT education programme for different population. So that we can progress ourselves in IT industry and IT enabled services.

Now after Literacy our mission will be e-Literacy so as to educate the common man of the country with basic usage of computer and Internet, so that we can make the life of Indians comfortable. We need to invite all the forces closely associated with the IT industry to achieve our goals.

In order to plan the manpower with IT education, we have presented the existing IT education system available in the country and they are suitable for which population of the country.

* **Course Coordinator (DAC), Mumbai Educational Trust's, Institute of Information Technology, Bandra (W), Mumbai—50 Email: prasadk_iit@met.edu**

Key Words: IT (Information Technology), ITC (Information Technology & Communication), LP (Learning Population i.e. the population in the age group of 2 to 21 years), PP (Productive Population i.e. the population in the age group of 2 to 21 years)

PREAMBLE

21st century will be called as century of IT revolution. This century will witness the growth of IT industry itself and the automation of all non-IT industries using ITC. All services, industries, work places will be IT enabled. So we will not be able to ignore the importance of IT education while planning the manpower of 21st century. Now IT education may be the basic IT education leading to know a person about the usage of the Personal Computer and Internet or it can be in-depth knowledge of Software Development Life Cycle. Now this IT education must be provided to every Literate Citizen of the country. After Literacy the e-literacy has to be the mission of the country. In this chapter we will discuss the issues pertaining to imparting the IT education to "The Productive Population of the country" i.e. the population in the age group of 22 to 60 and "Tomorrow's Productive Population of the Country" " i.e. the population in the age group of 07 to 21. Here we have called these groups as Productive Population (PP) and Learning Population (LP). Here is a case study rather a success story of one of the districts of the country, which has to be the vision for every district of the country.

MALAPPURAM—A SUCCESS STORY

A rural e-learning project that the state government of Kerala has launched a year ago has made *Malappuram, India's first e-literate* district. People who used to undertake long bus journeys to pay bills now walk across to any of the 600 information kiosks that have sprung up across the district. The *kiosks*, called *Akshaya Kendras,* offer multiple e-services including payment of electricity, water and telephone bills, registration of complaints in police stations, birth and death certificates and internet telephony. The government has tied up with the State Bank of India for the payment getaway. Mohammed Bashir, a 62-year-old banana merchant, can manage the mouse under his shivering palm.

"Initially it was a problem. Now I know how to handle the computer," says Bashir, who sends an email to his son in Dubai.... Each Akshaya Kendra is equipped with computers, printers, fax machines and photocopiers. It has now facilities for DTP, printing, computer rental, browsing, chatting, and Internet telephony among others. "It has not been an easy task for us. But our unique experience has succeeded well. Now our mission is to replicate the Malappuram success story across the state," says Kerala IT Secretary Aruna Sundararajan; who overlooked the project. Akshaya now aims to generate self-employment opportunities for nearly 45,000 people and enhance the income of those who possess basic computing skills. Already, hundreds of youth in Malappuram have become entrepreneurs thanks to Akshaya. The Kerala government has titled the project 'Bridging The Digital Divide'.... (Source: *http://in.rediff.com/money/2004/aug/19spec.htm)*

IT EDUCATION

We will classify IT education in 5 different categories with different purposes and Target Audience. The following Table- -22.1 gives the details of the Type of IT education, Purpose etc.

Identified Manpower of the Population Which Must Undergo IT Education

We will consider that age group of the population of the country, which can undergo IT training. We select the age group from 7 years to 60 years. Generally we see that the Age group 7 to 21 is in its learning phase so we have named this group as Learning Population (LP) and after 21 this age group becomes the Productive group so we will call this as Productive Population (PP). We have summarised the required details of these population in the following Table—22.2.

Table—22.1 Classification of IT Education

Sl. No.	Type of IT Education	Purpose	Target Audience	Where this can be imparted? or being imparted
1	2	3	4	5
1.	Basic IT education	To use PC effectively	Every citizen who want make effective use of PC	Primary, secondary schools, All organisations, every citizen working in organised/unorganised sector...
2.	Formal IT education	To make career in IT industry	Students going for graduation or Post Graduation	BCA, B Sc (IT or Comp. Science), MCA, B.E. (IT or Computer Science), MIM, MBA (Systems), M Tech or ME (in IT) etc.
3.	Orientation Programmes	To learn how IT can be effectively utilised in Non IT domain	Students of Non IT discipline	Non IT disciplines of education like BA, B Com, BE (Non IT like Mechanical, Civil etc.)

(Contd...)

1	2	3	4	5
4.	Bridge programmes/ courses	Non-IT disciplined students interested in migration to IT industry and IT graduates interested in specialisation	Students who have graduated in B Sc (Non IT), B Com, BE (Non IT like mechanical Civil etc.) BA etc.	MCA, MBA (Systems), C-DAC, NCST, DOEACC conducted programmes or specialised programme offered by many private institutions in the country
5.	International certification programmes	To specialise in specific tool or technology or core areas of IT like network security or microsoft technologies …	Anybody who is functional in IT or a student of IT and want to specialise in specific areas	Online Certification Programmes like Brainbench or Prometric centres…

Table—22.2 Population and suitable IT education programmes

Category of Manpower	Learning population (LP)	Productive population (PP)
Age group	7-21 Yrs.	22-60 Yrs.
Population (2001 census)	*350 Million (*ref Fig 22.1*)	*620 Million (*ref Fig. 22.1*)
Literate population @ 65.38% (ref Fig. 22.3) (2001 census)	228 Million	405 Million
IT education programmes to be imparted/can be imparted	1. Basic IT education (compulsory) 2. Formal IT Education 3. Orientation programme 4. Bridge programmes/courses 5. International certification programmes	1. Basic IT Education (compulsory) 2. Orientation Programme 3. Bridge programmes/courses 4. Formal IT education 5. International certification programmes
Remark	All IT education programmes can be imparted to LG.	Programme No. 3, 4 & 5 are less suitable for PP but can be imparted as per the choice and willingness of an individual

(*Approximate calculated values from the graph)

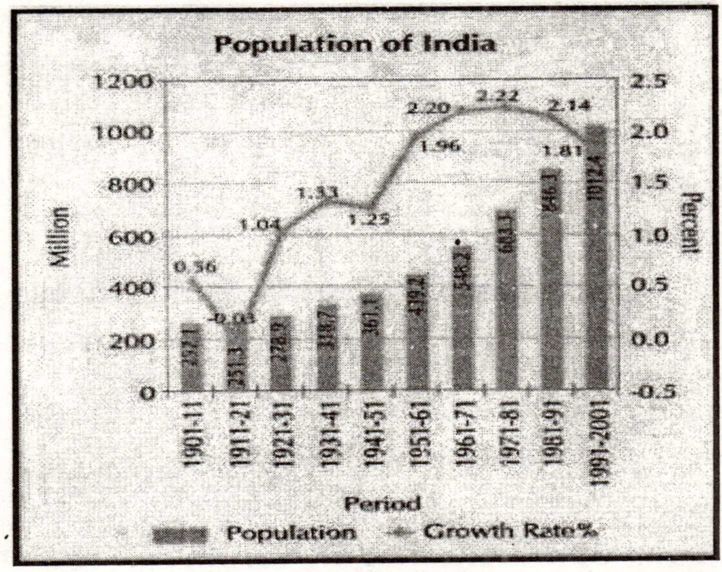

Fig. 22.1: Population age-wise

Sources: National Commission on Population, Govt. of India. http://populationcommission.nic.in/npp.htm

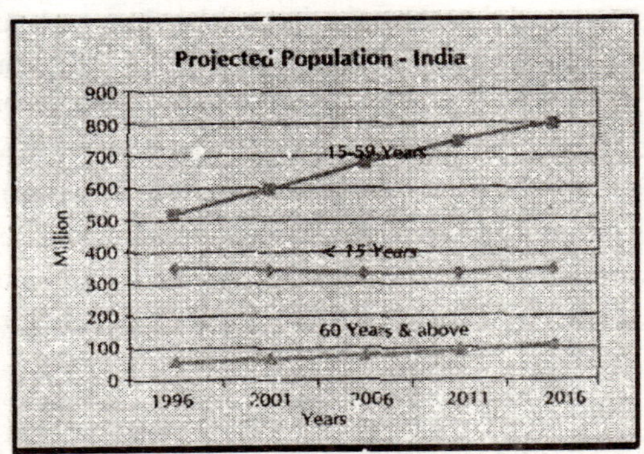

Fig. 22.2: Year-wise population of the country

Sources: Registrar General of India

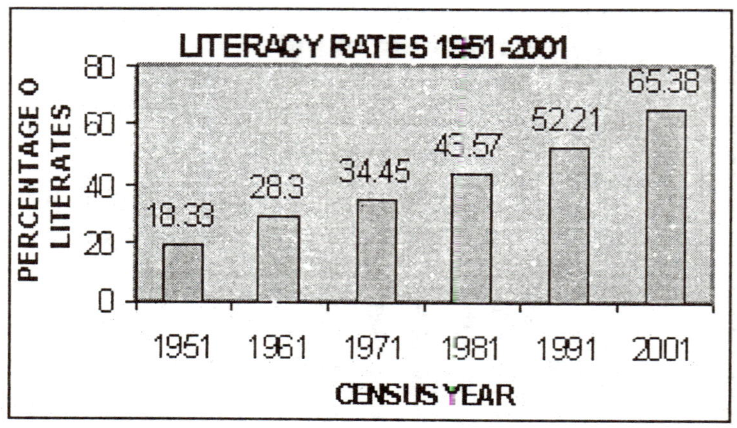

Fig. 22.3: Year-wise literacy rate of the country

FACTORS OF IMPORTANCE IN IMPARTING THE IT EDUCATION; CHALLENGES AND WAYS

Basic IT Education to Learning Population

This must be made compulsory for learning population in Primary and Secondary schools. This is going to become pre-requisite when Learning Population will become productive population. As per from Table—22.3 we can see that total no of Primary and Upper Primary Schools are 664041 and 219626 respectively where the majority of the learning Population learns. Out of which 90.92 and 76.41% (Tables—22.4 and 22.5) schools belong to Government and Local Bodies and these schools are financially not in a position to offer the basic IT education. To some extent given govt. aided schools, which count to 3 and 8.5 per cent for primary and upper primary schools respectively; may not afford IT infrastructure cost. In this case Govt. should take intuitive to invest in IT infrastructure. Some IT giants or corporate world can adopt such schools. Some companies do such efforts.

Table—22.3 Growth of recognised educational institutions from 1950-51 to 2001-2002

Years	Primary	Upper Primary	High/Hr. Sec/Inter/ Pre. Jr. Colleges	Colleges for General Education	Colleges for Professional Education (Engg., Tech., Arch., Medical & Education Colleges	Universities/ Deemed Univ./Instt. of National Importance
1	2	3	4	5	6	7
1950-51	209671	13596	7416	370	208	27
1955-56	278135	21730	10838	466	218	31
1960-61	330399	49663	17329	967	852	45
1965-66	391064	75798	27614	1536	770	64
1970-71	408378	90621	37051	2285	992	82
1975-76	454270	106571	43054	3667	**3276	101
1980-81	494503	118555	51573	3421	**3542	110
1985-86	528872	134846	65837	4067	**1533	126
1990-91	560935	151456	79796	4862	886	184
1991-92	566744	155926	82576	5058	950	196
1992-93	571248	158498	84608	5334	989	207

(Contd...)

1	2	3	4	5	6	7
1993-94	570455	162804	89226	5639	1125	213
1994-95	586810	168772	94946	6089	1230	219
1995-96	593410	174145	99274	6569	1354	226
1996-97	603646	180293	103241	6759	1770	228
1997-98	619222	185961	107140	7199	2075	229
1998-99*	626737	190166	112438	7494	2113	237
1999-2000*	641695	198004	116820	7782	2124	244
2000-01*	638738	206269	126047	7929	2223	254
2001-02*	664041	219626	133492	8737	2409	272

Table—22.4 Percentage of primary schools under different management

Year	Govt.	Local Body (LB)	Govt. + LB	Private Aided	Private Un-aided
1973-74	50.88	42.47	93.34	5.01	1.64
1978-79	38.96	55.03	93.99	4.42	1.59
1986-87	41.37	51.71	93.08	4.34	2.57
1993-94	44.63	47.47	92.10	3.78	4.12
1996-97	47.78	43.88	91.66	3.34	5.00
2001-02*	47.45	43.47	90.92	3.07	6.01

Table—22.5 Upper primary schools under different management

Year	Govt.	Local Body (LB)	Govt. + LB	Private Aided	Private Un-aided
1973-74	50.71	26.86	77.57	17.75	4.67
1978-79	40.31	38.13	78.44	16.90	4.66
1986-87	42.79	32.33	75.12	16.30	8.58
1993-94	45.94	33.51	79.45	9.53	11.02
1996-97	46.41	29.13	75.54	10.25	14.20
2001-02*	47.36	29.05	76.41	7.81	15.77

Basic IT Education to Productive Population

Productive population of higher age group is reluctant to undergo IT education programme. Most of the people have fear of computer. We need to educate them to overcome these types of problems. Until and unless the use of computer is not there in their daily life like in offices, banks, public places they will not be encouraged to learn the computers. Some pressure has to be built up on this population or some incentives have to be given for taking the basic IT education. The incentives can be like while filing the Income tax return some percentage of discount can be offered provided that the person has undergone basic IT education programme. While taking up the new job in Govt. or private agency the IT literacy of the person should be checked then only he/she should be appointed. Instead of visiting to govt. offices for payment of bills, online bill payment should be encouraged.

Formal IT Education

Formal IT education should cover the fundamental things required for programmer or Software Engineer like Computer Organisation, Programming, RDBMS, Software Engineering, Operating System Concepts, Data Communication and Networking concepts. These courses should follow the technological standards set by ISO. For e.g. Instead of teaching compiler specific C++ compiler independent standard C++ should be taught. Formal IT education should prepare the base for professional career. This can be well taken by those students who want make their career in IT industry.

Orientation Programme

Orientation Programme should be offered to all those students who want make their career in Non-IT sectors. This programme will orient them; how to use IT in their career of domain and will help in doing the RD work in their domain area. For e.g. Student of Medical College should be oriented in such way that how Computer is widely used in Medical field, right from scanning the patient till the predictions of illness and the operations. Students of commerce can be oriented how software is used for maintaining the books of accounts. Orientation programmes can be well offered as elective in the final year of his/her graduation. Even orientation programme can be prepared for working professionals and they can be educated to use Computer in their routine life.

Bridge Programmes

These are the specially designed programmes for all those who have graduated in Non- IT discipline and are interested in making their career in IT. Every year, approximately 19 million students are enrolled in high schools and 10 million students in pre-graduate degree courses across India. Moreover, 2.1 million graduates and 0.3 million post-graduates pass out of India's non-engineering colleges. While 2.5-3 per cent of them find jobs in other fields or pursue further studies abroad, the rest opt for employment in the IT industry.

(*Source:* http://www.tatatelecom.com/experienceindia/advantage/strength.asp) Because of the strong knowledge base of mathematics and science and mastery over quantitative concepts coupled with English proficiency; the graduate student become eligible for software developer of programmer kind of job provided that he is completing the Programme like C-DAC's DAC, NCST, DOEACC certification examinations and many other Bridge programmes provided by the private players of the country. Bridge programmes should be designed in such a way that it should provide the basic knowledge viz. programming fundaments, RDBMS, Software Engineering, Operating System Concepts, and Data Communication and Networking concepts. This course should fulfil the requirement of industry.

Even regular Formal programmes cannot train the students in some specialised area like Indian Language System and Application software development (Localisation Problem), E-business Systems, Cryptography and Data Security, Multimedia Technology, Healthcare and Bio-medical Systems, E-Governance, Cyber law and IPR issues, Net-Centric Computing including Web application etc., Quantum Computing, 3G/4G Communication, VLSI Design, Fibre Optics Communication, Digital signature certification, Data mining, Networking Technology, GIS Applications, E-Learning, Content Development for Distance Education, Embedded Software/Technology. For this combination of Bridge Programmes and Orientation Programme can be provided.

International IT Certification Examinations

These are the examinations conducted internationally by some companies which have a tie up with the key IT industry giants involved in designing and developing the IT tools and technologies. This certification provides the accreditation to a candidate; about his/her proficiency in particular technology for which he/she is tested. All students undergoing formal or Bridge IT programmes should be encouraged to take up the international certification examination. This certification is helpful for his employment.

We would like to summarise the level of recommendation of each Training programme for these two groups (see on Table—22.6).

WAY AHEAD, STRENGTHS OF OUR POPULATION AND SUGGESTIONS

Strengths of the Population

The Indian Education System: Boon for Learning Group of the Population

The Indian education system places strong emphasis on mathematics and science, resulting in a large number of sciences and engineering graduates. Mastery over quantitative concepts coupled with English proficiency has resulted in a skill set that has enabled the country to take advantage of the current international demand for IT. Strong analytical and logical skills of the people make learning it easier.

The Largest English Population of the World

Today 2 million-strong English-speaking work force is to the credit of India and it is increasing day by day. This has proved to be our strength against other Asian countries like China and Japan. So the demand for Indian IT Software Professional is there from all over the world.

Demographic Advantage, the Country will be having in the Next Decades

In the period between 1996-2016, population in the:

(a) Age group 15-59 will increase from 519 to 800 million;

(b) Age group < 15 yrs will decline from 353-350 million; and

(c) Age group > 60 yrs will increase from 62.3 to 112.9 million.

Thus we will have strong manpower of 800 million of Productive Population that can be utilised to accelerate socio-economic growth. So the upcoming India is young and energetic. But the challenge is that we need to Invest adequately in Human Resource Development (HRD)/skill development.

Table—22.6 **Level of Recommendations**

Sl. No.	Type of IT Education	Level of Recommendation and Target Audience	
		Learning Population (LP)	Productive Population (PP)
1.	Basic IT education	Compulsory (HR)	Compulsory
2.	Formal IT education	For only those students who want make their career in IT (HR)	Not recommended (NR)
3.	Orientation programmes	Recommended for those students who are from Non-IT background (HR)	Recommended, this should educate the professional how he can use computer in his routine work (UTI)
4.	Bridge programmes/ courses	Recommended for those students who are from Non-IT background and want to make career in IT or students who have done formal IT training but want to make specialisation in IT subject. (HR)	Not recommended (NR)
5.	International certification programmes	Recommended only for those who have completed the formal IT education and/or bridge programme (HR)	Not Recommended (NR)

Recommended, UTI—Up to an individual)

Suggestions for Encouraging the IT Enable Manpower

PC Penetration

Penetration of personal computers is an indicator of the diffusion of IT in various sectors of the economy. It was 3.43 per thousand (in year 2003). Policy has to be designed so that penetration of PC in the market should increase. To meet this objective, personal computers have to be made freely importable; customs duties on import of PCs have to be lowered, so that a common man can afford to purchase a PC like Television sets.

Maximum Use of IT in Govt. Services

IT should be used to its fullest extent in day-to-day operational activities where *"Aam Janata"* involved. This will automatically encourage people to use IT to its fullest extent. Some incentives should be given for utilising online facility.

Online Examination Form Filling and Online Examination Conduction

Govt. bodies or universities should use Online Examination Form enrolment purpose and should conduct the online examination. So that lot of energy, efforts, time money will be saved.

Tax Benefit for Those Undergoing Basic IT Education Programme

Instead of spending money on basic IT education of the Govt. or private professional some discount should be given in tax per se Income Tax for doing basic IT education programme. This type of scheme can be applied for specific age group per se 35 to 55.

Scholarship and Prizes

Scholarship and prizes should be given to those who have extraordinarily contributed to IT research or Innovations. Opportunities should be made available in India to all those who go outside for lucrative jobs.

After the Literacy Mission e-Literacy Mission Should be Started

e-Literacy is as important as Literacy for the country. Now the mission for e-Literacy should be started. During the next census i.e. in 2011, e-Literacy rate should be counted.

MET'S THRUST OF BUILDING IT MANPOWER

We at MET league of Colleges; are studying the existing IT education methodologies as presented in this chapter and requirement of the industry. In collaboration with the IT Industry we are designing an IT Bridge Courses also. We do offer Basic IT education Programme for beginners; house wife's, senior citizens. As a social and moral responsibility towards the society we offer Freeship programme which funds the education of two academically qualified but economically backward students.

REFERENCES

1. National Commission on Population, Govt., of India, URL: http://populationcommission.nic.in/npp.htm
2. The Article "IT Literacy— The New Social Cause Punita Jasrotia/New Delhi", URL: http://www.expressitpeople.com/20020318/cover.shtml
3. The News Article-"Malppuram the First r-Literate District of the Country" URL: http://in.rediff.com/money/2004/aug/19spec.htm)
4. Official Web Site of Dept. of Education, Govt. of India URL http://www.education.nic.in/htmlweb/edusta_pt3.htm#Literacy
5. Official web site of Registrar General and Census Commissioner, India URL: http://www.censusindia.net/
6 Official web site of UGC URL: http://www.ugc.ac.in/inside/statistics.html

23

Effective Approaches and Models in Manpower Planning for Drawing Manpower Balances During 10th Plan

*N. V. Bhandarkar**

ABSTRACT

After independence, the Govt. of India followed the part of five year plans beginning in 1961-62. All states followed the same part. Considering the world economics circumstances , the Govt. of India set up planning commission which considered to have broad economic sectors viz. public sector and private sector. The public sector consisted of central and state departments and their undertakings and co-operative sector while private sector consisted of organised and un-organised establishments. Public sector had almost most of the path and remaining part was engaged for organised and un-organised sector. This was start of captive economy. The Govt. of India strikingly emphases laid on industrial expansion which relied large demand for technical manpower. This necessitated of Technical Education . Up to fifth plan very isolated efforts was made for forecasting demand technical manpower for bigger project during formulation of 6th plan, the Govt. of India and planning commissions considered to have regular forecasting system. The working group on Technical Education recommended to establishments of National Technical Manpower Information System (NTMIS) which was accepted

* **Sankalp –Siddhi, Plot No. 33, Vaibhav Colony, Rajiv Nagar, Nashik 422 009**

by Ministry of Human Resources Development(MHRD) and this task was assigned to the Institute of Applied Manpower Research which is having large part of experts. It is now a lead centre for forecasting technical manpower. In order to have more effective model, country-wise coverage of technical manpower, it has established 21 Nodal Centres of which 17 Nodal Centres look after flow dimension and 4 for stock dimension. This work is being done since 1983-84 till this date. Thus , it will be seen that IAMR New Delhi and Nodal Centres have becomes a large store houses. This system covers all disciplines and levels.

In this chapter an attempt has been made for finding out more effective model for employment generation of Technical Manpower in public sector during 10th plan two years of 10th plan are over. the Govt. of India has already prepared and published it. This documents have 3 volumes which indicate achievements made during 9th plan, dimension and strategy, sectoral polices and programmes, state plans details. However, due to change of guard at National levels, there will be revision of priorities and programmes. Even on this situation, methodology for forecasting will not be effected for estimation of Technical Manpower. This will be useful for central as well as state plan. This enable to help the planners, administrators and technical educationists. Details of basic data to be use for computational purposes. There will be various steps as pointed out and explained as under:

Stock of manpower.

Baseline stock (i.e. 9th plan End).

Baseline stock adjudged for attrition at the end of 9th plan.

Stock of Technical Manpower available at the beginning of 10th plan.

Adjusted stock, one will have to add outturn of every year. For remaining period 10th plan will have to be extrapolated up to end of 10th plan.

Labour force likely to be available at the end of 10th plan from adjusted data trends will be determined.

Finally one will know the gross availability of Technical Manpower.

It will give idea about imbalances in certain disciplines and levels.

All details, steps and methodology to be used is described in this chapter.

Since methodology for forecasting requirements in private sector is already presented in the National Conference of NTMIS at Rourkela.

Sources: Government of India's 10th plan, NTMIS data and various instructions received from planning commission from time to time.

INTRODUCTION

This methodology for planning technical manpower balances during 10th plan. It deals with appropriate utilization, improvement and presentation of human resources for achieving economic and social goals. Manpower planning involves and evolution of existing technical manpower assessment for forecasting in terms of quantity and quality for achieving the stipulated objectives and taking suitable measures for ensure that the technical manpower is available when required for decentralized levels (state level).

Details of basic data to be used for computational procedure for estimation of selected manpower components which are presented in the following para of this chapter. The Govt. of India has already published its 10th plan document. Probably stocks , 10th plan might be ready shortly. For estimating 10th plan requirements, it is absolutely essential to have data of 9th plan. The data required is as under which also available with Nodal Centres as far as many state is concerned.

Item I: Baseline stock adjudge at the beginning of 9th plan—This is first stage for assessment of stock of manpower position at the given time is baseline year. Various steps involved are.

Item II: Labourforce/Economically active stock -Labour-force Economically active stock for each category of Engineering by applying state specific labourforce participation rate on the stock of manpower of concerned category. Estimate of labourforce participation rate for selected technical manpower. These rates are calculated by Department of statistics and National sample survey of Govt. of India. Adjust stock at the beginning of 10th plan by making suitable allowances for attrition (National worked out attrition rate of engineering is 1.5 for degree holders and 1.0 for diploma holders.

Item III: Components of Labour force viz. Employed, Unemployed and seeking for jobs.–Since NTMIS is working from 1983-84 it will be possible as the components like employed, unemployed and seeking for jobs can be available from NTMIS depending upon the baseline year (2001-2002) Alternatively Employment Exchange data is also available but this data has various limitations and infirmities so data produced by NTMIS which is collected by Nodal Centres will be more useful.

Item IV: Net Availability—Net availability at the end of 9th plan period consist of backlog of unemployment at beginning of 9th plan and net addition availability during the plan period. This means net availability at beginning of 10th plan will be available by excluding attrition rate this will be use as availability at the beginning of 10th plan.

Item V: Requirements total—gross additional manpower requirement—This requires some additional clarifications which are as under:

(i) Gross additional requirements has two components:

(a) Manpower for new programmes included in 10th plan. Manpower to meet replacement due to attrition of existing employed stock. Total to these two components is regarded as gross addition requirements (Now manpower likely to be generated in 10th plan minus attrition and requirements);

(b) In addition to these two components, it has two minor components namely unfilled vacancies and leave reasons.

(ii) Total requirements: total requirements at the end of 9th plan would consist of total employed stock will be as described in item I,III & IV (as above under item 4).

METHODS OF ESTIMATION

(a) *Direct Enquiry Method:* Under this method, the requirements of manpower are estimated by collecting data furnished by the employer for this purpose. The Nodal Centre located in Board of Apprenticeship Training will have to play an important role for collecting this data. They will have contact industries (higher officers). In addition to this Nodal Centre will have to estimate teaching manpower required by existing institutions and as per AICTE Act 10 (a) manpower requirements at the end of 9th plan. Nodal Centre located at BOAT will examine new programmes in 10th plan documents prepared by the states.

(b) *Programmatic Approach:* Compared to above approach, the programmatic approach will be more realistic as a department head will be involved in pointing out as how much manpower is actually generating during 9th plan and how many technical manpower will be generated by these programmes, projects. They are likely to implement programmes and projects during 10th plan, a separate study for private sector will have to be undertaken by BOAT or DTE so that both public and private sector will no more realistic estimates for different sector economy including small scale industries. In order to undertake such steps, a high power Task force will be necessary. This task force will be able some data from Employment Exchanges which study both sectors in alternate year. To estimate technical manpower, NTMIS data will be useful.

(c) *Global Approach:* This method involves establishing a relationship (either by linear or log linear) based on particular years observations between the employment (dependent variables) and some suitable independent economic variable viz. investment or state domestic product as constant prices. One development or expansion target during 10th are known, the likely magnitude of requirement is estimated on the basis of relationship. By this method to availability by the end of 10th plan will be estimated.

(d) *Normative Approach:* Most of Govt. departments, co-operative have develop and implemented. For technical education, AICTE has prescribed norms for Engineering education viz. for one engineering course, it requires

1: 2: 4 i.e. one Professor, 2 Assistant Professors and 4 Lectures. Co-operative sugar factories, spinning mills have also some norms depending on crushing and spinning capacity.

Item VI: *Manpower Balances:* The sequence of steps described under items 1 to 5 above would furnish the basic data to draw manpower balances i.e. of demand/requirement and availability/supply of manpower of specified categories. The results obtained 5 items described above can be used for drawing manpower balances.

Estimates of additional manpower availability can be made by subtracting the total requirement at the beginning of the 10th plan from the estimates at the end of 10th plan. This will also to know the new disciplines and levels , also it will show emerging and decaying disciplines and levels. Thus the Administrators, Planners and Technical educationists will take proper corrective measures.

24

Impact of Programme on Technical Institutions

Debabrata Maji[*]

INTRODUCTION

Till the end of the Second World War there were few Engineering Colleges in India. Prior to Independence in 1947, there were 38 Engineering Colleges with intake capacity of 1850 students per year. After attaining Independence rapid expansion in Technical Education took place, and today India has more than 700 Colleges and Institutions of Engineering and Technology with over 1,30,000 students intake capacity per year out of which 70 per cent Colleges and Institutions are self financing and are providing courses up to Post-graduate level in respect of one billion population by 2003.

Programmes to improve the quality of Engineering and Polytechnic teachers in respect of their expertise and capabilities were started in 1959 with the introduction of teachers' Technical Training Programme in certain selected centres. In 1970, the Quality Improvement Programme was introduced in its present form. The main purpose of the Quality Improvement Programme was to keep the teachers of Engineering Colleges familiar with the up to date development of new concepts and research in their respective fields

* **North Eastern Regional Institute of Science and Technology, Nirjuli (Itanagar) - 791 109, Papum Pare District, Arunachal Pradesh**

of specialization. The various techniques through which this was thought to be achieve included Refresher Courses, Symposia, Seminars, membership of various professional societies, deputation of teachers aboard for on-the-job training and research, and participation of Engineering educators in Engineering Conferences etc. Besides, the Quality Improvement in Engineering Education was sought to be improve in the following distinct ways:

(a) Through short duration Quality Improvement Programmes and Courses which are conducted during Summer/Winter vacations every year for various fields of Engineering and Technology for duration ranging from 1-4 weeks;

(b) Improvement and upgradation of curricula through Curriculum Development Cells established at leading Technical Institutions; and

(c) Sponsoring of Engineering teachers working in various Engineering Colleges for higher studies leading to M.Tech. and Ph.D degrees at Centres of Excellence in various selected institutions in the country.

ACHIEVEMENT

Summer and Winter QIP Schools

These efforts have shown some tangible results in respect of Quality improvement in the Engineering Colleges.

In 1985 as many as 179 Short Term Courses (presently called STTP) on various areas of emerging technology were sponsored by the Indian Society for Technical Education (ISTE) and the Ministry of Education, Government of India for the benefit of Engineering Colleges and Polytechnic teachers. The participation in each of these courses has been restricted to 30-40 participants. But, on an average about 20 participants have participated in these courses. Although exact figures are not available, it would be reasonable to infer that over the last one decade at least 14000 or more Engineering educators would have got benefited from this exposure to continuing education programme.

The result of this exposure to advanced courses under short duration programme has been that the teacher on his return from such participation has given a better account of his/her teaching in the class. Although no standard method of assessing the impact of such Quality Improvement Programmes on the teaching capabilities of the teacher has been devised so far, their is general consensus among education administrators and academic Heads of the Department that the quality of the teacher in the classroom improves in more than one ways by the exposure of the teacher to short duration Continuing Education Programmes.

Apart from imparting new knowledge to the teacher, these programmes have also exposed the teachers to a wide variety of faculty contacts in different locations in the country which broadens his/her outlook and heightens his/her appreciation of the country's social milieu in general, which is so important for the profession of teaching.

Such programmes have been successfully run in the country for some good reasons. There are a large number of teachers and experts highly qualified in their respective fields who would like to share their knowledge and know-how. Equally, there are teachers who are keen to update their knowledge in a competitive job market. Secondly, the programmes are fully subsidized and the participants have to make a minimal sacrifice from their meager incomes. Thirdly, because the programmes are held in different parts of this vast country they provide a means for the participant to travel to distant areas and meet engineers and see the local Industries and have a feel of the actual problems. Also, progressive academic Institutions have liberally sponsored candidates for participation in such programmes. There are others however, who have equally misused the prerogative of sponsoring for administrative control of their engineering employees or for given undue favours to some and denying the same to others.

Evaluation of participant learning in such programmes has been attempted with varying degree of success. Not all participants are equally motivated and it is difficult to tailor a programme to every level of knowledge and skill. Attempts are being made, however, to evaluate the impact of these programmes both in respect of the benefit to the individual teacher participant and to the Institute which had sponsored him. The sponsoring employers often insist that the participant share his/her acquired know-how with his/her colleagues as well as students in cocurricular seminars and formal courses. The participants themselves provide an evaluation of the course, which serves as feedback for course improvement and modification. Ultimately through this mechanism of a 'free market', quality, relevance, and early applicability of new knowledge to career development shall be evaluated constantly and courses not relevant rejected by the perspective participants.

QIP Programme for Teachers Leading to Higher Academic Degrees

Another continuing education programme for teachers of Engineering Colleges which began in 1970 provides special incentives to teachers for pursuing regular courses of studies leading to higher academic qualifications like M. Tech. and Ph.D. Degrees. Teachers sponsored for such programmes are given study leave with full emoluments by their employer and are given in addition to this, an allowance of up to Rs. 600.00 per month during the tenure of the Post-graduate programme by the Institute where he/she pursues the course. Such research fellowships are fully funded by outright grants by the Central Government. The number of staff members sponsored for such programme by a college depends upon the size of the faculty as well as the qualifications of the staff at the time of initial recruitment. Such programmes were, in particular, greatly needed because of the rapid expansion of technical education in the sixties and the recruitment of Engineering teachers with first degrees and some industrial experience only.

These programmes have been found very useful by the participants and employers and have greatly aided in making the Engineering Colleges, located in the various regions of the country, centres of Excellence from where the other members of the Engineering profession engaged in Government enterprises or private industry obtain their share of continuing education through various means.

The North Eastern Regional Institute of Science and technology, Nirjuli, Arunachal Pradesh, which was established in 1984 made use of this facilities for Post-graduate education of its faculty in a phased manner. Between 1984 and 2003, 8 teachers were sponsored for M.Tech. and 22 for Ph. D. Programme which represents about 20 per cent of the total strength of the faculty of the Institution.

It would be correct to say that such programme have been beneficial. But, there have been some understable human problems, which reviewed later.

Curriculum Development

The Ministry of Education and Culture, Government of India established Curriculum Development Cells at a few Institutes in the country with the objectives of framing and developing model syllabi and curricula for the core courses and the various engineering courses of a four year degree programme which could be recommended to all the engineering institutions throughout the country. The efforts of the various expert committee and the various discussions and seminars held by the Curriculum Development Cells culminated in the publication of Model Curriculum and Syllabi for core subjects of the four year B.E. degree course in June 1981. These syllabi were recommended for adoption to all the Principals, Directors, and Vice-chancellors and Directors of technical education in the states for adoption and implementation in the respective institutions throughout the country.

This exercise has gone a long way in identifying in bringing some uniformity in the various B.E. programmes as well as made the programme a little more logical in their approach. It is, however, not yet been assessed, nor is there any mechanism established to do so whether these Model syllabi have been adopted in toto or in a modified form. It would be an interesting study to find out the deviations/variations in the various schemes throughout the country and find out the basis of such variations in each case. In a vast country like India, the relative merit of these modifications arising out of personal/institutional/locational factors would serve as a useful feedback to the design and improvement of the curricula in future as well. The author is not aware of any broadbased comparative study of the syllabi and curricula followed in various engineering colleges in the country.

ASSESSMENT OF IMPACT

Problem of Teacher

In respect of Quality Improvement Programmes for teachers leading to their achieving higher academic degrees, there have been some understable human problems.

The needs of the employing organization have not always been in tune with those of the engineer employee. The employers insist on a legal contract with the employee, which among other things stipulates that the employee shall serve the institution for a period of three years after getting his/her education and higher degree. If he/she chooses to serve elsewhere then he/she has to pay back his/her full salary for the period of training and an additional penalty.

The absence of proper personnel development policies in the staff structures of technical Institutions has led to frequent movement of staff in search of higher positions and better working conditions than those available in their parent organisations. This is a type of 'Brain Drain' from the underdeveloped institutions to the developed ones within the country itself.

Discrimination in sponsoring faculty members for higher degree programmes by the employer has also given rise to difficulties in laying down consistent personnel promotion policies.

Lack of uniformity in the application of these legal sanctions favoured those who got away into better positions without paying anything while others had to pay back all the money under law. Many Technical institutions have had to seek legal remedies in the courts against its former staff. This is neither conducive to promoting neither excellence nor academic freedom.

Quality Improvement vis-a-vis Institute Infrastructure

Some of the other problems in engineering colleges, which will remain intractable and therefore are a hindrance to Quality improvement, Programmes of the colleges are discussed below:

The average cost for training of a student in the IIT's, NIT's (formally REC's), State Government Colleges, private Colleges, varies between wide extremes. So much so, that between a private college and an IIT the ratio of expenses per student would be of the order of 1:20. Even between the NIT's and the IIT's the ratio is the order of 1:5. Inspite of this we are taking up a uniform quality and uniform sustem in all the institutions. Obviously, this is an ideal, which is impossible to achieve irrespective of the inputs through Quality Improvement Programme. The cost of subsidies by the Government influences the infrastructure facilities, which includes well-organized libraries and well-equipped laboratories. Just as these facilities are used for training of the students so also the staff for their self development needs these. The Libraries should provide, besides textbooks, important standard journals. Similarly the laboratory should contain, in addition to routine experimental equipment, some basic research facilities. If a teacher wants to introduce a course, or is interested in doing research, he/she should be able to find 75 per cent of his requirements to do his/her work in his/her own college. If such facility is absent, no quality improvement is going to take place.

Service Conditions

Further, the service conditions in respect of academic freedom should be the same at all the institutions. This is not so at the moment and the major engineering colleges in the country have not taken the full benefit of any of the three Quality Improvement Programmes mentioned above. In respect of implementation of Quality Improvement Programmes there has been no uniform policy throughout the country, which has impeded the fullest utilization of these programmes. If opportunities for participation in seminars and symposia and short-term QIP during vacations are not liberally made available to the teachers in all colleges the benefit of QIP is denied to such teachers as well as students in those institutions.

India is a country demeaned by the out-mode caste system. There is a tendency in every walk of life to grade systems into four castes. Once colleges have been labeled in this manner this classifications is used to deny the basic amenities to the students and teachers in these colleges on the plea that the college belongs to the lowest category. This is demoralizing and tends to diminish motivation for Quality Improvement amongst the otherwise excellent faculty and good manpower resources in some of the colleges.

National Policy in regard to the various technical institutions in the country should, therefore, ensure that similar facilities, and equal opportunities, are provided at all the institutions and a sense of healthy competition is encouraged amongst them. Presently, there is a wide gap between an IIT and an Engineering College in the matter of teaching norms, promotional avenues to the teaching staff, and the various other multifarious inputs, both financial as well as infrastructure, which make the healthy competitive development impossible.

Shortage of Teacher

Due to deputation of teachers for Quality Improvement Programmes for higher studies, there has been a shortage of teachers in the classroom. The vacancies created by deputation under QIP can not be filled on a permanent basis and the ad-hoc staff does not usually deliver the good as desired. Sometimes the situation is so grave that work almost comes to a standstill. Leave vacancies are difficult to fill and are not attractive enough to young engineering graduates. The teachers on duty are overloaded; each one teaching two or three courses in a semester while their counterparts in the top-tier institutes may be handling one course or they may not be even teaching at all, if they may show guiding research or consultation work. To fill the vacancies created due to foreign assignments fresh graduates on ad-hoc basis are appointed. The vacancies created by QIP cannot be filled as they are on regular pay rolls. The ad-hoc staff joins late and they can leave their service whenever they like. The student community openly compares against the ad-hoc staff for their lack of interest in their jobs. At any time not more than 20% of the sanctioned staff is allowed to leave the departments. However, to provide for their teaching work an additional 20% of the regular staff at Lecturer and Assistant professor levels should be sanctioned. Recruitment to fill the vacancies should be done very early on priority basis so that the teaching work of the department may not suffer under any circumstances. Promotional avenues and the staff development schemes as they exist in a top-tier Institute should be introduced in all the Colleges.

Promotional Avenues

Promotional avenues for teachers are inadequate, particularly for those who have obtained higher degrees under QIP and have long professional experience. This has caused lot of frustration amongst the teaching staff. The Personal Promotion Scheme introduced towards the end of the 6th Five-Year Plan has not been implemented uniformly throughout the country. This has caused further cynicism amongst the teachers who have served the cause of Engineering education for more than two decades giving their best efforts for Quality Improvement Programme in every way.

Quality Improvement Programmes everywhere should be followed-up with sustained efforts to nurture Quality Improvement on a continuous basis. This has not happened throughout the system.

It is well known that every engineering teacher desires that his/her research work should be presented as a paper at a national or International Symposium. The preparation of the papers as per the instructions of the organisers is quite a hard and expensive job. The teachers in the colleges meet this expenditure from their pockets. Participation in Seminars and Symposia educate the teacher and expose him to the current developments in the subject. The official sanction to sponsor the teacher, and bear the registration fees, TA and DA is not always given, and it discourages the teacher very much. Adequate funds should be provided to meet this kind of expenditure as it surely contributes to the self-development of a teacher. Often in these colleges a teacher is not provided even with a well-furnished room. Either he/she will be sitting with many other teachers or in the Laboratory. Economy measure or ban on purchases of furniture's, etc. prevents him to get basic amenities. The authorities should liberalize these items and building grants to meet such urgent requirements. In the absence of these basics QIP flounders.

Adverse Effects of Degree-oriented QIP

The teachers selected for QIP by the IIT for a Master's or Doctoral degree are expected to stay at the IIT for two or three year's duration for study and research. The teacher is paid salary by the college and the IIT pays him Rs. 500.00 per month as stipends out of QIP grants. Generally, the teachers extend this leave period by another six months through earned leave and commuted leave. During this period no substitute even on ad-hoc basis is given to the department. The subject of higher study by the teacher is often in no way related with the needs of the department. It meets the ends of his/her guide only. It is a paid holiday with additional emoluments of course to do research and to improve oneself. The teachers in the colleges want to avail it, and the professors in the IIT's also want that colleges should continuously supply them with teachers to carry out their research programmes. An adverse effect of this is the remaining teachers do any such work only when some of them receive additional payment to do similar work. Another effect of this is the misery of the departments, which cannot arrange to meet the teaching load, and the students suffer on this account. As one regular teacher complained: "this (QIP) Scheme is going to be a continuous burden on the college, and the remaining teachers are treated as mute donkeys". Some of the departments of a College, which were flourishing heads and shoulders, above an IIT department before the QIP and foreign assignments programmes began, are now famished with lack of adequate staff; fall in standards; and student in-discipline and restlessness.

There is yet another adverse effect of this programme. If a teacher is found to be brilliant and outstanding, the IIT tries to absorb him. The other QIP scholars quote such cases gleefully saying that the Government relaxed the 3-years bond in those cases. The state of mind of a returned QIP participant is often reluctance and disinterested in the development works of the college, and he/she says dejectedly that he/she has to spend two more miserable years in that colleges, before he/she can venture to get a foothold in a top-tier institute which provides far superior infrastructure and staff development facilities.

The present QIP is like transplanting a plant and nourish it in a different environment. When returned to its old place the plant naturally rejects the old environment and withers away in due course. The QIP scholar, having intimately seen the work-load norms, freedom, facilities and other comforts as enjoyed by the IIT teachers, shows a frustrated and harassed feeling in the discharge of his normal duties although he was previously a very helpful and cooperative teacher willing to do assigned work.

The best alternative to QIP is to improve the working conditions and facilities in the same college for the teachers to develop themselves through research and continuing education. They can be sent as participants to short term summer schools in the subjects in which the department feels deficiencies and provide incentives to deserving teachers for their contributions. If necessary, the teachers may be sent to conduct some experiments of their research work or study a particular laboratory equipment or instruction method to an IIT during summer/winter vacations without disturbing the normal functioning of the departments during a session.

IMPACT OF MODEL CURRICULA

The Model Curriculum and Syllabi for core subjects for the four-year degree programme in engineering was published in June 1981. The model syllabi for four year degree courses engineering was published in November 1981, subsequently in April 1984, a model list of laboratories experiments and equipment was published for the four year programme. These documents have been circulated amongst the various technical institutions in the country over the last few years.

By and large these syllabi have had the effect of stimulating the faculty into action in respect of modifying and improving their own courses in the respective disciplines and institutions. Where the institutions are autonomous, and are the only institutions affiliated to a University, the revision of curricula and syllabi has been easier. In most other colleges, however, it has been extremely difficult to make basic changes because a large number of colleges are affiliated to a single university and there are lot of arguments and resistance to making changes which do not suit the faculty. In fact, there is always some amount of inertia in the faculty's thinking, which does not allow quick change. Lot of time lag occurs thereby.

The model syllabi proposed under QIP did not carry the weight of either statutory direction, or even an outstanding academic basis. Some of the syllabi and courses offered in many institutions in certain disciplines of engineering are far better in content, and in their logical approach to the training of an engineer. These have not been considered by the Curriculum Development Cells, which drafted their syllabi on the contributions of a few professors's chosen at random. Also the absence of a practical bias in these courses is evident. This is due to the fact that most scholars who contributed in these efforts had not generally possessed practical industrial experiences of sorts in the profession of engineering itself.

The administrative structure in most of the affiliating institutions in the country is so rigid and the financial constraints so many that it is practically impossible to bring about a change in the laboratory systems and the syllabi according to the guidelines provided in the model list of April 1984. Unless these impediments in the path of progress and development are removed forthwith it is difficult to ensure any impact of the quality improvement programmes on the quantity and content of academic courses at the grass roots level. Even in some of the better placed institutions AICTE model list of 1960 has not yet been fully installed either due to the paucity of funds or due to administrative slackness or both.

It is therefore, suggested that the model list in respect of equipment is supplemented with a pattern of financial grants, in terms of cost of equipment at the current market prices, which every institution must receive during 1985-90 in order to be able to bring some uniformity and improvement in the quality of technical institutions. When this input is assured, it would not be difficult to ensure that by and large the curriculum and syllabi, evolved by the QIP and by the local experts in the institutions are implemented and made to give better results.

CONCLUSION

The QIP launched by the Government of India in 1970 has by and large awakened the institutions to quality consciousness. Teachers have been well trained under this programme. A few institutions have also improved the quality of equipment, syllabi and training which has resulted in better quality output from institutions. However, there have been some adverse affects of the Quality Improvement Programme on the institutions which have been elaborated in this chapter and which can be remedied by the suggestions made herein.

25

The Collaborative Role of Technical Institutions and Manufacturing Sectors in the Challenging Scenario of Technical Manpower Planning

*Tanmoy Maity**

ABSTRACT

In a country with a potential of large human capital, the formal education, training and on-the-job learning are essential for obtaining skilled workforce and management. Collaborative work is a burning need to the new area of technical manpower planning. In this chapter the collaborative role of the technical institutions and the business houses are explored in the present country situation. Also for examples, some existing collaborative systems in advanced countries are reviewed in this chapter. Here, some suggestions are also made to establish a direct need-based links to the technical institutes in our country with the business world. There is still a big gap between technology development in the institute laboratory and taking it to the market as a product. The manufacturing sectors need to form collaborative partnerships with technical colleges and universities to build networks and clusters of

* **Assistant Professor, Department of Electrical Engineering, College of Engineering & Management, Kolaghat, West Bengal - 721171, E-mail: tanmoy_maity@yahoo.com**

excellence to win competitive advantage from widening scope of technology. It also benefits them from the rising cost, increasing complexity.

Key Words: Collaboration, Technical Institutions and manufacturing sectors, technical manpower.

INTRODUCTION

With the advent of globalisation and opening up of Indian economy to outside world, competition among manufacturing industries has become hard. They are in a challenging situation of cost and quality. To solve their engineering problems thy look up now to the quality technical manpower from existing technical and engineering intuitions. But, in the present situation due to various reasons either there is the closure of lot of traditional manufacturing sectors in different parts of the country or there is a tremendous brain-drain towards lucrative software industry. Better interaction between Technical institutions and manufacturing industry is the need of the hour. As the progress of manufacturing still sets the tone for the overall business cycle and the health of this sector is very much at the core of India's socio-economic fabric, a long-term collaboration is needed between institutes and manufacturing organizations for the purpose of achieving specific business objectives by maximizing the effectiveness of each participant's resources. This will not only provide exposure of industrial atmosphere to engineering students and subsequent placement of young graduating engineers in the sectors but also will change traditional relationships to a shared culture without regard to organizational boundaries. The relationship is based upon trust, dedication to common goals, and an understanding of each other's individual expectations and values. There is an urgent need to prepare engineering students for jobs in manufacturing sectors, by exposing them to newer technologies and engineering methodologies. Expected benefits include not only the improved efficiency and cost effectiveness but will increase opportunity for innovation, and the continuous improvement of quality products and services.

In the past 10-15 years there have been considerable developments in the perception of innovation processes. One of the findings from recent research on innovation systems is that there is a considerable variation between national innovation systems in terms of the extent to which firms interact with different collaboration partners and in terms of whether collaboration is pursued with domestic or international partners.[1] Investigating patterns of inter-firm collaboration is also useful in order to highlight these differences between national innovation systems.

MANUFACTURING SECTORS

Amidst a worldwide change in the way the manufacturing sector is being defined, it is acquiring a whole new dimension. Manufacturing can be defined as physical or chemical transformation of materials into products on a large scale using machinery and/or capital equipment.[6] A part of production and many of the low value added jobs are being transferred to the developing world through global manufacturing networks. Manufacturing is moving, slowly but surely, from mass-production to mass-customisation.[5]

More significantly, the fall in manufacturing activity in the recent past corresponds to a dramatic increase in the services sector—not only in India, but the world over. Suddenly, manufacturing was out of fashion and services—spanning software, finance and a host of other sectors—became the rage. Today the manufacturing is more knowledge intensive than many other knowledge intensive business. Manufacturing is no longer confined to a factory; it has gone much beyond that.

Now, the need of manufacturing organizations is to turn into commercial success of the scientific and technological knowledge in the universities and research organisations. As the companies develop new products and processes, they can determine clearly which activities they will undertake individually, which in collaboration with other firms, which in collaboration with educational or research institutions.[3] Also, they need to form collaborative partnerships not only with technical colleges and universities but also with others like vendors, customer etc. to build networks and clusters of excellence to win competitive advantage from widening scope of technology. It also benefits them from the rising cost, increasing complexity. They should make use of scientists and engineers as a source of expertise. Ultimately the people are the key resource to be considered in order to measure knowledge capital. Business must encourage and support all their employees continually to develop their skills and qualifications. They should introduce knowledge management for creating values from the organisation's intangible assets. Knowledge management aims to asses how knowledge creates shareholder value and to estimate how much to invest in knowledge creation.[4]

TECHNICAL INSTITUTIONS

In a country with a potential of human capital, the formal education, training and on-the-job learning are essential for obtaining skilled workforce and management. Collaborative work is central to the new knowledge economy. The role of the institutions in this context is:

- To establish a direct links with the business world. They should focus the need of industry at large and train graduates with skills to meet that need;
- To keep an eye towards the education considering the cost and competition to re-skill and train the freshers under employment in the firms;
- To change of overall culture of the present learning environment. To promote and encourage innovativeness. To establish the requirement of industrial experience among the faculty members;
- Most of the institutions are reluctant to develop modernised curricula. It is sluggish type, not upto the mark. A budget allocation and formation of committee is required for every institute to modernise the curricula regularly at every year;
- A need of better equipped laboratory. There is still a big gap between technology development in the institute laboratory and taking it to the market as a product;
- Quality of education includes not only training for students but also for faculty, professionals, management of engineering colleges and more. They also play the

part of an information storehouse so those students can access required information. Some of their other initiatives are: awards for faculty, student competitions, scholarships, and emphasis on research;

- To establish a competitiveness among the institutions.

COLLABORATION—EXAMPLES

Many advanced countries have different collaboration system. Strategic Research Programme is designed to stimulate R&D between industry and university researchers in the area of advanced systems. The Strategic Research Programme supports large-scale, long-term research or research projects of up to two years in duration.

Also, they have Industrial Fellowship Programme that supports the salary costs of university faculty in advanced systems disciplines hosted by companies for a period of 2 weeks to 2 years. The programme fosters the transfer of knowledge by providing direct contact between industry and university staff and exposing academic researchers to the industrial environment.

There is the Technology Development Fellowships programme which is transferring the technical expertise in colleges and institutes to the high-tech industry. It also seeks to provide new opportunities for students to gain experience solving real-life industry technical problems.

The mission of the Advanced Systems Institute of BC, Canada (ASI) is to create partnerships and collaborations between academia and industry which further the research and commercialization of advanced systems technologies developed throughout the province and to position British Columbia as a global leader in advanced research and technologies.[2]

CONCLUSION

In a developing country like India with inequalities in income distribution, there is a burning need of promoting manufacturing sectors. As India is moving towards the global competitive edge, the collaborative work can derive the system quality, cost competitiveness, and delivery capability in manufacturing sectors through application of appropriate technology and continuous innovations in products and processes. However, not only the industry and institutes but also the government together must work to create a passion for manufacturing and to facilitate its role in economy and society.

REFERENCES

1. Jesper, Lindgaard, Christensen, Collaboration Between Manufacturing Firms and Knowledge Institutions on Product Development-evidence from Harmonised Surveys in Australia, Denmark, Austria, Norway and Spain. Sept. 2000.
2. http://www.asi.bc.ca.html
3. Houghton, J. P., Sheehan, A Primer on the Knowledge Economy, Centre for Strategic Economic Studies, Victoria University, Feb 2000, pp. 1-21.
4. Cappellin, R., Territorial Knowledge Management: Towards a Metrics of the Cognitive Dimensions of Agglomeration Economics, Int. Journal of Technology Management, 16/26, 2003, pp. 303-325.
5. Future of Indian Manufacturing—The Economic Times:// www.timesb2b.com/etigManu/index.html

26

Mechanical Engineering Education and Employment Scenario in M.P.

Meena Gupta[*]

ABSTRACT

Mechanical Engineering is concerned with all types of machinery's in industries and all aspects of their mechanism and functioning and owing to this, Mechanical Engineering has touched to its height and increased its importance in the light of industrial and technological globalization. The present study attempts to analyze the trend in educational facilities created for Mechanical Engineering viz., number of institutions, actual intake and outturn comparatively overall facilities in Engineering Education in M.P. An attempt has also been made to discuss some important parameters like activity status, earning differentials absorption pattern, absorption rates and estimated size of unemployment to look at the labour market situation of Mechanical Engineering. The scope of the study is limited to Degree and Diploma holders in Mechanical Engineering from Engineering colleges and polytechnics.

There has been in the past decade (1993-2003) significant growth in Mechanical Engineering at Degree level while at diploma level it remains to be constant. At Degree level it shows a mismatch between demand and supply positions of Mechanical Engineers. The study indicates that labour market for Mechanical Engineers do not provide an

* **Project Officer, NTMIS Nodal Centre, Bhopal.**

encouraging picture. This is reflected by the absorption pattern of degree and diploma holders. The time series analysis shows that in most of the years a significant proportion of fresh degree and diploma holders were found to be looking for jobs even after two years of passing their examination. The size of the backlog of unemployment at both degree and diploma level was found to be high.

INTRODUCTION

Mechanical Engineering is one of core discipline introduced in the engineering educational institutions right from the beginning of engineering education in the state. In tune with the emphasis that is given to accelerated growth of the industrial scenario and to bring about economic growth and development of a lot of emphasis had been given to develop Mechanical Engineers right from the starting of the plan era. As a result, over the years, there has been a considerable expansion of Mechanical Engineering education at Degree level. At present (as in 2003) out of 56 degree colleges offering courses in Mechanical Engineering as many as 38 institutions, accounting for about 68 per cent of the total institutions, facilities are available for under-graduate level course in Mechanical Engineering. The number of polytechnics in the state is 46 out of which 33 (about 72 per cent) offer courses in Mechanical Engineering at diploma level. The intake capacities at degree level course have also gone up significantly while at diploma level course it found to be constant. Such significant stride in the development of this core discipline has also brought in other issues viz. the employment of graduates of course at different levels.

The data and information available in the National Technical Manpower Information System indicate that the labour market for this category of engineers is not very encouraging in the State. The study is therefore an attempt to trace the development that has taken place in the facilities for Mechanical Engineering Education both at under-graduate and diploma levels and also capture the signals that emerge from an analysis of labour market situation for them.

OBJECTIVES OF THE STUDY

The study has been assigned the following objectives:

1. To analyze development of facilities for education in Mechanical Engineering in terms of:
   (a) Number of Institutions, year-wise and level-wise;
   (b) Intake, year-wise and level-wise;
   (c) Outturn, year-wise and level-wise;
   (d) Teacher-Student ratio year-wise and level-wise.
2. To analyze the labour market situations of Mechanical Engineers in terms of:
   (a) Activity status of fresh graduates, year-wise and level-wise;
   (b) Extent of absorption, year-wise and level-wise;
   (c) Earning differentials, year-wise and level-wise;
   (d) Size of unemployment, year-wise and level-wise.

METHODOLOGY

The methodologies used for the analysis are the same as adopted under the National Technical Manpower Information System (please see Appendix—I).

Trends in Facilities for Education

Mechanical Engineering Education is not only a general but also most important field having no area untouched where its utility is not taken into account. Looking to this view an attempt has been made to analyze the growth of facilities in Mechanical Engineering. A growth profile of institutions offering courses at under-graduate and diploma levels can be seen from Table—26.1(A) and 26.1(B) respectively. Currently (as in the year 2003) there are 56 degree colleges including universities department and 46 polytechnics in the state. Of these institutions, at the under-graduate level course in Mechanical Engineering is offered in as many as 38 institutions where as 33 polytechnics offer course at diploma level. In other words it implies that of the total number of institutions offering under-graduate course in engineering as many

Table—26.1(A) Growth profile of facility available in mechanical engineering at degree level in MP

S. No.	Year	Total Institutions	Total Intake Actual	Institutions Offering Mechnical Engg.	Actual Intake of Mechanical Engg.
1.	1993	13	1901	11	510
2.	1994	14	1911	12	510
3.	1995	19	3115	14	840
4.	1996	22	3241	17	872
5.	1997	27	4118	20	1044
6.	1998	28	4145	21	995
7.	1999	30	6778	23	1483
8.	2000	30	6880	21	1105
9.	2001	33	6461	22	1128
10.	2002	45	10213	28	1670
11.	2003	56	9110	38	2270

Table—26.1(B) Growth profile of facility available in mechnical engineering at diploma level in M.P.

S. No.	Year	Total Institutions	Total Outturn	Institutions Offering Mechnical Engg.	Outturn of Mechanical Engg.
1.	1993	37	2659	31	687
2.	1994	38	2453	31	542
3.	1995	44	2828	32	790
4.	1996	45	2679	33	811
5.	1997	52	2071	40	653
6.	1998	53	3333	38	959
7.	1999	55	2135	39	561
8.	2000	46	2205	33	633
9.	2001	46	2719	33	652
10.	2002	46	2878	33	702
11.	2003	46	2775	33	455

as 68 per cent of them offer facilities for education in Mechanical Engineering while at diploma level about 72 per cent of the total polytechnics in the state have facilities for offering course in Mechanical Engineering. During the decade 1993-2003, the total number of engineering educational institutions has increased by more than four-fold where as the institutions having the facility for Mechanical Engineering has increased by more than three-fold in the state. A huge number of degree institutions (23) were introduced in the year 2002 and 2003.In the year 1999 there were 42 polytechnics offering Mechanical Engineering education in the State which was the highest and after dividation of Chhatisgarh state, eleven institutions were transferred to Chhatisgarh state and remaining 33 polytechnics offering Mechanical Engineering till 2003.

Analysis of Intake

The time series data on actual intake at degree level in Mechanical Engineering are given in Table 26.1A while similar information at diploma level in Table 26.1B. It can be seen from the Table 26.1A that actual intake at State Level in the year 1993 was 510 which increased to 2270 in the year 2003 accounting for about more than four-fold increase in actual intake over the period. When we compare the actual intake of Mechanical Engineering with overall actual intake in engineering education, data indicates that in 1993 about 27 per cent of overall actual intake was Mechanical Engineering and in 2003 it was about 25 per cent which shows that the proportion of Mechanical Engineering remains to be constant. Though the actual intake into 2000 was reduced owing to dividation of Chhatisgarh State but establishing new institutions in the year 2001 fulfilled it.

The data as can be seen from Table—26.1(B) reveals that there was no change noticed on account of growth of facility for Mechanical Engineering at Diploma Level over the period 1993 to 2003. However, the overall intake into diploma courses was increased by 29 per cent over the period.

Table—26.2(A) Outturn of mechnical engineers at degree level in the state of M.P.

S. No	Year	Total institutions	Total outturn	Institutions offering mechnical engg.	Outturn of mechanical engg.
1.	1993	13	1823	11	528
2.	1994	14	1651	12	499
3.	1995	19	2123	14	493
4.	1996	22	1849	17	523
5.	1997	27	1679	20	450
6.	1998	28	1707	21	412
7.	1999	30	1732	23	382
8.	2000	30	2553	21	527
9.	2001	33	2821	22	638
10.	2002	45	2050	28	180
11.	2003	56	3439	38	617

Table—26.2(B) Outturn of mechnical engineers at diploma level in the state of M.P.

S. No	Year	Total institutions	Total outturn	Institutions offering mechnical engg.	Outturn of mechanical engg.
1.	1993	37	2659	31	687
2.	1994	38	2453	31	542
3.	1995	44	2828	32	790
4.	1996	45	2679	33	811
5.	1997	52	2071	40	653
6.	1998	53	3333	38	959
7.	1999	55	2135	39	561
8.	2000	46	2205	33	633
9.	2001	46	2719	33	652
10.	2002	46	2878	33	702
11.	2003	46	2775	33	455

Analysis of Outturn

Data relating to outturn from degree and diploma level programmes in Mechanical Engineering during the period from 1993 to 2003 are presented year-wise in Table—26.2(A) for degree level programmes and Table—26.2(B) for diploma level programmes. It can be seen from the table that the outturn from degree level, which was 523 in 1993, is expected to be order of 617 in the year 2003. It can also be seen from the table that the overall outturn at degree level was increased from 1823 to 3439 over the period 1993–2003. At the diploma level the outturn in the year 1993 at aggregate level was 2659 as can be seen from Table—26.2(B).

Teacher Student Ratio

The Teacher student ratio is a useful parameter for understanding the quality of instructions being imparted in an educational institution. If there are too many students per teacher, the quality of instructions is bound to suffer. On the other hand if there are too few students per teacher it will amount to wastage of national resources and low utilization of teachers. It is in this perspective that analysis of teacher-student ratios in technical educational institutions would be useful. Taking into the account of this view a time series analysis of teacher student ratio in the Mechanical Engineering education in M.P. has done separately for degree and diploma level institutions and presented in Table 26.3(A) and 26.3 (B) respectively. The data reveals that in degree level institutions it was ranging between 1:10 to 1:19 over the period from 1993-94 to 2001-02 whereas in diploma level institutions it ranged between 1:17 to 1:27 which is quite large in comparison to degree level institutions.

ANALYSIS OF LABOUR MARKET

There are a number of parameters, which can be considered in the context of labour market analysis of a particular category of manpower in general and degree and diploma holders in Mechanical Engineering in particular. However, in this section we have considered only four parameters, which we considered very important. These are i) activity status, ii) absorption rates, iii) the earning differentials and iv) the estimated size of unemployment.

Table—26.3(A) Teacher-student ratio in mechanical engineering in degree institutions

S. No	Year	Total Enrollment	Actual Strength of Teacher	Teacher Student Ratio
1.	1993-94	–	–	–
2.	1994-95	2227	182	1:12
3.	1995-96	1954	187	1:10
4.	1996-97	2617	164	1:16
5.	1997-98	3072	164	1:19
6.	1998-99	2711	173	1:16
7.	1999-00	2711	159	1:17
8.	2000-01	2797	147	1:19
9.	2001-02	2730	178	1:15

Table—26.3(B) Teacher-student ratio in mechanical engineering in diploma institutions

S. No.	Year	Total Enrollment	Actual Strength of Teacher	Teacher Student Ratio
1.	1993-94	–	–	–
2.	1994-95	2516	134	1:19
3.	1995-96	2753	140	1:20
4.	1996-97	2694	154	1:17
5.	1997-98	3866	160	1:24
6.	1998-99	3403	125	1:27
7.	1999-00	3016	126	1:24
8.	2000-01	3012	126	1:24
9.	2001-02	2954	116	1:25

Table—26.4 Distribution of mechanical engineers by activity after 2 years of their passing out

Batch Year	Engineer at Degree Level					Engineer at Diploma Level				
	Paid Job	Self Employed	Unemployed	Other Activty	Total	Paid Job	Self Employed	Unemployed	Other Activty	Total
1993	190	23	91	7	311	284	15	132	57	488
%	61	7	29	2	100	58	3	27	12	100
1994	256	14	56	27	353	209	23	168	103	503
%	73	4	16	8	100	42	5	33	20	100
1995	262	12	23	2	299	308	31	200	62	601
%	88	4	8	1	100	51	5	33	10	100
1996	302	1	32	4	339	343	24	240	58	665
%	89	0	9	1	100	52	4	36	9	100
1997	254	1	139	56	450	289	14	297	53	653
%	56	0	31	12	100	44	2	45	8	100
1998	228	25	90	69	412	386	26	392	155	959
%	55	6	22	17	100	40	3	41	16	100
1999	166	31	100	85	382	214	12	205	130	561
%	43	8	26	22	100	38	2	37	23	100
2000	241	11	148	127	527	167	30	273	163	633
%	46	2	28	24	100	26	5	43	26	100

Activity Status

The data on activity status of fresh graduates and diploma holders in Mechanical Engineering who passed out during the period 1993-2000 have been shown in Table 26.4. Analysis reveals that in most of the years More than 55 per cent fresh graduates were succeeded in getting placement in to economic activities within two years of passing their examination. The proportion of fresh graduates who have chosen the self-employment was between 0 to 8 per cent as noticed from the activity status of pass-outs from 1993 to 2000 batches. A considerable proportion of fresh graduates was found to be looking for job even after two years of their graduation.

The activity status of diploma holders who passed out from 1993 to 2003 shows that 40 to 57 per cent of them were got absorbed into the economic activities whithin two years which indicates a low employment opportunities in comparison to degree holders. Only about 1 to 5 per cent diploma holders were found to be self-employed. And more than 33 per cent were unemployed even after the two years of passing their examinations.

From 1998 batch it has also been noticed that the proportion of graduate and diploma holders who have reported to engage in other activity has gradually increased till 2000 batch.

Pattern of Absorption

In the discussion that follows an attempt has been made to present the pattern of absorption in percentage, of degree and diploma holders in Mechanical Engineering getting absorbed in one year and two year (see Annexure–I for the Methodology adopted for estimating Absorption rates). Even after two years if significant proportions of degree and diploma holders were found to be unemployed and were looking for job it only indicates the mismatch that exist between demand and supply of these categories of engineers in the labour market. In order to see how the situation has changed over a period of time we have also tried to present in this section the situation that obtained for degree holders and diploma holders in Mechanical Engineering who passed out in the year 1993 to 2000. The comparative picture so obtained is presented in Table—26.5 and 26.6 for degree and

Table—26.5 Absorptin pattern of mechanical engineers (1993-2000) in M.P.

		Time Taken for Getting First Employment								
Batch Year	Level	<3 mth.	3-6 mth.	6-9 mth.	9-12 mth.	12-15 mth.	15-18 mth.	18-21 mth.	>21 mth.	Total
1993	Degree	16	21	25	3	3	2	61	128	259
	Diploma	20	11	44	47	39	21	18	100	300
1994	Degree	32	78	80	18	28	5	14	14	269
	Diploma	40	67	50	12	15	4	12	41	241
1995	Degree	110	30	24	15	27	2	32	22	262
	Diploma	72	14	68	59	35	41	7	26	322
1996	Degree	79	56	27	50	60	1	7	8	288
	Diploma	116	44	28	34	58	8	48	7	343
1997	Degree	69	19	44	21	9	9	14	70	255
	Diploma	83	74	8	16	11	7	19	85	303
1998	Degree	62	72	19	6	23	6	10	30	228
	Diploma	106	41	35	27	55	11	12	99	386
1999	Degree	26	23	13	20	34	1	14	35	166
	Diploma	18	63	20	11	34	6	8	54	214
2000	Degree	44	24	22	8	26	46	45	93	308
	Diploma	26	17	24	17	27	18	20	49	198

Table—26.6 Estimated absorption (in %) of mechanical engineers

Batch Year	Degree Holder		Diploma Holder	
	Within 1 year	Within 2 year	Within 1 year	Within 2 year
1993	22.78	43.68	32.76	62.97
1994	66.52	100	44.77	64.86
1995	63.36	91.5	42.17	71.48
1996	66.44	90.26	38.35	64.03
1997	38.94	54.72	30.97	41.81
1998	46.6	67.84	26.41	42.53
1999	27.78	52.9	26.84	47.47
2000	25.34	57.4	18.22	36.88

diploma holders. As far as the fresh graduate concern, the data reveals that there were no any specific trend noticed. More than 90 per cent graduates of 1994 to 96 batches were got absorbed within two years, and thereafter absorption rates come down and only about 53 to 67 per cent graduates of 1997 to 2000 batches were placed in the job within two years.

In case of diploma holders it can be seen from Table—26.6 and 26.7 that percentage of absorption is low in comparison to degree holders in almost all the years. Absorption rates of diploma holders also show that the employment opportunities are being gradually decreased over the years.

As done in the case of degree holders in Mechanical Engineers we have tried to capture the change in labour market for diploma holders in Mechanical Engineering over a period by presenting similar information for those who have passed in the 1993 to 2000.

It can be seen from the table that employment opportunities for diploma holders by and large deteriorated over the years.

Analysis of Earning Differentials

The data presented in the Table—26.7 on emolument earned by fresh degree and diploma holders in Mechanical Engineering by year-wise are based on the survey of graduates who passed out in the years 1993-2000. It can be seen from the table that degree holders earn significantly higher emoluments than those diploma holders in Mechanical Engineering do. The average monthly emolument was highest for the 1998 batch (Rs. 13760) while lowest for the 1994 batch (Rs. 5076). Year-wise minimum and maximum emoluments varies over the period.

In case of diploma holders the average emolument earned by them is significantly lower than those of a degree holders are. Further, emolument earned range from the highest of Rs. 4069 in the year 1999 to low as Rs. 2948 in the year 1994.

Analysis of Estimated Size of Unemployment

The size of unemployment is yet other indicator of labour market imperfection of a particular category of engineers. At the state level, for instance, it is estimated that as at the end of 1993

Table—26.7 Average monthly emoluments (in rupees) of mechnical engineers at their first paid employment (1993-2000)

	Degree Holder			Diploma Holder		
Batch Year	Minimum Emolument	Maximum Emolument	Average Emolument	Minimum Emolument	Maximum Emolument	Average Emolument
1993	3000	5812	5219	1532	3807	3025
1994	4129	9137	5076	1821	3769	2948
1995	4750	8047	6271	1958	6070	3770
1996	2500	291721	12065	1737	3864	3202
1997	9954	16888	12993	1811	4757	3010
1998	9166	20883	13760	2612	4415	3613
1999	3000	13476	11030	2313	6135	4069
2000	6458	12125	9139	2759	4615	3709

Table—26.8 Estimated size of unemployment of mechnical engineers (1993-2000)

Batch Year	Unemployment at the end of Year	Size of Unemployment (*)	
		Degree	Diploma
1993	1997	813	702
1994	1998	128	566
1995	1999	184	560
1996	2000	205	679
1997	2001	602	1327
1998	2002	466	1171
1999	2003	425	853
2000	2004	462	806

(*): Excluding the outturn of that year.

813 degree holders in Mechanical Engineering would have remained unemployed while the figure for the diploma holder is about 702 can be seen from Table 26.8. While at the end of 2000, 462 graduate and 806 diploma holders in Mechanical Engineering would have remained unemployed, which indicates that, the labour market for Mechanical Engineers almost satisfactory over the period 1993 to 2000.

SUMMARY

There has been significant growth in the facilities in engineering education in general and Mechanical Engineering education in particular. Of the total number of 56-degree college in as many as 38 institutions a course in Mechanical Engineering at under-graduate level is offered. In the case of diploma level courses of the total number of 46 polytechnics in as many as 33 institutions a course in Mechanical Engineering at diploma level is offered.

In tune with the growth in the number of institutions offering courses in Mechanical Engineering at under graduate level the intake in Mechanical Engineering course at under-graduate level also increased significantly while at diploma level it was remains same .For instance, in the year 1993 the intake at under-graduate level in Mechanical Engineering was 510 which increased steadily over the years and stood at 2270 in 2003. At diploma level the intake was of order 1390 which shows no any remarkable increase.

The outturn from degree level in Mechanical Engineering is expected to be about 617 in 2003 indicating an increase of 89 over the period from 1993. In the case of diploma course in Mechanical Engineering the outturn in 2003 is put at 455.

Analysis of labour market for Mechanical Engineers does not provide an encouraging picture. A significant proportion of fresh degree holders were found to be looking for job even after two years of their graduation. The situation is more acute in the case of diploma holders. Emoluments earned by degree and diploma holders in Mechanical Engineering varied significantly according to batch years and also between the two levels.

As at the end of 2004, the backlog of unemployed degree holders in Mechanical Engineering was put at 462 while that diploma holder 806. Therefore, it can be concluded that employment prospects for degree holders in Mechanical Engineering are more encouraging than for diploma holders in M.P.

Annexure I

Methodology Adopted in NTMIS for Estimating Absorption Rates.

For estimating rates by discipline and level the following steps are involved:

1. Distribute the employed fresh engineers of the given category by time taken for the first employment viz. 0-3 months, 3-6 months, 9-12 months, 12-15 months 15-18 months and 18-12 months based on the data gathered from tracer study of the given batch;
2. Divide the number of engineers who got absorbed as given above by the total number of engineers available for employment. The number available for job is the sum total of those who are found to be employed and those unemployed and are looking for jobs on the reference date;
3. Convert the proportions so arrived into percentages and cumulate them with respect to time;
4. Plot on a graph paper the cumulated percentages taking time on the X-axis and the absorption in percentage on the Y-axis;
5. Draw a free hand curve through the points so plotted and extended the curve up to the point where 100 per cent marked on the Y–axis is met;
6. Read out from the graph the absorption rates i.e. P1 in the first year (0-12 months), P2 in the second year (12-24 months), P3 in the third year (24-36 months) etc. In this case as can be seen the absorption in the first year viz. P1 IA actual.

Procedure for estimating Annual Absorption and Size of Unemployment of a given Category of Engineers.

The methodology adopted for estimating the size of unemployment of a given category is as under.

Annual absorption rates of fresh engineers of the given category of a particular batch are estimated separately as per the methodology mentioned in Appendix-III. The rates thus worked out when applied to the total number available for jobs relating to the batch yields the number of engineers getting absorbed in different years as illustrated below.

Let P1, P2, P3, P4 be the rates of absorption in the first, second, third year etc. respectively of a given category of engineers and A, B, C and D be the engineers belonging to the same category available for employment out of the outturn relating to the years of Y1, Y2, Y3 and Y4 respectively. Then the size of unemployment at the end of Y5 is worked out using the mathematical model described below:

Absorption in Year

Year	Engineers available for employment (labour force)	Y2	Y3	Y4	Y5	Estimates of unemployment at the end of Y5 (excluding Y5 outturn)
Y1	A	A x P1 = (A1)	A x P2 = (A2)	A x P3 = (A3)	A x P4 = (A4)	A-(A1+A2+A3+A4)=A′
Y2	B	–	B x P1 = (B1)	B x P2 = (B2)	B x P3 = (B3)	B-(B1+B2+B3) = B′
Y3	C	–	–	C x P1 = (C1)	C x P2 = (C2)	C-(C1+C2) = C′
Y4	D	–	–	–	D x P1 = (D1)	D-(D1) = D′

In the above model it is assumed, for illustration, that all graduates of a given category will be absorbed in four years and in that case A′ would be zero. If the speed of absorption is more than what is assumed, then depending on the speed of absorption there will be less number of rows in the model. For, instance, if all the graduates of a given category in a given batch who are available for jobs are fully absorbed, say in two years, there would be none belonging to the batches of Y1, Y2, Y3 and Y4 who would comprise of these who passed out in the year Y5 and are still looking for jobs after the year Y5. If, on the other hand, a particular category is found to be taking more than four years, say 5 years, the estimated size of unemployed persons belonging to this category as at the end of Y5 will have a component of those who passed in the year Y1 and are still looking for jobs (as after Y5) and so on.

The summation of the column numbers A4, B3, C2 and D1 as shown in the model will provide estimate of total number of persons belonging to a particular category of engineers getting absorbed in one year in general and in the year Y5 as in the model presented.

The last column in the model provides estimates of the residuals of the outturns belonging to the relevant batches who are yet to be employed as at the end of the year Y5 (excluding the outturn of the year Y5), Therefore, the summation of the figures A′, B′, C′ D′ provides estimate of the unemployed persons of the given category of engineers as at the end of the year Y5.

27

Planning for Higher Technical Education in Changed Scenario

*C T Bhunia**

ABSTRACT

Due to adoption of liberalized economy policy in India, the scenario of higher technical education has changed. The private participation is one of the major changes. The changes have brought many advantages, but at the same time have resulted in many imbalances in different forms. This chapter investigates these and suggests a few solutions to remove the limitations so arrived at.

Key Words: Changed higher education, Imbalances, Solutions

INTRODUCTION

After adoption of open economy and the participation in GATT agreement, the higher education in India has taken a new shape. This is mainly due to overwhelming participation and initiatives from the private sectors. But the government policies and regulations apparently lack directions to achieve the benefits out of the would-be and vision-based regulated private participation. The natural consequence has resulted in the

* **Recent past Director, Bengal Institute of Technology and Management and presently Professor, Dept of Computer Science & Engineering, Indian School of Mines (Deemed University), Dhanbad-826004, Email: ctbhunia@vsnl.com**

imbalances in different forms in the higher education. Before we look into the important imbalances, a general look into the issues arising out of introduction of GATT agreement, a natural attribute of the privatization is desirable.

Review of General Aspects of Technical Education in GATT Scenario

India ranked 141 out of 173 countries in the overall education index in the year 2000. India ranks below even most developing countries in terms of enrolment per 100,000 inhabitants.[1-3] Out of several other parameters behind such a poor position, one was the non-availability of higher education institutes. With private participation, the opportunities of higher studies increases, and this may increase the enrolment figure comparable to other developing countries. Several educational commissions including Kothari Commission argued for active industry and institute interaction for effective research and development. The private institutes sponsored by the industry houses can more efficiently and meaningfully realize the industry institute interaction for fruitful achievements. At the same time, the resource crunch for R & D activities may be overcome by the industry sponsored institutes. Although debatable it is often said that private sectors are more disciplined and efficient than the govt sectors. This being a case, it is expected that the education will be more efficiently and in more disciplined way be imparted in the private institutes. It is undoubtedly that a corporate culture will prevail in the private institutes that are absent in public institutes. Due to financial crunch, the students of the developing countries could not study at the universities of the developed countries. But due to GATT, the universities of the developed countries are opening branches at the developing countries that will provide a scope to the students of the developing countries to study at the universities of the developed countries at a relatively low cost. Adam Smith said, " It is not from the benevolence of the butcher .. or the baker that we expect our dinner, but from there regard to their own interest." Here lie all theories of investment by private sectors. Profit or in gentle word return on investment as often told in the education sectors, is the ultimate motive. The profit motive has natural attraction for quality degradation. Low teacher-student ratio of the existing private institutes in general has this reflection. However profit only motive is dangerous and counter productive in education sectors. As a consequence of ever-increasing marketization of higher education due to GATT, the basic disciplines like physics, chemistry, mathematics, languages, philosophy, history and geography etc are not offered in the private institutes and universities. The private investment still is oriented to courses of market demand. This will create an imbalance in the higher education system. In India most of the private engineering colleges offer courses in Computer, Electronics and IT; and hardly mother engineering like mechanical, electrical, civil etc. The imbalance so created will have adverse effect in future both in terms of availability of engineers at proportional level and in related expertise & development. The high tuition fees of higher education in private sectors will encourage only affordable societies to opt for. The meritorious poor students will not benefit from higher education opportunities offered by the private institutes. Is not GATT creating a further gap between haves and haves not in higher education? Generating scope for higher education for affordable students at the costs of non-affordable but meritorious students is bound to cast poor figure on quality on outputs and cause poor productivity.

Main Issues

The main issues revolve around two things: (a) how to make government to establish institutes of technical higher education as state sectors and (b) how to remove the major imbalances arisen out of the participation of private initiatives. In the present work a few possible solutions are suggested.

CREATING STATE SPONSORED INSTITUTES BY INNOVATIVE APPROACHES

The solution lies in proposed Institute-Cum-Industries (I-C-I).[4-10] The I-C-I will consist of two departments, namely industry departments and institute departments. The role of the industries department will be to implement commercially viable projects in which the final year degree/post-graduate students will be the major and main contributors. The completion of the projects in the full last year of the respective courses will be mandatory for awarding degree to the students. What is the harm if a group of final year degree students of electronic discipline is asked to design a fully commercial PC set as compulsory part of their degree course? Is it not possible to ask a group of post-graduate students of electronics that the complete design and installation of a packet switched network for a resign is mandatory for getting degree? The industry department will also conduct the practical classes for the degree and post-graduate level students under the supervision of the concerned faculty member and diploma modules may also be conducted in the industry department. The faculty members may be allowed to conduct their research work in the industry department with full library for which there will be a separate section. The intake to the proposed I-C-I shall comprise 10th passed students as in modular scheme, thereby combining two innovative ideas. However education structure will be somewhat different from the modular scheme as indicated below:

1. 1.5 year will be the duration for certificate course. For vertical mobility students, 0.5 years more will be the required to be put in by students terminating studies in the industry section.
2. 1.5 years will be the duration for the diploma course, and only top 60 per cent students of certificate course will be admitted to provide they secured more than or equal to certain percentage of aggregate marks in the certificate course. For students terminating their studies at diploma level will have to undergo 0.5 years additional industrial training in the industry section for getting their degree.
3. 3 years will be the duration of the degree course and admission procedure will be as in diploma level but based on both the results of certificate or diploma. The specialized course will be offered at the first year of the degree course. The special papers will be allotted 50 per cent of aggregate marks of total marks.
4. 1.5 years will be the duration of the P.G. course out of which 0.5 years will be for theory class, 0.5 years for

the projects and 0.5 years will be kept reserved for research (extension of project) in respective specialization with the condition that based on this research at least one paper must be published by individual student/group in order to make them eligible for the award of the degree.

In the ICI theory, duration has been fixed for certificate (base)/and diploma courses on the basis of the requirements of "know-how", while for degree and post-graduate courses the duration has been fixed on the basis of the needs of "know-how". The industry section will earn revenue for running the institute as well as for investment in R & D. By this the developing countries can overcome the financing problem of higher education and research. Therefore a single institute shall provide technical manpower needs at all levels for which conventional system requires to 3 institutes. This reduces the investment on technical education without affecting productivity. The objective of producing better skilled technical engineer is embedded in modular concept where diploma and degree students get continuous exposure to technical field respectively for 4 and 6 years rather than 3 and 4 years as in conventional systems. However I-C-I shall be slightly different of modular type. For vertical students whereas duration of base and diploma will be each 1.5 years, for degree students it will be 3 years. Terminating students have to go 0.5 years rigorous training in industry section at each module to make them eligible for certificate or diploma. Duration has been suggested keeping in mind that for base and diploma requirement is of "know how" whereas for degree it is "know why"; and is consideration of production of better skilled human resources at all the levels. Out of the two departments of I-C-I, namely industrial department and institute department, the roll of the industrial department will be to earn IRG by implementing commercial viable projects and consumer products of high quality whereas final year students will be the major contributors. Practical classes and productive research shall be conducted at industry section. There shall be financial advantage in merging industry section with laboratories and in using students as skilled persons in an environment of learn while doing. The proposed model is a new one and caters to meet the need of developing countries[11] to face technological challenge of developed countries. Dr. Colombo said, "...the most important resources in today's world is human intelligence, creativity and ingenuity. Education and training must be number one priority in any sound development strategy." I-C-I is an instrument of this strategy for India. The partial solution to I-C-I is being experimented in the project of NERIST (North Eastern Regional Institute of Science and Technology).

SOLUTIONS FOR IMBALANCES

True, the private initiatives have out scored (fig 27.1)[12] the government initiatives in higher education but the avenue so opened remains confined in degree and post-graduate level engineering and management education, and in a very limited way in medical education. Again then, the private initiatives in engineering education at present is mainly restricted to the market oriented courses (fig. 27.2) of Computer Science and Engineering, Electronics Engineering, and Information Technology. Heft ill attention has been noticed in the disciplines like Civil, Chemical and Mechanical engineering that are actually mother engineering. The basic disciplines of science in higher education like physics, chemistry, mathematics, philosophy and economics etc are not offered in the private institutes and universities. This will create an imbalance in the higher education system and the imbalance so created will have adverse effect in future both in terms of availability of scientists and engineers at proportional level and in related expertise and development. A plan and regulation from the regularity authorities of Ministry of Human Resources Development and All India Council for Technical Education is the need of the hour to stop further widening of the imbalance. The regulation may be of the form of approving the private institute only when, the institute agrees to run at least a mother engineering course per each three or less market demand courses, and one master programme in the basic science per each five market driven courses.

The availability of good Directors/Senior Teachers (particularly at the level of Professors), in general, in private institutes has become difficult task. The attraction of secured permanent and higher status job of government institutes/ universities is one of the reasons behind this, although another reasonable attraction is that the government servants are usually preferred for prestigious position of brand institutes/universities at the level of Director/ Vice Chancellor. Equally competent and qualified Professors in the private institutes/universities are often ignored. This further is sometimes compounded when the authority of private institutes/universities do prefer Professors of government institutes/universities for such positions in their institutes/ universities. In general the teachers in the government institutes/ universities are more qualified and competent, but there are teachers in private sectors also who are no way inferior to the teachers of the government establishment. To make for the imbalance of availability of good Directors/ Vice Chancellors and teachers between government and private institutes/ universities, the teachers must be looked beyond his affiliation but on his teaching, research and administrative competency and ability. A plan of action in that direction is absent now, and for proper and equal opportunity to the private initiatives it has become imperative to begin with a plan. It would not be unsound if the proposal for the grading of Professors of all institutes approved by MHRD/AICTE is introduced purely on the basis of the achievement and points so earned. This may be done in line with accreditation of institutes currently being done for the institutes/ universities. For grading of professors at different level purely based on points a reference table is suggested (Table—27.1).

The present imbalance among the graduate level engineers, post-graduate level engineers and doctorate level engineers is alarming due to sudden huge increase in intake capacity of degree offered by increasingly number of private colleges. The problem has further compounded due to the fact that in post-graduate level engineering education, on average 21 per cent sanctioned seats remain vacant and then 31 per cent is the drop out. The decline trend in Ph D in engineering is shown in fig. 27.3. The major reason for this is that the students take the post-graduate studies and the Ph. D as stopgap arrangement before getting suitable job. Neither the post-graduate education nor the Ph.D. has been seriously thought of higher education in leading to meaningful research and development. Sometimes Ph.D. has been taken in general as a means for teaching jobs in the institutes/universities and for promotional purposes, rather than as a aim to become future international researcher/scientist for the development of the subject and the technology. The solution needs a thorough review of degree and post-graduate level education in engineering. Today the subjects are becoming more and more interdependent and interdisciplinary in nature. An engineer of any branch in today, needs to have knowledge and skill in three more interdependent subjects namely environmental engineering, computing and electronics and communication engineering including Internet access besides other common subjects of communicative languages, cost analysis (economics), management, basic electronics engineering, electrical engineering, engineering physics, engineering chemistry, mathematics, workshop and drawing. There is an idea to change the admission procedure for engineering education in the changed scenario. The students may be admitted with no branch. After two years of common studies, based of grade points earned and choice, the discipline may be allotted. This will give a better opportunity for studying the basic subjects with vigour and seriousness that is mutely lacking to the students admitted on disciplines wise based on the score of entrance test. Similarly there is a thought to revise engineering education in the form of integrated 5 years M Tech course after 10+2. Those who want to opt out with a job after 4 years study may do so, but they will be entitled to get B Tech degree after completion of project on job. The proposals need debate at the appropriate fora.

CONCLUSION

In this chapter we have reviewed the scenario of the higher technical education in India in particular and in the developing countries in general in view of private initiatives and GATT agreement. It is noted with concern and facts and figures wise the problems and imbalances that has been resulted in the changed scenario. Attempts have been made in this paper to suggest a few remedial solutions for the existing problems keeping in mind the strategic need of more and better technical manpower generation for the developing countries[13-18] to meet the global challenges in the age of LPG (liberalization, privatization and globalisation). The concept of ICI has been moving long back as a cost effective and efficient approach for implementing state sponsored technical higher education. The NERIST project may be converted into an ICI for which several attempts were made but yet to materialize. Other solutions for making private institutes to offer B Tech programme in mother engineering, post-graduate courses and basic science courses may not face difficulty for implementing if vision and mission often noted by the private agencies in their applications made for approval to AICTE are accepted. The proposal for introduction of the national gradation of Professors may be debated over different academic for a before final acceptance.

Table—27.1 Points proposal

(A) Educational Qualifications FULL POINTS = 25

Items on educational qualifications		Full point	Division of points based on grade of Universities/Institutes offering the degrees			
			***** University	***** University	*** University	** and unaccredited Universities
D Sc/D Engg		5	5	4	3	2
Ph.D		5	5	4	3	2
M.Tech	With 75% marks	5	5	4	3	2
	With less than 75% marks	3	3	2	1	1
B Tech as in M Tech						
10 + 2		5	5 for first class	3 for second class	1 for pass grade	

(B) Research and Development: Full Marks 25

Items	Full points	Remarks
Per five or more publications referred journals in the last ten years	5	For less than 5 points will be proportional
Per twenty or more articles in reputed magazines in the last ten years	5	For less than 20 points earned will be proportional
Per 20 or more papers in national/International seminars conferences etc. in last ten years	5	-do-
Per 2 or more books authored and published in the respective field in last ten years	5	For less than 2 books it will be proportional
Per 2 or more sponsored research projects in the last 5 years	5	-do-

(C) Experience: Full Marks 25

Items	Full points	Remarks
For 5 years or more as full Professor	5	For less than 5 years proportional point be earned
For 5 years or more as HOD	5	-do-
For 5 years or more as Dean	5	-do-
For 5 years or more as Director/Deputy Director/Pro VC/VC	5	-do-
For member of national level board for 5 years or more	5	-do-

(D) Others: Full marks: 25

Items	Full points	Remarks
Getting award of national/international level award	5	One or more but one is the ceiling
Chairing 5 or more technical session at the international level conference outside India	5	For less than 5 it is proportional
Editors of referred technical journals for 5 years or more	5	-do-
Working in foreign lab on Fellowship for a period of 5 years or more	5	-do-
Conduction summer/winter schools for 5 times or conducting of seminar etc. national/international level 5 times/Fellowship of IEEE for 5 years	5	-do-

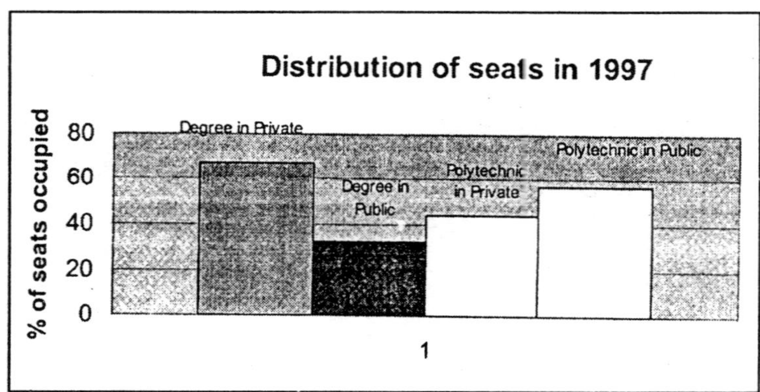

Fig 27.1: Distribution of seats on different categories of institutes

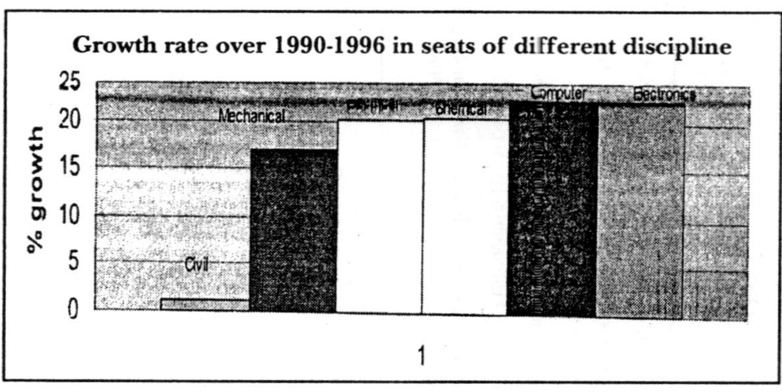

Fig 27.2: Growth of different categories of institutes

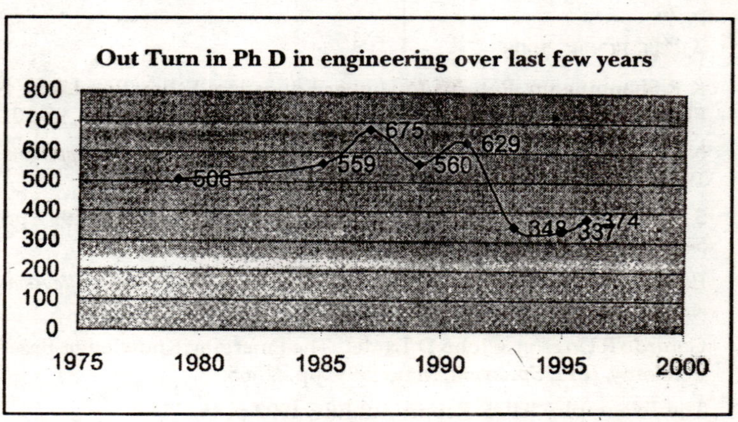

Fig 27.3: PhD Statistics

REFERENCES

1. B B Bhattacharya and C T Bhunia, Threats and Opportunities in the Higher Education in the Context of GATT, Communicted to *University News* in 2003.
2. C T Bhunia, Overcoming High Cost of Higher Education, *University News*, June'2003, pp. 6-12.
3. C T Bhunia, Hybrid Approaches in Higher Education, *National Seminar on Manpower Development and Utilization*, NIT, Rourkela, 2004, p. 5.
4. C. T. Bhunia, Institute Cum Industry, *University News*. Aug'94, pp 11-14.
5. C. T. Bhunia et. al., A Model Structure of I-C-I of Electronics and Computer Engineering, Proc ISTE *National Seminar cum Workshop on Management of Technical Education*, Bhopal, 1995, pp. 1-7.
6. C. T. Bhunia et. al., I-C-I revisited, *University News*, Nov. 1995, pp. 1-4.
7. C. T. Bhunia, Person Power Development - Why and How, *CSI Communication*, Feb. '97.
8. C T Bhunia et al , *Technical Education and Training for the Information Age, Productivity*, Vol. 39, No. 4, pp. 579-587.
9. C T Bhunia, Institute-Cum-Industry Revisited, *University News*, Association of Indian Universities, Nov' 20, 1995, New Delhi, pp. 1-4.
10. C T Bhunia, Higher Education Restructuring and Productivity, *University News*, Association of Indian Universities, Jan'3, 2000, New Delhi, pp. 1-4.

11. Bill Ratterec, The Prospects for Teachers, *UNESCO Courier*, April, '96, p. 26.

12. AICTE BOOK, 1998.

13. K R Shanmugam, Returns to Higher Education: Estimating Using A Flexible Functional Form, *Productivity*, Vol. 39, No. 1, pp. 1998, 97-101.

14. Nancy DiTemase et. al., Degrees and Diversity At Work, *IEEE Spectrum*, 1994 pp. 38-40.

15. S Basu, Education for 21st Century, *University News*, Nov, 1995 pp. 5-6.

16. Edward Said, Academic Freedom Involves Risk and Danger, *The Asian Age*, 19 July, 1999, pp. 12.

17. Gerardo R Ungson & John D Trudel, The Emerging Knowledge-Based Economy, *IEEE Spectrum*, May, 1999, pp. 60-65.

18. The Telegraph, "HDR Report', 13 July, 1999 p. 15.

28

Technical Manpower Planning in India

Issues and Concerns with Special References to Andhra Pradesh

*D. Madhusudana Rao**

INTRODUCTION

Pandit Jawaharlal Nehru, the first Prime Minister of independent India, visualized a dream that our country should be in the forefront in the use of latest scientific technology in all fields of activity. In spite of financial difficulties faced by this poor nation after independence, he laid solid foundation for the development of Science and Technology in our country. As Chairman of the Planning Commission of India, he pioneered his mission to establish IITs and RECs, in Technical Education and many Research Laboratories like BARC, ISRO, ICAR, CSIR, CLRI etc. which have developed into centers of excellence attaining international standards today. Our countrymen could excel in all fields of activity, with the scientific and technological background developed in India, throughout the globe. His vision led to creating durable scientific talent in the country.

Technical Education recorded phenomenal growth in the last 57 years. From a mere 91 degree and diploma level institutions in

* **Training and Placement Officer, Directorate of Technical Education, B.R.K.R. Bhavan, Tank Bund Road, Hyderabad– 500 063, E-mail: dmrao9@hotmail.com**

1947, the number reached 12360 in 2004.[13] At the national level, since independence, the intake of Engineering Colleges increased from 3200 from 44 Engineering Colleges to 3,80,000 from 10265 Engineering, MBA,MCA and Pharmacy Colleges in 2004, while in respect of Polytechnics, the intake increased from 3400 from 47 Polytechnics to 3,42,000 from 2095 Polytechnics. The increase is more than 100 times in both cases. Growth in Andhra Pradesh is also similar and the number of institutions and their intake in A.P. from 1996 onwards is presented in Annexure II.

Computer boom of 90s might have necessitated creation of more technical manpower to support the software industry. Many self financing institutions started with courses like ECE, EIE., IT and related faculties apart from large number of MCA/MBA/ Pharmacy institutions, to support the enhanced activity, which is more pronounced in the last decade.

Growth in any field is welcome if it is balanced. But the present scenario is one that is greatly suffering from imbalance. Traditionally, 1:2:4 pattern was followed for Engineers, Supervisors and Technicians in training as well as employment in organizations. But recently the pattern got reversed. While the intake in Technical Institutions increased tremendously at the degree level, the bottomline almost stagnated, causing negative impact on human resources management at all levels, particularly in manufacturing sector. While a degree candidate is available for the salary of a diplomaholder, the industry seldom speaks about this imbalance, but certainly reiterates the shortcomings in our education and training.

Chairman, AICTE, noted that two-thirds of national admissions are concentrated in 4 States, viz., Tamil Nadu, Andhra Pradesh, Maharashtra and Karnataka[1]. This pattern is causing regional imbalance in the establishment of Technical institutions in the country. Proposals for new institutions from States below national average are not forthcoming, and the candidates from those States are migrating to other States in their search to further their career in Technical Education.

ROLE OF GOVERNMENT IN TECHNICAL EDUCATION

On the administration side, the Governments at the Centre and States, through AICTE, Departments of Technical Education and Universities encourage healthy growth of Technical Education and offer educational and research facilities to the needy. Technical Education's priority over general education was more pronounced in 90s than before.

Governments also act as regulators in Technical Education, by insisting on standards of training. To start or run a technical institution, the required infrastructure, viz., Land and buildings, qualified staff, equipment, books, amenities have to be provided for obtaining recognition by AICTE, which is mandatory. A new concept of accreditation of technical institutions has been done through NBA, an affiliate of AICTE to ensure quality of training imparted in their institution.

Government of India and State Governments are spending huge amounts from the public exchequer on creating Technical Manpower. IITs, NITs (formerly RECs), Technological Universities, Academic Universities offering technical courses, Engineering Colleges, Polytechnics, Vocational Institutions, Industrial Training Institutes are provided funds for maintenance under Non-plan and growth schemes under Plan.

During the year 2004-05, Govt. of Andhra Pradesh has provided Rs.199.43 crores under this head as against Rs.101.54 crores in the previous year. Even in Self-financed institutions, Government provides significant funds on Scholarships to weaker sections of society through its welfare departments. Subsidy on transport, Pratibha scholarships to talented students of the State are also funded by Government.

DATA AND METHODOLOGY

(a) Need for the Study

In view of the importance of this vital sector, as well as to provide accountability to the Government for the funding and direction provided by it, there is need to study the orientation of training provided and employment of technical manpower in the country. Degree and diploma institutions today stress more on "*awareness*" than "*on the job exposure*". To some extent, they are justified in this argument since one does not know where the trained candidate will be absorbed. But on the placement side, industry shows more urgency on putting the graduates and diploma holders from Technical Institutions directly on the job. The controlling agencies, viz., AICTE, Universities, Directorates of Technical Education or Academic Boards who monitor academic performance of institutions, need to emphasize on quality of training provided in all the technical institutions so as to produce best talent. A study of these aspects will throw light on future plans on this field.

(b) Objectives of the Study

In India, the need for collecting and updating data on any topic is rarely realized, though some of the Statistical wings, Universities and reputed organizations collect and assimilate the data collected. Accuracy of data gets less importance due to presentations at short notice. Percentage of error in collection and presentation of data including population census, is going wider, thereby conclusions drawn on any study are unfortunately not accurate. Objective of this study is to stress both need and urgency to develop a strong national technical manpower database.

The National Technical Manpower Information System (NTMIS) or Institute for Applied Manpower Research (IAMR) under the guidance of AICTE have been doing good job in collecting data from all technical institutions. But we need to develop a methodology to continuously update the information regarding placements, which alone will guide our planners to plan properly as to the future needs of technical manpower in the Country. At the sametime, for the success of this vital national project, accountability of recognized technical institutions is essential. There should be stringent penalties on the managements (private or Government) like reduction of intake in popular courses should be levied for callous attitude, inaccuracies in data collection and entry of data in the website and for failure to keep to the schedule of the project.

(c) Data and Methodology

Necessary data required for the purpose is collected from secondary sources. It is reinforced by discussions with staff of Technical Institutions and Industry. Data is collected from journals of ISTE, websites of AICTE, ISTE, DTE, SONET, SBTE&T etc.

(d) Present Employment Scenario

Some reputed organizations absorb the cream from the best institutions with twin objectives. One is to maintain their reputation as best organizations in the country offering high pay packets and to develop their research base and the other is to retain best talent with them. Such absorptions through campus interviews can benefit only very few, may be about 10 per cent. The rest of the trained manpower look to opportunities by responding to various advertisements, applying to innumerable organizations by spending time and money testing their fortune. Sometimes it may extend to months and years, leading to reduced sharpness of their skills. While organizations want experienced hands, passed out candidates need a place to get proper exposure. Through Apprentices (Amendment) Act of 1973 and 1986, Government of India is bridging the gap through BOAT, a wing of MHRD. It provides on-the-job training as apprentice.

But the apprehension of industry to accept fresh graduates and diplomaholders is on the following lines:

1. The cost of exposing fresh graduates and diploma holders to actual work environment is very high compared to their productivity in the organization. As expressed by the entrepreneurs in computer industry, the risk involved in taking the raw candidates with poor knowledge is extremely high;
2. The time needed by these candidates for adapting to the work environment is long;
3. After joining the organization whether as apprentice or employee, better prospects elsewhere are attracting them. As a result, their turnover is high, causing dislocation of the work assigned to them;

4. Continuous unauthorized absence from work leads to uncertainty, and hampers organisation's targets, goals and needs;

5. Creativity of the candidates in work environment is short of the requirements of the employers;

6. Cost of recruitment is very high. Some organisations are adopting more cautious approach and are insisting on bond from candidates and sometimes retain their original certificates.

A beginning in apprentice placements has already been made. Gradually industry implemented the social objective by accepting the fresh graduates and diploma holders as apprentices and train them for one year. Many apprentices are absorbed in the same organization on regular basis.

METHODOLOGY SUGGESTED

Researcher has some difficulty in obtaining accurate data. To achieve his objective, a questionnaire on employment of Technical personnel may be filled by the technical student as proposed below. The same student will be exposed to real life situation very soon. His experience in data collection will enrich him to upgrade his knowledge and skills in the next two or three years of his study.

1. As part of the curriculum, five students at III semester level of BTech/MCA/MBA/Diploma shall be formed as a team and asked to spend just two days under the supervision of their staff member. An area consisting of a particular area is allocated to the team, to collect data and *immediately feed the data to the website* existing or opened for the purpose. Cross verification shall be done by senior staff of the same institution immediately. Delay creates confusion as was noticed in Janmabhoomi survey conducted by students in Andhra Pradesh. In some areas, resurvey had to be conducted. Each institution may be provided a password to ensure identity and to fix up responsibility for errors in data collected and entered into the website.

2. We have about 1,32,000 technical students out of which a minimum of 1,00,000 are available in Andhra Pradesh at III semester stage (Early II year stage) and at least 20,000 teams can be constituted. They will have to handle data of about 3,00,000 to 5,00,000 technical manpower in Andhra Pradesh. Ultimately, each team of students need to register not more than 25 employees in their area. The only difficulty is identification of personnel left over or entered twice at individual or organization level.
3. Data of employees working in other States are collected by adopting this method throughout the country and the same can be listed when needed. However, in respect of employees working in other countries, initial information has to be collected from their parents or family members here and the balance through e-mail.
4. Each geographical area may contain about 2 to 4 mandals in that District and allocated to one Polytechnic or Engineering College or MCA or MBA college located in or near the area. We now have 909 institutions (excluding 51 pharmacy institutions). Location of employee's official Headquarters shall be taken as the basis for registration of an employee by one institution identified for the survey.

The telephone directory, local directories of various local, state or national professional bodies, associations of employees, Government Treasury or Bank from which salaries are drawn, can be used to locate technical personnel. In respect of urban areas, as the area will be wider with excessive concentration of technical personnel, the allocation can be in terms of wards or divisions instead of mandals.

A model format containing bio-data of technical personnel is presented hereunder:

ANNEXURE—I

REGISTRATION OF TECHNICAL PERSONNEL IN INDIA/ ANDHRA PRADESH CHAPTER

Education	Ph.D.	M.Tech.	B.Tech/BE	Diploma

Or equivalent qualifications recognised by AICTE

1.	Name			
2.	Father's name			
3.	Date of birth	Date	Month	Year
4.	Designation			
5.	Address (Office):	Name of the Organisation		
		Area		
	Employed or Self-employed	Mandal		
		District		PIN
6.	Address (Residence):	Area		
		Mandal		
		District		PIN
7.	School—SSC or equivalent	Name of the School		
	Year of passing	Mandal		
		District		PIN
8.	Junior College (Intermediate)	Name of the Jr. College		
	Year of passing	Mandal		
		District		PIN
9.	Polytechnic (Diploma)	Name of the Jr. College		
	Year of passing	Mandal		
		District		PIN
10.	Engineering College (Degree)	Name of the Engg. College		
	Year of passing	Mandal		
		District		PIN
11.	Engineering College (PG Degree)	Name of the Engg. College		
	Year of passing	Mandal		
	Specialisation:	District		PIN
12.	Income per year (Optional)			

For successful collection of data, the income column may be made optional and made assessible by the student researcher. Normally any employee tries to avoid the income statement. The collection of other vital information need not be jeopardized for the sake of income details.

It is not out of place to mention that suitable software for entry of data, may be developed to facilitate assimilation of information collected quickly from the website. The format of website has to be as per the needs of the planning at National and State levels, and published. We have the technology to develop websites with the information as required by different agencies.

Similar method can be adopted to register students leaving the institution after completing their course and obtaining their Certificate, Diploma or Degree should be insisted to enter the data onto to the website and inform their status to their alma meter every year as on January 1st. All the technical institutions will be able to update their records of their alumni. As a token of their involvement with their parent institution, they can also extend their help in the development of the laboratory facilities, as is done in western countries. Through this method, even students leaving the country for higher education and employment can be spotted.

GROWTH PATTERNS IN ANDHRA PRADESH

Growth of Technical Education in Andhra Pradesh at Diploma, Degree levels under the purview of AICTE have been presented in the Annexure II. The statement explains the growth of number of institutions and the intake in different types of institutions in the last decade.

From the Annexure—II, it is clear that the growth of the graduate institutions had its boost in the last decade particularly in the last 5 years. While degree institutions grew by between 557 per cent to 1183 per cent from the mean 305 to 363 per cent, growth at diploma level is merely 46 per cent, even after taking into account single course institutions, i.e., pharmacy institutions, a clear indication of stagnation at that level. Imbalance in the growth is clearly reflected from the statement.

ANNEXURE—II

GROWTH OF TECHNICAL EDUCATION IN ANDHRA PRADESH

Sl. No.	Year	Poly-technics		Engineering Colleges		M.B.A. Colleges		M.C.A. Colleges		B. Pharmacy Colleges		Total Colleges	
		No.	Intake	No.	Intake	No.	Intake	No.	Intake	No.	Intake	No.	Intake
1.	1996-97	93	14910	37	10455	57	2145	44	1330	6	310	237	29150
2.	1997-98	94	15850	57	14155	81	3000	75	2270	20	890	327	36165
3.	1998-99	100	16705	89	19773	92	3825	99	3020	21	970	401	44293
4.	1999-00	103	17580	102	25064	109	4660	153	4890	24	1190	491	53384
5.	2000-01	103	17860	107	30896	110	4680	162	6395	24	1190	506	61021
6.	2001-02	104	19410	174	46090	143	7274	236	10075	26	1410	683	84259
7.	2002-03	104	19410	217	62710	160	9039	263	12795	28	1510	772	105464
8.	2003-04	120	21210	225	65960	205	11270	270	13495	31	1770	851	113705
9.	2004-05	136	21725	243	79815	217	13360	313	17060	51	3000	960	134960
10.	Percentage Growth	46.2	45.7	556.8	663.4	280.7	522.8	611.4	1182.7	750.0	867.7	305.1	363.0

ANNEXURE—III

REVENUE DIVISIONS, MANDALS AND TECHNICAL EDUCATION INTAKE IN A.P.

Sl. No.	Name of the districts	No. of Revenue Divisions	No. of Revenue Mandals	Number of Institutions BTech	MCA	MBA	Polytechnics	Total	Average Mandals per institute
1	2	3	4	5	6	7	8	9	10
	Zone I								
1.	Srikakulam	3	37	3	2	2	3	10	3.70
2.	Vizianagaram	2	34	5	3	1	3	12	2.83
3.	Visakhapatnam	3	43	11	16	15	8	50	0.86
	Zone II								
4.	East Godavari	5	59	10	16	7	6	39	1.51
5.	West Godavari	3	46	9	19	8	6	42	1.10
6.	Krishna	4	50	9	12	8	10	39	1.28
	Zone III								
7.	Guntur	3	57	9	21	8	7	45	1.27
8.	Prakasam	3	56	9	5	3	5	22	2.55
9.	Nellore	3	46	10	12	6	6	34	1.35
	Zone IV								
10.	Chittoor	3	66	10	14	13	8	45	1.47
11.	Kadapa	3	50	5	5	2	6	18	2.78
12.	Anantapur	3	63	6	6	4	3	19	3.32
13.	Kurnool	3	54	5	3	2	6	16	3.38
	Zone V								
14.	Adilabad	5	52	4	0	0	2	6	8.67
15.	Karimnagar	5	56	10	4	5	3	22	2.55
16.	Warangal	4	51	10	15	14	6	45	1.13
17.	Khammam	4	46	9	7	7	4	27	1.70
	Zone VI								
18.	Mahboobnagar	5	64	7	12	3	3	25	2.56
19.	Nalgonda	4	59	16	18	8	4	46	1.28
20.	Rangareddy	3	37	49	69	42	17	177	0.21

(Contd...)

1	2	3	4	5	6	7	8	9	10
21.	Medak	3	45	12	5	1	3	21	2.14
22.	Nizamabad	3	36	8	3	0	3	14	2.57
	Zone VII								
23.	Hyderabad	2	16	17	46	58	14	135	0.12
	Total Institutions	**79**	**1123**	**243**	**313**	**217**	**136**	**909**	**1.24**
	Total Seats			**79815**	**17060**	**13360**	**21725**	**131960**	

In the districts of Adilabad, Srikakulam, Kurnool and Anantapur density of employees is thin. It may be necessary to allocate more than four mandals per institution.

List of Districts, number of Revenue Divisions and Mandals, number of technical institutions in each District are presented in Annexure-II.

Districts like Srikakulam, Vizianagaram, Anantapur, Kurnool, Adilabad, Mahboobnagar , the ratio needs to be slightly more, viz., upto 4 mandals per institution. Density of employees per mandal in these districts is also less, though it is necessary to cover more area geographically.

OBSERVATIONS

1. Registration of graduates and diploma holders *whether employed, self employed or unemployed* should be made mandatory and made as per Medical Council of India but should be made free. Registration should be simple through technical institutions and website once in a year. This can be notified by AICTE or authorised agencies of State Government. The data collected by various institutions as suggested above shall to be updated once in a year. January 1st of the year shall be the base date for registration.
2. The cost of collecting data can be funded by Governments and AICTE through IAMR and NTMIS. Proformas can be printed and sent to all the institutions for processing at their end. Information is fed to website

and so the filled in proformae can be preserved for future use and the same can be shared by all the agencies which are in need.

3. In manpower planning, the methodology adopted by employment exchanges in Andhra Pradesh is not in conformity with the actual needs and national goals. A candidate is registered at any time and even a *student on rolls of an institution* can be registered as unemployed thereby inflating the number of unemployed. Seniority in registration is also accorded to such candidates. It is necessary to have a fresh look on this policy to remove distortion.

4. Technical personnel at all levels form the backbone of the country's economy. Sky is the limit to their scope. Opening up of the economy to the outside world has thrown many challenges to the country. In this perspective, there should be no time lag in facing the global challenges and improve the country's GDP.

5. Discussions have been held to address the problems of the industry, which seeks support from the Government to compete at the national and international levels. Mostly, they want tax incentives and timely financial support from financial institutions. Banks, as custodians of public money, have their own stipulations in sanctioning loans and advances. The ultimate goal of providing employment to the technical manpower can be achieved only with a healthy economy. A special study on the needs of the industry should be conducted to ensure healthy growth of manufacturing and service sector.

6. Industry, which looks to institutions of higher learning, have a responsibility to the institutions. Institutions need moral support from industry. Each industry can adopt some institutions and guide them on a continuous scale. Industry-Institution Partnership Cells created under AICTE programme are trying to fill the gap. But much more is needed for the realization of the nation's

goals. Industry can support the activities of the Institutions and develop them to suit their needs. This effort alone will generate the best talent out of our technical institutions.

Need of the hour is commitment on the part of all players in the field, the students, the teachers, the Government , Government's agencies and particularly, the industry should contribute for generation of better technical talent in the country and achieve the vision of Pandit Jawaharlal Nehru.

Abbreviations Used

IITs	Indian Institutes of Technology
RECs	Regional Engineering Colleges
NITs	National Institutes of Technology
BARC	Bhabha Atomic Research Centre
ISRO	Indian Space Research Organisation
ICAR	Indian Council for Agricultural Research
CSIR	Council for Scientific and Industrial Research
CLRI	Central Leather Research Institute
MHRD	Ministry of Human Resources Development
BOAT	Board of Apprenticeship Training
AICTE	All India Council for Technical Education
ISTE	Indian Society for Technical Education
DTE	Directorate of Technical Education
SONET	Society for Networking of Technical Education
SBTE & T	State Board of Technical Education and Training, Andhra Pradesh
IAMR	Institute for Applied Manpower Research
NTMIS	National Technical Manpower Information System
NBA	National Board for Accreditation of AICTE
GDP	Gross Domestic Product

REFERENCES

1. Journals of Indian Society for Technical Education, 2004.
2. Newsletters of Indian Society for Technical Education, 2001 to 2004.
3. Website of AICTE—www.aicte.ernet.in
4. Website of ISTE—www.isteonline.com

5. Website of DTE—www.dteap.ac.in

6. Website of SONET—www.apsonet.org

7. Website of SBTE & T—www.sbtet.ap.in

8. Website of NTMIS—www.jntu.ac.in/ntmis

9. Website of apinfo—www.apecinfo.com.

10. Prof. R. Natarajan Chairman, AICTE, in his article "Some Contemporary Issues in Technical Education" in the Jounral of ISTE, Jan-March 2004, Vol. 27, No. 1, pp. 1-5.

29

Effective Implementation of the Scheme of Apprenticeship Training in India Issues, Prospects and Solutions

*S. M. Sundaram**

ABSTRACT

Technical Education equips manpower with Human Resources requisite Technical Knowledge, skills and competencies required, which by itself will not be complete unless its two complements, namely the learning of fundamentals at the institutions and acquiring the practising skills at the work spot are balanced. The latter can be acquired through training, of which Apprenticeship Training forms an important component. This chapter discusses the various aspects of Implementation of Apprenticeship Training for Engineering Graduates and Diploma holders in Engineering and Technology.

INTRODUCTION

Education being the principal tool for development of human resources has a direct contribution towards achievement of economic goals and objectives of the nation. This is more so in the field of technical education, which equips manpower with human resources requisite technical knowledge, skills and competencies required for production of goods and services make demand not

* **Deputy Director of Training, Board of Apprenticeship Training (SR) C.I.T. Campus, Taramani, Chennai 600 113, India, smsundaram54@yahoo.co.in**

only on the technical skills but also on a conglomerate of other skills, a significant part of which is related to the total humanistic growth of the man. Such conglomerate of technical and humanistic skills cannot obviously be mastered through pure academic learning of concepts in formalized and institutional courses and in isolation of actual work situation. It, therefore, naturally follows that technical education will not be complete unless its two complements, namely, the learning of concepts at the institutions and acquiring the practising skills at the work spot are balanced. The latter can be acquired significantly through formalized or informalised programmes of training of which Apprenticeship Training forms an important component.

By and large the Apprentices (Amendment) Act, 1973 seeks to organize facilities on a nationwide scale in actual world of work, that complement of learning related to application of concepts acquired in the academic world through formalized Apprenticeship Programmes.

Right from the provisions for assessing and notifying Apprenticeship Training, supervision and evaluation of training, every section of the Act and Rules do place emphasis on the qualitative aspect of the training. The Act not only visualizes active participation of the business and industry, but also spells out the obligations of the industry, to ultimately produce competent technical manpower needed by them. While the industry is required to do its best to organize apprenticeship, the apprentices, i.e., the fresh Engineers and Technicians are also required to fulfill a number of obligations to diligently acquire the practical skills.

CHALLENGE OF TECHNOLOGY

As we are aware, Technology is changing at a rapid rate than what was forecasted. New sources of energy have to be exploited. The new thrust for use of relevant and appropriate technology and the socio-technical problems, which are becoming more and more complex, would need multi-disciplinary approach in solving problems. The professional disciplines of Civil, Electrical, Mechanical, Chemical etc., need to overlap and integrate new skills to educate future Engineers and Technicians. The problems of equipping them to face the new challenges have implications both to the technical institutions who produce these products and to the industrial community, which use these products. Professional and vocational oriented education is complete and effective only with properly planned and closely related practical training in the actual field of activity. Such training provides the students a clear awareness of the world of work, the practices, procedures and techniques that are followed in the field situation. It also includes them the attitude and competency to identify, appreciate and propose solutions through analysis and application of theory. In many cases, it is difficult even to understand the subject in the absence of exposure to the relevant practical situations. Lack of such a practical training is the chief reason for the inability of many of our educated young Engineers and Technicians "to deliver the goods" in their careers and to contribute to new development and productivity in their fields. The employers complain that they have to provide for long period of training for their fresh entrants before they become productive. Thus there is a need for integrating education with actual work experience of theory with practices; and of knowledge with skills and at the same time developing the right attitude and value systems.

HISTORY OF APPRENTICESHIP TRAINING IN INDIA

Apprenticeship is one of the oldest social Institutions. From time immemorial, every master craftsman, builder, sculptor and weaver or a model worker had his own apprentices, usually his son to whom he passed on the "art and skill of his trade". In the medieval period in Europe, apprenticeship had formalized and became the normal method of entry to a craft guild. In our own country, we had the Acharya or the Guru-Sishya concept. The industrial revolution in Europe brought more organized apprenticeship system. Apprentice Act was introduced in various countries like Denmark (1921), France (1915), followed by Britain and Germany. In our country, the first Apprentice Act was passed in the year 1850 which as mainly intended for "enabling poor children and orphans to learn trades and crafts and by which, when they came to full adult age, they may gain a livelihood". The next phase was the starting of systematic apprenticeship by the Indian

Railways. This was followed by the Defence Department, which provided apprenticeship in the various ordnance factories. In the private organizations too, like Tata Iron and Steel Company Ltd., Jamshedpur, a training Institute was established in the year 1921 and apprenticeship schemes was started. The progress attained by the Indian Railways, the Defence Organisations and the Steel Plants is largely due to the continuous supply of skilled and trained hands from their apprenticeship systems for manning the various technical and managerial positions. When India became independent in 1947, the country embarked on a comprehensive programme of national development through successive five-year plans. This led to the establishment of a chain of Industrial Institutes and expansion of technical education system in the country.

At the same time, in pursuance of the recommendations of the Scientific Manpower Committee, the Ministry of Education, Government of India started a training scheme known as Practical Training Stipend Scheme in 1949-50 with the object of providing practical training to fresh graduates and diploma holders, which would ultimately lead them to gainful employment. The value of stipend was Rs. 150/- p.m. for Engineering graduates and Rs. 75/ - p.m. (later revised to Rs. 100/- p.m.) for diploma holders. The stipend was tenable for a period varying from one to two years depending upon the training establishment and the training programme. The stipend was allotted to the Institutions on priority basis based on out of turn of graduates and diploma -holders and the candidates were selected for stipend on the basis of marks obtained by them in the final examination. Those selected, made their own arrangement for practical training with the assistance of their institutions. The scheme was revised in 1953-54 after a review, in which facilities for practical training were secured by the Ministry of Education and the candidates were selected and posted by them, The industrial establishments, who took part in this scheme on a 50-50 basis, and in some cases the entire stipend was met by the Government. The response on the whole, from the industry to the scheme was encouraging. As the scheme gained momentum and more and more candidates sought apprenticeship, the administration of the scheme was transferred to the Regional offices of the Ministry as and when they were established in the four regions. The total number of trainees under this scheme was about 2800 in the year 1966-67. It will be worthwhile to look into the industrial progress of the country at this juncture. The second and third five-year plans gave accent to development of Heavy Industry and expansion of Power and Transport System. The Technical Education system also was expanded rapidly and more and more technical institutions were opened in different parts of the country. Thus the outturn of engineering graduates and diploma-holders grew at a very rapid pace; however, the industrial progress did not keep pace with this and thus there was an acute unemployment situation among the engineering graduates and diploma-holders prevailing in the country during 1967-68 and the Ministry of Education launched a crash programme to provide training to as many engineering graduates and diploma-holders as possible. As on June (30-6-2002) about 20696 apprentices are undergoing Apprentice Training in Southern Region under the Act. At this juncture, in order to streamline and administer the Scheme which had assumed larger proportions, the Ministry set up four Regional Boards of Apprenticeship Training in the four Regions of the country. These Boards had representation from the Industry, State Governments and the Technical Institutions apart from the Central Government who financed the entire Scheme. The manner of administration of this scheme was still the same except that the rates of stipends were raised from Rs.150/-p.m to Rs.250 p.m. for engineering graduates and Rs.100-p.m. to Rs.150p.m. for Diploma-holders. Current rate of stipend are given the latter part of this chapter.

Industrial Needs

Industrial needs are the realization of the present day technological know-how and then adoption to find the solutions to the socio-economic needs. Continuous upgradation in materials and processes to bring out competent products is the desired industrial evolution. Full automation, computerisation etc. has changed the phase of industries. Industries have to adopt the latest technologies always and hence have to give training to their personnel continuously. They also have to get engineers with the latest know-how.

Industry Institute Interaction

A term often heard today, this has great relevance. Engineers with all theoretical knowledge come out only as engineering scientists. They become real engineers only if they are able to assimilate the problems of the industries and to find solutions for them. This is possible only with a good interaction and such an interaction can yield the following steps:

— Industry Sponsored PG Programmes
— Industry Sponsored R&D Programmes
— Consultancy programmes for industries by institutes
— Training to industrial personnel in industries
— Training to faculty in industry
— In plant training to students
— Industrial projects to students
— Apprentice training to passed out graduates
— Placement to some graduates

The first four steps help industries to get latest expertise from the industries at low cost, which in turn help institutes to generate some revenue. The other step helps the institute to give a sort of practical training to the students making them real engineers.

The interaction is very important as then only good curriculum will emerge out. Industrial training of students in the form sandwich course practised in Germany has yielded good results.

A Curriculum for 21st Century

Curriculum for 21st century should be so oriented to take a total view of social, economical, managerial and environmental problems and to adopt the latest technological advancements. The team to prepare curriculum should include industrialists, R&D, experts, from government departments etc. in addition to the academicians.

APPRENTICES (AMENDMENT) ACT 1973

As the number seeking apprenticeship facilities grew more and more, it become difficult to obtain voluntary participation of the industrial community. Those who were already taking apprentices were requested to take more and more, with the result the optimum point was reached. Hence the Government thought of amending the Apprentices Act 1961 that was originally meant for the apprenticeship training for Craftsmen Trainees and Trade Apprentices. The Act was amended in the year 1973 to provide for training of Graduates and Diploma-holders in Engineering/ Technology and the amended Act came into force in June 1975.

Since the Act came into force, 101 subject's fields of Engineering/Technology are notified under the Act. The training establishments prescribe a training programme which has to be approved by the Regional Central Apprenticeship Authorities, even though a contract of apprenticeship has to be entered into between the apprentice and the employer, a provision has also been made in the contract for termination without cost if the apprentice gets gainful employment during the tenure of apprenticeship period. He could also be released from the training scheme on medical grounds, on production of suitable certificate from a Civil Surgeon.

The Training Places Secured Under the Act Have Been Divided into Three Categories:

(a) The Central Sector which includes the Central Government Departments and the Central Government undertakings;

(b) The State Sector which includes the State Government Departments and State Government undertakings;

(c) The Private Sector.

The Act also envisaged that the industrial establishments should ensure that a proper person possessing the requisite qualifications is placed in charge of the training of these apprentices.

Recent Amendment to the Apprentices Act

In order to provide for continuous and sustained efforts for training of the products of the vocational stream, the Government of India amended the Apprentices Act 1961 in September 1986 by introducing a new category of Apprentices called Technician (vocational) Apprentices. The amended rules were notified in September, 1987 and later in April, 1988, 20 vocational courses were notified as designated subject fields for the purpose of training under the Amended Apprentices Act and as on date 94 vocational courses has been brought into the preview of the Act.

Under the scheme, those who pass out of the vocational stream in the notified subject fields will be eligible for training for a period of one year. Minimum monthly stipend fixed by the Government is Rs.1090/- p.m. 50 per cent of which, will be reimbursed by the Central Government in arrears, on quarterly basis to the training establishments. However, employers are at liberty to pay a higher rate of stipend, but the reimbursement of the Government share will be limited to the minimum rates only.

ISSUES, PROSPECTS AND SOLUTIONS

Even though the Act is meant primarily for providing the "initial work experience" for the emerging Engineers and Technicians, certain practical problems have cropped up, while implementing the provisions of the Act and these issues can be divided into four major heads, namely:

- Issues concerning the apprentices
- Issues concerning the industrial establishments
- Issues concerning the Technical Institutions and Apprenticeship Training the four partners to the Apprenticeship Programme.

These are enumerated below:

Issues Concerning the Apprentices/Students

Create Awareness of Career Knowledge

On an extensive discussion with many of the passed students, it is found that there is lack of career knowledge among them.

They seem to rely mostly on the information and opinion of the immediately passed out students and their colleagues. In fact many have not even given any thought to the problem of after education, what? But, curiously, everybody wants a comfortable, well paid and secured job; but does not know how to go about getting it. They are also not aware of their own aptitudes and preferences and in which type of job they would be successful. For example, when a student passes out from an Engineering College or Polytechnic, he is known as a Civil Engineer, Mechanical Engineer, Electrical Engineer, etc. depending upon the subject field in which he qualified: but the industry looks at Engineers and Technicians in a different way. They employ them as Production Supervisors/ Engineers, Maintenance Engineers, Construction Engineers, Designers, Quality Control Engineers, etc., depending upon the application of Engineering/Technology in functional areas. This division or the basis of functional application is rather unknown to the emerging Engineers and Technicians. Unless, they are given a change to get practically experienced in an industry in all these functional areas at least for a short duration, they will not be able to know the various requirements of these jobs and here comes the apprenticeship training handy where they are given a chance to see for themselves the application of Engineering/Technology in the actual work spot and hence they are in a better position to take a decision as to which functional area would be suitable to them. This incubation period of one year of training is necessary for the emerging Engineers and Technicians in order to make them healthy later, but the fact is somebody must tell them about this.

In this connection the Board of Apprenticeship Training (Southern Region) with the collaboration of the Directorate of Technical Education of the concerned State has been conducting Career Guidance Programmes for the final year students in which eminent experts from the Industries, Public Service Commissions, Defence Services and other Agencies discuss with the students career opportunities open to them. Mock interview sessions on how to face interviews are also conducted as part of the Programmes. These Programmes have been found to be very effective and useful for the students. Hence, it is requested that all Heads of Institutions would take this opportunity of arranging in their Institutions, such Career Guidance Programmes so that the students are well prepared to select appropriate areas for their career. This knowledge coupled with one year of training will definitely help an Engineer to choose a career suitable to him.

Improvement of Employment Prospects

Since it is not obligatory on the part of Industrial establishments to offer employment at the end of Apprenticeship Training, many emerging Engineers and Technicians prefer and entry point with a possibility of employment prospects to an open ended training like apprenticeship Training. It is found that many promising passed out students do not come up for apprenticeship training, especially, in those places where the stipend payable is the minimum prescribed or where the prospects of immediate employment is not there, like the Government Departments/ Undertakings, etc.

In this connection, it would be necessary to appeal to all the establishments to dovetail their manpower planning system in such a way that the requirements of technical personnel of these categories can be met with their own trained apprentices and in places where there are regulations for recruitment, the establishments may take up with the authorities that these regulations can be modified in the case of apprentices. Already such modifications exist in the case of Central Government undertakings and in some State Government undertakings.

Difference in the Standards of Technical Institutions

The level of education and standards of assessment among Institutions/State/Region vary widely. This calls for special attention when organising training in an industry. The Programme devised to suit the students of one institution or State will not be adequate for a different group. In the absence of a common standard, it is difficult to evolve a single pattern of training programme. The same difficulty is experienced in the case of industrial establishments also, as all of them do not have the same facilities for training even in a particular discipline. This is more true in the case of small and medium establishments, as in the cases of broad based disciplines like Mechanical Engineering, etc., where under one roof will be difficult to obtain practical experience of all aspects Engineering/Technology.

Provision of Facilities for Related Instruction During "In-plant Training"

"On the job" training or in-plant training depends for its success mainly on the line managers and their assistants taking keen interest in the trainees. Usually the line manager is too busy with his routine problems to devote time to the trainees. Under such circumstances, in-plants training get reduced to a mere observational one, where the trainee soon loses his enthusiasm and ends up with a negative attitude. Even though the Act Provides for employment of a suitable person as "Training Officer" in practice, this is seldom done in that way. Apart from a few companies, where there are full-fledged training departments, many of the establishments delegate this function to one of their engineering staff. In many cases the person so appointed is from the junior management cadre who would not be in a position to take any decision by him. There are also occasions where the technical areas are so specialised which a small band of training personnel cannot comprehend fully and impart training. They are also not aware of the appropriate training techniques and approaches for effective "on the job" training. It is, therefore, essential for establishments to encourage line managers and their assistants to develop themselves as "trainers" by undergoing special Programmes conducted by professional organisations. It is, in this context that the Board of Apprenticeship Training can play a useful and effective role, in arranging Programmes for Trainers in Industries, as well as Institutions.

Supervision of on the Job Training

The concept of dignity of labour is unfortunately not fully appreciated by many emerging Engineers and Technicians and hence when they go to the shop floor, they put themselves on a high pedestal and are reluctant to put their hands on the job for fear of getting their hands dirty. They also develop a feeling of "infradig" with the result that they do not ask searching questions to the shop floor personnel for fear of being "exposed", due to all these; they are looked down upon by modern workers. Even in a small number of freshers show this attitude, the whole band of trainees are denied co-operation affecting all of them. Sometimes, old time supervisors who are less qualified academically, but well experienced in the line are reluctant to co-operative with freshers, just because of certain complexes. Occasionally, skilled workmen and old time supervisors join hands (may not be by design) to make it difficult for freshers to learn. The line managers must be aware of these conditioning factors in organising and supervision effective in-plant training. Training Modules may be prepared in consultation of Industrial Establishment for effective implementation.

Stop Gap Assignments to Trainees

In many cases, it is seen that trainees are used as observers, tracers, work-study assistants, data collectors, etc., taking them out from the scheduled training plan. While these special assignments may be necessary as part of the planned training approaches, it might not be useful for the trainee if he does only this work day-in and day-out. Hence, it would be necessary to draw a well-balanced Training Programme and this pre-planned Programme evolved with care and approved by authorities should never be changed, truncated or abridged. However, special assignments can be included in the Training Programme deliberately as an integral part of training with specific and results. It will be appreciated, if in designing open ended Training Programmes, as is done for the apprentices under the Act and where the chances of absorption in a specific job function is not apparently visible at the time of organising training, this aspect is borne in mind.

Quantum of Stipend

There is a general feeling among the apprentices that the quantum of stipend paid to the apprentices does not help to make both ends meet. Even though, the stipend is only a maintenance allowance, distinct from wages and salaries certain basic needs may have to be met with. It is a matter of great relief that the Government of India announced increases in rates of stipend payable to Apprentices from 18.05.2001. They are:

1.	Engineering Graduates	-	Rs.1970/- per month (For Post-Institutional training)
2.	Sandwich Course students from Degree Institutions	-	Rs.1400/- per month
3.	Diploma Holders	-	Rs.1400/- per month (For Post-Institutional Training)
4.	Sandwich Course students from Diploma Institutions	-	Rs.1140/- per month
5.	Vocational Certificate Holder	-	Rs.1090/- per month

It is open to the establishment to pay stipends at rates higher than the minimum prescribed. However, the reimbursement of Central Government share would be limited to 50 per cent of the rates prescribed above i.e. the reimbursement would be confined to Rs.985/- p.m. in respect of a graduate apprentice, Rs.700/- p.m. in respect of a technician apprentice, Rs.700/- p.m. in respect of a technician apprentice and sandwich course student from degree Institutions, Rs.570/- p.m. in respect of a sandwich course student from Diploma Institutions and Rs.545/- for +2 Vocational apprentices.

Knowledge of Training Methodologies and Approach

Many a time, the apprentices enter an industry without knowing what to do with the training programme, even in cases where well drawn up training Programmes exist. In fact, they have not been properly attuned to seek, search, analyze, develop and go in depth into the industrial problems. A "prop" is invariably necessary to make a beginning in many cases and in this; the technical institutions can play a useful role by properly conditioning the final year students on approaches for training. Here again the Career Guidance Programmes drawn up by the Boards of Apprenticeship Training will come in handy.

Issues Concerning the Industrial Esablishments

1. Establishments who have a Training Department of their own and believe in training as an on going activity for development of human resources of the enterprise;

2. Establishments, which do not have, separate Training Departments (either because they are not big enough to have such out-fits or by design), but provide training through the line managers or their assistants;

3. Establishments who neither believe in training as on going activity nor have any training out-fit of their own. These establishments engage the trainees, just to fulfill the obligations under the Act and do not bestow generally any attention in trainees and apprentices.

A planned Training Programme will be successful only when all concerned, contribute their share to the total spectrum of activities. Thus it would be necessary for the establishments, in their own interest, to bestow attention on training, commensurate with their size and activities. Even if they are not able to bestow special attention, the can at least fulfill the obligations under the Act and send the quarterly Progress Reports of the apprentices in the prescribed form and make correctional efforts to improve the apprentices performance by periodical reviews. It would be appreciated, if the industries can take this, as a part of their normal obligation towards Apprentices.

Special Situations

There are occasional problems for the industries because of labour situations like strike/lock-out conditions or profitability/ market situations like loss of profit/market etc. Even though, these happenings form a part of the industries, time cycle, because of the need for growth and stability, the training should not get truncated; in fact, good training interventions might pull the establishment out of the wood. In some cases, there are attempts to put off selection and engagement of apprentices for some reason or other. This should be avoided in the general interest of training of apprentices.

Integration of Practical Training in the Degree Course

In the National Policy on Education, the Government of India as early as 1968 had recommended that practical training should form a component of the curriculum of the undergraduate courses in Engineering/Technology. In pursuance of the above, the

Government of India has been taken up with the various Universities and Technical Institutions the possibility of providing integrated practical training within the curriculum itself in the various degree courses in Engineering/Technology. In view of the fact that the Apprentices (Amendment) Act 1973 provides an opportunity for provision of training with stipend in industry, this aspect was pursued in detail with technical institutions as well as with the industry to find out the various modalities of bringing about this training. Meetings were held on that a period of at least six months of training in the Penultimate semester would provide adequate industrial orientation to the degree students. However, certain provisions possibility once training under the Act is undergone either as pattern, acted as a disincentive to further progress in this type of training. This has been subsequently amended and now the students who passed out from institutions under Sandwich Pattern are also eligible for further training under the Act with the prior approval of Apprenticeship Authorities. It would be necessary to find out alternative approaches to provide for integration of practical training within the curriculum, itself so that engineering education will be complete with its practical component.

Training of Sandwich Students

Sandwich pattern of Technical Education in which the industrial exposure of appropriate nature and content sandwiched between the institutional learning, is supposed to make the learning more effective because the student is given an opportunity to verify and reinforce his academic knowledge in actual work situations. However, this requires active and willing co-operation and Collaboration of the industries, which provided training facilities.

However, in the core subject fields like Civil Engineering, Mechanical Engineering and Electrical Engineering, the sandwich type of education cannot be extended on extensive scale as the facilities for industrial/practical exposure is rather limited. But in the case of process or product oriented subject fields like Chemical Engineering, Sugar Technology, Leather Technology, Polymer Technology, etc., the practical training can be matched to the theoretical inputs and specific tailor made training programmes could be evolved.

The placement for industrial training for these students is covered under the Apprentices Act. The mode of collaboration includes the tripartite efforts of the Institutions, Industries, and the Board of Apprenticeship Training. The Institutions will start the dialogue with the Board for getting the required number of placements in the Industries situated nearby. The Board in its turn calls on the Industries and arrange for training. The Institutions are informed about this and placements of students are done by the Board. Once the apprentice joins the Industry the usual formalities like filling up of Apprenticeship Contract Registration Card (ACRC) etc. are done through, by the industries with the Board.

While certain Industries prepare a programme of apprenticeship in consultation with the Board and the Polytechnic, other assign specific work experience related to the nature and content of the knowledge possessed by the students. Rotational training is also undertaken wherever industries have major sections/departments. The Board helps in formulating broad specific training objectives, facilities to be provided for the students and the type of feedback required, to guide the trainees in "in plant training". In some cases, small projects connected with the apprentice's working knowledge are also prescribed to create motivation and self-confidence in trainees.

This type is in vogue in Andhra Pradesh and Tamil Nadu. In Karnataka, a beginning has been made. It would be necessary to introduce sandwich type in certain specific areas like Printing Technology, Polymer Technology etc.

Role of the Technical Institutions in Effective Implementation

There was a time when the Institutions believed that their responsibility ended with the declaring of the results of the final examinations and once the student passes out of the Institutions, they have nothing to do with him. But the situations have changed today and the institutions are playing a major role in the career development of students. In many cases, there are Training and Placement Officers who look after their career planning of the passed out students. But, it is found that in many cases the Training and Placement Wing has not been properly equipped with instruments for locating, monitoring and reviewing career opportunities available to the students. Here again, the Technical Teachers Training Institute along with the Boards of Apprenticeship Training can play a useful role for bringing the relevant parties together to improve the training and placement work of the technical institutions. As technological change has been taken place to employability skills required to carry out the work successfully get changed. The requirement of skills are Technical knowledge, technical skills, mechanical skills and most important is the behavioral skills. Technical instruments must be considerable as this and develop these skills in Engineers and Technicians during their course of study.

ROLE OF NTMIS IN TECHNICAL EDUCATION

The Technical Manpower Information System collects and analyses Technical Manpower Information on a yearly basis from all Engineering Colleges in India. The NTMIS gathers data on Student intake and out-turn from all the Engineering Disciplines. It also conducts follow-up Surveys every year to find out absorption of Engineering Graduates/Diploma Holders in various Employment Establishments. The NTMIS thus provides panel data to study supply and demand aspects of Technical Manpower in various Engineering Disciplines. The statewise data available from NTMIS adds further impetus to the data system for planning at State-Level. The various data collected from Southern Region are set out in Annexures.

CONCLUSION

The responsibility for generating adequately trained manpower for meeting the increasing needs of the country cannot obviously be that of Government alone. It has to be a combined effort of the industry through its training activities and the technical institutions, which prepare the young men and women in their pre-employment stage and the Government, which gives policy, provision and protection. Organised training through Apprenticeship Training Programme for providing the much-needed "initial work experience " for the emerging Engineers and Technicians has come to stay. It should be ensured that there is adequate and continuous exchange of ideas, experience, equipment and expertise between the industry and institution both at student and teacher/manager levels so that there is co-operation, collaboration, co-ordination and cohesion. Well designed and organized training will definitely pay in the long run and it is and obvious must for the economical and social progress of our country.

30

Withering Polytechnics
Some Remedial Measures

*K.V. Subbarao**
*B.Vijaya Kumar***

ABSTRACT

Polytechnics serve the society with skilled manpower. But the polytechnics now face a lot of challenges, if not extinction. This is attributable partially to the non-adaptability of the syllabi to the demands of industry, insufficient hands-on training on modern technology and to some extent to the competition from the Engineering graduates. For overcoming this malady, the curriculum should be visited as frequently as possible incorporating the aspirations of industry as well as the technology, adoption of Polytechnics by the industry for hands-on training and more educational avenues for the working Polytechnicians are some of the remedial measures to infuse life into the Polytechnics.

Key Words: curricula, diploma holders, Polytechnics, vocational education.

* **Sr. Lecturer in CCP, Government Polytechnic for Women, Nellore–524 003, E-mail: rao_kvs2000@yahoo.co.uk**

** **Lecturer in CCP, Government Polytechnic, Nellore– 524 005, E-mail: bhattaramvk@rediffmail.com**

INTRODUCTION

For industrial growth and prosperity, the need is to produce highly professional and competent engineers. This could be achieved by imparting quality teaching to students. Towards this, some norms and standards of engineering education need to be laid down so as to educate the students with appropriate skills suitable for a rapidly changing industrial scenario. There are Craftsman (I.T.I.s), Diploma level (Polytechnic), Graduate and Post-graduate level (Specialisation and Research & Development) stages. The output of these institutions is to cater to the various needs of the Industry right from the skilled workman to the Top Level Management. Over the years, the policy of the Governments of the more industrialised economies is to maintain the ratio between the graduate, technician and craftsmen is of the orders of 1:3:5; the same is considered by the Government of India to be a healthy ratio and facilities for education are also provided for in that order. From secondary education onwards, the five-year plans enabled education to include vocational training as well. Education is increasingly sought to be made relevant to work, to enhance employment opportunities. Even the technical training imparted is to be increasingly related to industry. Quality in education, along with the necessary focus on vocational training, is expected to solve the twin problems of the need for manpower and of unemployment.

POLYTECHNIC EDUCATION

Diploma level courses are for the training of middle level manpower needed for a wide range of professional duties, for application of knowledge in field operation, in production and construction, testing and development etc., and such functions are offered in 291 polytechnics all over the country with an annual enrolment capacity of about 50,000 students. They offer a variety of specialization in engineering and technology as well as in a few non-technological fields. In Andhra Pradesh, there are 121 polytechnics both in governmental and private sector with an intake of around 21,300 students offering engineering, non-engineering and sandwich technician courses.

Table—30.1 Outturn of diploma-holders during 1990-2000

Sl. No.	Discipline	Out turn During the Year										
		1990	1991	1992	1993	1994	1995	1996	1997	1998	1999	2000
1.	Civil Engineering	1915	2016	1785	1839	1462	1977	970	832	1265	497	1985
2.	Mechanical Engineering.	1745	1851	1850	2095	1734	3606	1470	1775	2136	988	1942
3.	Electrical Engineering.	749	818	832	790	755	1574	768	686	1460	914	1874
4.	Electronics Engineering.	1369	1664	1425	1672	1782	3472	1274	1626	1956	1506	2312
5.	Chemical Tech.	24	31	3	16	33	30	21	52	51	–	162
6.	Metallurgy	60	71	28	50	77	115	51	85	140	–	158
7.	Mining	116	111	116	127	93	218	58	60	65	65	121
8.	Architecture	234	142	152	131	73	215	57	107	100	35	138
9.	Automobile	194	182	255	197	207	402	224	207	283	221	294
10.	Sp. Dip. in Elect.	98	92	95	103	96	162	80	77	78	–	84
11.	Mechanical (SW)	23	14	10	12	10	36	14	34	28	–	25
12.	Sugar Tech.	8	14	13	3	19	65	28	19	43	–	47
13.	Textile Tech.	3	15	2	15	19	38	16	25	34	–	45
14.	Leather Tech.	7	15	12	13	3	27	18	14	26	–	51
15.	Printing Tech.	44	56	40	24	49	57	40	45	45	38	47
16.	Ceramics Tech.	35	2	8	15	36	68	33	41	48	–	52

(Contd...)

1	2	3	4	5	6	7	8	9	10	11	12	13
17.	Computer Engineering	49	228	87	149	144	517	298	423	680	614	841
18.	Pharmacy	370	373	380	371	362	184	306	398	–	504	517
19.	Hotel Management	17	15	33	32	35	57	32	21	38	29	32
20.	Costume Design	5	18	9	41	19	56	25	37	28	26	23
21.	DCCP	698	749	82	132	296	838	181	222	466	344	408
22.	Elect. & Inst.	35	27	31	33	30	–	67	–	156	268	54
	Total	**7798**	**8504**	**7248**	**7860**	**7334**	**13714**	**6031**	**6786**	**9126**	**6049**	**11212**

Source: Statistics of NTMIS, Hyderabad.

The above table illustrates the outturn of diploma holders during the ten-year period of 1990-2000, while the number of Polytechnics numbered about 91 in the year 1999.

The employment generation for these diploma holders has not been in consonance with the outturn. The job opportunities for them have been evaporating. While, 6,031 came out of the Polytechnics in the State during the year 1996, only 1,638 could get employment in the State. The middle or low-income groups, which constitute the majority of the population, can afford the reasonable cost of Polytechnic education

REASONS FOR MALADY

(i) Andhra Pradesh State is lagging behind many other states in the field of industrial development. The index numbers of industrial production is self-explanatory. With regard to employment in factories, the total number of workers remained stagnant during the period 1995-96 and 2000-01. The number of industrial workers increased only from 8,23,979 to 8,25,827 during the same period recording only a marginal increase. It is argued that whatever the industrial growth taking place in the State it is without additional jobs. The number of notified vacancies decreased from 53,431 in 1980-81 to 10,919 in 2000-01[1].

(ii) With the policy of the State Government taking a paradigm shift towards higher technician education, the number of Engineering colleges has registered phenomenal growth. The number that stood at 100 during the year 1999 with 91 Polytechnics supporting them has risen to 218 having an intake of 60395 seats supported by 121 polytechnics as on date. Thus, the number of engineering graduates coming out of the portals of these institutions has touched the peak. The result is that the healthy ratio of 1:3 between Graduate and Diploma engineers has been totally shattered.

(iii) As the industrial employment on the decline, the polytechnic student is aghast with the closure of further educational avenues. There are only 1200 seats available

in the University Engineering Colleges for the 12000 and more of the diploma holders coming out of the Polytechnics every year.

(iv) The Industry, on the other hand, has plenty of technical manpower at hand – both the graduates and diploma-holders hobnobbing for the limited employment opportunities – and has the higher bargaining power. The Graduate engineers vie for even the lower salary packages for their own survival and the industry turning away the diploma holders. While the certificate holders from I.T.I.s retain their share in the employment ladder, the slow and steady proliferation of graduates into their domain leaves the poor diploma holders high and dry. The emphasis on "hands on training" cannot be under-rated. An uneducated boy working at a motor mechanic shed will have more talent and ease to tackle the problems (repairs) than a highly qualified in the same field. Practical training is and will continue to be the sine qua non of polytechnic education and introduction of new crafts in place of those abolished ones in workshops is the need of the hour.

(v) The quality of technician education, for long, has been considered not to the aspirations of the industry. According to President, Confederation of Indian Industry, "Our Vocational Education—Polytechnics and I.T.I.s—are outdated. Companies have to be involved to ensure that right skills are imparted in terms of training"[2]. Though the syllabi and curricula of diplomas are revised every five years, in view of the rapid changes in technological innovations and global competition, it is considered late. By the time the student with a diploma visits the industry, he realises that the technology has undergone metamorphosis and the gulf between what he has and what is required is wide. Thus, there is need for a thorough revamp of the curricula and the instructional methods.

SUGGESTIONS

- The curriculum of Polytechnics should be revised as frequently as the industry demands, especially in technologies that undergo rapid developments. Such revisions mean the removal of redundant theoretical knowledge. For this purpose, there should be constant interaction with the Industry and assessment by the Polytechnics.
- The role of industry in deciding what they want is highly significant. Instead of crying foul or that the vocational education is not suited to it, it is the right of the industry to participate in the revision of the curriculum with its heart and soul to demand what they want.
- To strengthen the participation of the industry, the polytechnics should be adopted by the industry in providing the students with an opportunity to have hands-on training on the technologically advanced machinery so that the students know the practical facet of the theory and will adjust themselves to the industrial needs later. The industry, on the other hand, benefits from the talent right from the early stage itself in planning the manpower requirements. The instruction in the Polytechnics, thus, should make a provision for such practical training well before the completion of the course.
- On the employment side, the interests of the diploma students should be duly protected either by bringing out a suitable legislation or strictly restraining the entry of more qualified graduates and postgraduates for posts which can be occupied by diploma-holders.
- When there are plenty of opportunities at stake for everyone on the land to prosecute the type of education one needs, why should it be denied to the Polytechnic students? For those unfortunate diploma holders who seek employment for obvious reasons but have the thirst for higher knowledge, the opportunities for higher

education should be enhanced. The imbalance in this regard should be set right and more avenues should be created.

CONCLUSION

With the controlling and monitoring body – All India Council for Technical Education – taking care of the quality of technical education both in Polytechnics and Engineering Colleges by infusing highly talented and educated teaching staff, the industry can expect a refurbished and rejuvenated technician coming out of the portals of the Polytechnics which, though not fully, meet the requirements of the industry to a greater extent.

REFERENCES

1. Pattern of Development in India—A Study of Andhra Pradesh—SER Division, Planning Commission Government of India.
2. Interview of Sri Sunil Kant Munjal, President, CII to N. Vidya Sagar, *The Times of India*, Dated June 23rd, 2004, p. 12, Bangalore ed.
3. Approach Paper on Tenth Plan.
4. National Human Development Report, 2001.

31

Low Enrolment of Women in Engineering and Polytechnic Colleges

*Shukla Mahanty**

ABSTRACT

The National Policy of Empowerment of Women was adopted in April 2001 to empower women as agents of socio-economic change on the basis of this policy, a number of strategies has been worked out as National Plan action. Higher Education is one of them, which highlights "Steps for eliminating gender bias in all educational programmes and to institute plans for free education of girls upto college level including professional levels, recognising the fact of the acknowledgement of an engagement with Science and Technology in higher education, and ensure their involvement in development projects with Scientific and technical inputs. Though women students are provided equal educational opportunity to different branches of education at different levels, women have very little preference to these because of social constraints.

INTRODUCTION

Traditionally this field was considered to be the men's. According to Tenth Five year plan 2002-2007.

* **Principal, Jamshedpur Women's College, Jamshedpur - 831 001, Email: principalshukla@yahoo.com**

Levels	1996-97		1999-2000	
	Women	Total	Women	Total
B.E./B.Sc. Engg/ B.Arch	0.05 (14.9)	0.33	0.08 (22.0)	0.36

Note: Figures within the bracket indicates percentage of total.

Planning commission 2002 only 0.05 million (14.9) women are in B.E/B.Sc. Engg./B.Arch in 1996-97 and in 1999-2000 only 0.08 million (22.0) women are in these courses.

Para-15.14.1 of the PDA, 1992 states "Opportunities for technical education for women at all levels will be suitably increased. Additional Polytechnics for women will be established under the world Bank assisted Technician Education Projects and concerted efforts will be made to increase the proportion of girls enrolling in polytechnics and engineering courses. Adequate hostel facilities will be provided to the girl students in technical and management institutions. Guidance Seminar for girls at the 10+2 stage will be organised through the State Governments, Boards of Apprenticeship Training and other selected institutions to make them aware of opportunities in technical education and potential for employment and self-employment.

An important area in technical education relevant to women participation is polytechnic education. One of the thrust area of the world Bank assisted Technician Education Project has been enhancing women's participation in polytechnics under the project, the overall percentage of women students in polytechnics has gone up from 11.29 per cent to 29 per cent. Sixty-eight new co-educational polytechnics, women's polytechnics and women's wings have been organised.

The State of Jharkhand was formed to fulfill the long-standing aspirations of the people of this region for development and a better quality of life. Some Govt. and private engineering colleges and polytechnic colleges are running their courses in Jharkhand. Bulk of women's enrolment in higher education even after so many years of efforts of Government continue to be on softer courses like Arts, Commerce, Science, and Education etc. Enrolment in Engineering and Polytechnic is rather very low.

Table—31.1 Women enrolment by faculty: 2001-2002

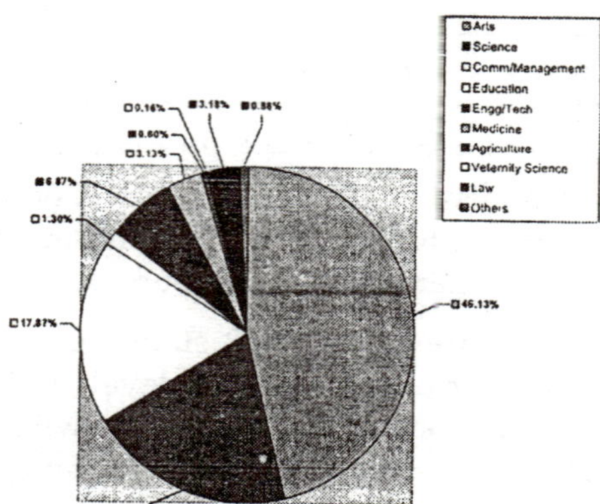

Sl. No.	Faculty	Enrolment	Percentage
1.	Arts	18,20,134	51.79
2.	Science	6,99,376	19.90
3.	Commerce/Management	5,81,993	16.56
4.	Education	5,939	1.69
5.	Engg/Technology	1,31,792	3.75
6.	Medicine	1,23,006	3.50
7.	Agriculture	9,137	0.09
8.	Veterinary Science	3,163	0.09
9.	Law	56,934	1.62
10.	Others	29,521	0.84
	Total	**35,14,450**	**100.00**

Source: UGC Annual Report 2001-2002.

Table shows that women enrolment in the faculty of Arts has been 51.79 per cent of total women enrolment only 3.75 per cent of total women is enrolled in Engg. and Technology.

Traditionally, the field of Science and Technology was considered to be the man's. Even today either at college level or at occupational level this is mostly dominated by the menfolk. There is a need to analyse the low enrolment of women in engineering and polytechnic in today's high world. Entry of women in these technical fields is of crucial importance to the ever-increasing demand in the field and to the economic development at State, national and international level. The present technical education responds not only to the scientific and technological but also to the subsequent social and economic changes in the society. But the entry of large proportion of women in these technical institutions is still a dream.

The objective of the study is to investigate the causes of low enrolment of women polytechnic and engineering courses. The study is also aiming at other factors like caste, place, and course of study, parental education and occupations, size of the family.

The present study has the following limitations too:

- The women students studying at two places, viz. Jamshedpur and Chaibasa district women's colleges.
- The women students studying at Govt. and non Govt. engineering and polytechnic institutions of Jamshedpur and Saraikela districts.
- This study is limited to a few independent questions in relation to their personal and family factors.

Table—31.2 The number and percentage of women students admitted in Kolhan commissionry in Jharkhand

Year	Womenrolment in Engg. in (%)		Women enrolment in Polytechnic (in million)		
	Govt.	Pvt.	Govt. women polytechnic	Govt. Co-ed. polytechnic	Private Co-ed. polytechnic
1999	0.0	0.0	5	Nil	Nil
2000	0.1	0.0	10	Nil	Nil
2001	0.9	0.0	30	Nil	2
2002	1.44	0.1	113	Nil	1
2003	2.00	0.6	130	Nil	3

From Table—31.2 it is clear that in Govt. engineering colleges women enrolment slowly shoots up but in Private Colleges the Scenario is very unsatisfactory. In Govt. Women Polytechnic the enrolment is nil and in private polytechnic institution enrolment scenario is better than private engineering colleges.

In order to analyze facts, the details of caste, occupation of the parent and annual family income were gathered by the sample for the investigation, which consisted women students in total by selecting 20 from engineering colleges and 80 from polytechnic institutions. Survey method of collecting the data for this investigation is also done in two intermediate women's colleges consisting 200 women students in total by selecting 100 from each women's college.

The Table—31.3 (see on next page) shows that in recent years backwards caste specially 'Mahato' caste is very prominent in enrollment. (27% of the total population is Mahto). The qualification of parents is Matriculation and Graduate. The percentage of dropout is also high because of their marriages during the course. Women students are interested in computer science or Mechanical courses but the seats are limited.

The enrolment has been increasing in 2003-2004 because the qualifying marks for women students has been lower than that of male students. Now Govt. women polytechnic institute has it's own hostel. Scheduled caste and scheduled tribes are less represented in these course because these require longer investment of resources in terms of time and finance and also socialization support and role models at home. Not a single student from rural educational background is enrolled.

But in engineering colleges the upper caste women enrolment is higher than SC/ST/OBC women enrolment. Only 2 per cent scheduled caste and scheduled tribe women were enroled in recent years. The parental education and occupation of women students in engineering is also very high in income and qualification both. In engineering, women students are interested in electronics, civil and computer science. Hostel facilities are available in Govt.. engineering college. Fees are very high in private engineering institution and that is the main cause for nil enrolment in these colleges. Most of the students are from urban area.

Table—31.3 Distribution of enrollment and performance of women polytechnic students in terms of caste

Year	Caste	Qualification	Parental education	Parental occupation	Drop out rate (in %)	Course offered	Place
2000	Gen-70 ST-01 SC-02 OBC-27	Matric	Father-non Graduate Mother non-Matric	Service	60%	Electronics	Urban
2001	Gen-65 ST-02 SC-04 OBC-29	Intermediate	Father-non Graduate Mother-non Matric	Service	40%	Computer Science	Urban
2002	Gen.-60 ST-04 SC-06 OBC-30	Intermediate	Father-Graduate Mother-non Matric	Service	35%	Computer Science	Urban
2003	Gen.-50 ST-04 SC-06 OBC-40	Intermediate	Father-Graduate Mother-Matric	Service	20%	Computer Science Mechanical	Urban

In Jharkhand after passing out from these courses job is not guaranteed until now. Women students and their parents are not interested to go far from their home town for any private services. They are interested in Government services more than private services. In these institutions not a single women student has failed during their course both in Engineering and Polytechnic.

The following steps may be adopted for better enrolment in women engineering and Polytechnic institution:

Creating education benefit consciousness, among all connected women intermediate colleges viz., the authority or management, faculty, students parents and the interacting society.

Treating the students as sovereign authority and creating a feeling amongst the faculty that the institution will be responsible for their campus selection.

Qualifying marks should be lower than the male students in competitive examination.

Separate Hostel facilities needed.

Better library and toilet facilities needed.

To avoid dropout of women students there should be counselling for parents and students.

In summing up it may be stated that women enrolment in engineering and polytechnic institution can increase if some efforts are done by Government and Society.

REFERENCES

1. Anbalaga, G., Academic Performance and Personality of Engineering College Students, Experiments in Education, 1984 Ahmad, K Equity and Women's Higher Education, Journal of Higher Education, 1979.
2. Bhanu S. and Tapatia, P.K. Effectiveness and Utilization of Job Oriented Education in Women's Polytechnics, Journal at Indian Education, 1989.
3. Chitins, S., Traditional Stereotypes and Roles of Women. A Report on A Study on Co-education and Professional Education As Factors Influencing the Attitudes and Outlook of College Girls in Bombay City.
4. Joseph, M.S. Characteristics of Women in Male Dominated Occupations, Competitiveness, Sex Role Orientation, Dissertation Abs.
5. National Institute of Educational Planning and Administration: Higher Education India: A Survey, NIEPA, N.Delhi.
6. University Grants Commission (2001-2002 - Annual Report, New Delhi.

32

Innovative Futuristic Impacts of Technical Education in India

*Ved Vyas Dwivedi**

*Roshan M. Shah***

ABSTRACT

Harnessing real time engineering resources and extending the budding technical skills for the betterment of quality tomorrow, needs, optimistically devised, precise degree of sequential dominations and globally unique minded devotions of virtually correlated industrious motivators. Tech education is moderately a long term influencing critically pertinent achievement. India is uniformly marching on the golden path to a developed nation supported by technically enthusiastic and socio-economic gap filling quite young brains, in surplus with other countries short. In the ultimate sense, fundamentally, eminent teaching professionals satisfactorily imparting the awareness of the healthy educational environment imprint entirely reflective impacts on community. Astonishingly the challenging curriculum development, its

***** **[AMIETE, AMIE, MIEEE, MTT-S], Lecturer, Dept. of Electronics and Communication Engineering, Charotar Institute of Technology, Changa– 388 421, Gujarat, Phone: 091 2697 247500 extn 221/234 Fax: 091 2697 247100. E-mail: vedvyasdwivedimtech@yahoo.co.uk**

****** **Asst. Professor, Dept. of Information Technology, Charotar Institute of Technology, Changa– 388 421, Gujarat, Phone: 091 2697 247500 extn 221/ 234 Fax: 091 2697 247100. E-mail: shahroshan@it.ecchanga.ac.in**

necessary delivery, evaluation methodology and restructured inter disciplinary interactive national syllabus including current and advance toolsets as per original suggestions gained from decades of experiences, we present here, will certainly regain the lost dignity from its scratch platform.

Key Words: Futuristic impacts, entropic knowledge, transparent methodology and system, p – cube, e-m engineering, tel-tech-education, total quality management, 3–D environment.

INTRODUCTION

In recent years, technology is the engine, capable of driving the growth and prosperity and giving it the necessary competitive edge. Almost never the properties required by business and enterprise goals consciously understood, fully articulated. Therefore decision maker must identify and effectively utilize their resources to solicit their goals/visions. As India vision to be developed nation by the year 2020, we are discussing the strategies about techno vision and striking mega mission, in aggregate, how agrees upon to lead India and India and Indo-Techs to the apex of safety, prosperity, environmental debates, sophistication in nano-bios, mysterious space-crust explorations, live quality stresses, digital information and communication society and globally integrated human and social aspects in principle.

The renovation, innovative-revolution, in engine (technology) and its applications are generating many of the virtually real a really virtual dream jobs. In the globalization race, pace many such jobs are held by non-traditional academic background people, but mysterious inter planetary visits to Mars could be made possible because of technical education e. g. one of our Indians (Late Miss Kalpana Chawala). A domain of once highly trained technicians became a friendly enough for non-technical workers.

Here we are discussing the roadmap of providing the technology access point to integrate the usage advantages and identification of knowledge like efficiency, satisfaction...and sharing the same to the demanders.

MERITORIOUS EFFECTS OF TECHNICAL EDUCATION

Technocrats are hard workers, thus reduce the socio economic gap by adopting latest technology encapsulated by affirmative effects tabulated under with.

Table—32.1 Affirmative effects

Dimensions	Methodology	Addressing?	Remarks
Proper time utilization	Planning	No	Experience
Remote technology emergence	Implementation	Yes	Tech Manpower
Universal security enhancement	Identify (Precision & Accuracy)	Yes	Tech Manpower
Gaining wide knowledge spectrum	Sharing	No	
Fruitful natural resources utilization	Applications Utilization	Yes	Tech Manpower Awareness
Transparency in entropic networking	Source Sharing	Yes	Tech Manpower
Excavation of typically critical challenges	Experience	No	
Easy and efficient communication, transportation,	Infrastructure	Yes	Tech Manpower
Sound analytical understanding of nature's secrecies	Research	Yes	Tech Manpower
Social awareness to good and bad or better and worse	Entropy	Yes	Tech Manpower
Technical knowledge – an internationally uniform currency	Globalization	Yes	Tech Manpower
Debated events like (p-cube) population, pollution, poverty elimination	Action plan	No	
Successful approach to inspire passive objects (bodies) to take part actively.	Inspiration	Yes	Tech Manpower
To do complex tasks effectively with utmost efficiency with least driving source.	Marriage with technology	Yes	Tech Manpower
Less job oriented manpower but self employment increased (number of–job seeker ↓, job providers↑)	Entrepreneurship	Yes	Tech Manpower

TECHNICAL FACTS IN FIGURES

Government Survey Report–2003: It has been predicted that the three richest countries by the year 2050 would be US, China and India. One of reasons has been the availability of employable and young technically technical educated population, which India would be surplus with other countries short. Even if countries, which would be short of employable young people, think of increasing their population now, they would still be 20 years behind! Lesson for India is to train and arm India's youth with the skills, which would be required in the coming years so that they become a useful and employable lot. This makes role of tech institutes and tech societies even more relevant in harnessing the resources of non-formal sector for generation of skilled and competent sound manpower.

One of the core competencies of India is Biodiversity resources, which combined with technology, will yield value-added products and lead India to be leader in technology.

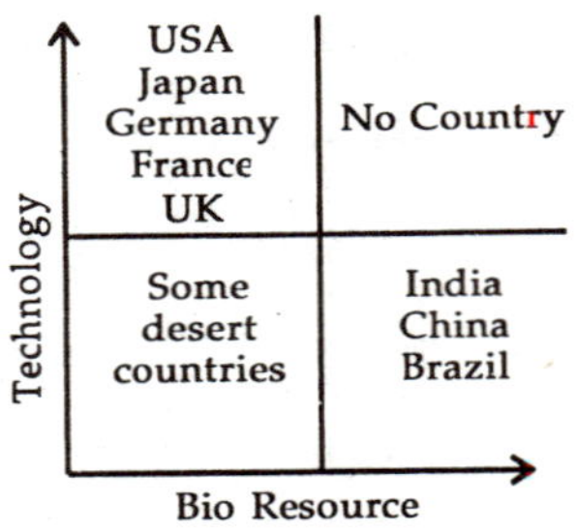

Fig. 32.1: Statistic development matrix

VALUE SYSTEM CHAIN—IMPORTANCE

Technology consists of stages like research and development, technology transfer, technology absorption, and production of products or systems with the desired performance, quality, and cost-effectiveness. Technology development can be achieved through two routes – (1) know–how and (2) know–why. In the case of India, progress in technology, particularly indigenous design, is the thrust area to enable India to become competitive with other countries.

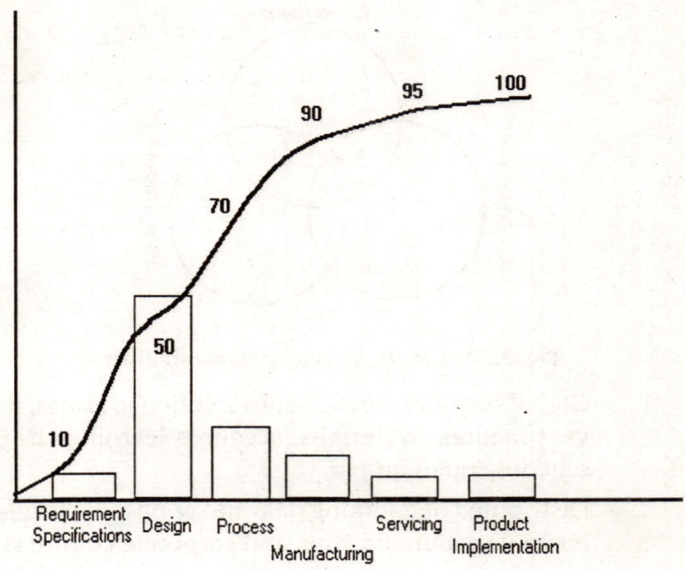

Fig. 32.2: Value chain in tech life cycle

CONCERN ISSUES

Need prior assessment with probabilistic forecasting: As the above graph shows the value chain for the quality improvement and wealth generation in percentages interrelating the bio resources on the platform of advantage and identifications of the tech requirements and the tech-education itself. The Syllabi, Methodology, Result, Sound Knowledge implementation,—

Time frame in nano-micro-macro to long span in interdisciplinary time—stress management and selling skills

Fee structure with respect to state govt.,

Faculty training and interaction—tele-education

Norms—AICTE, UGC

Standards—ISO, accredition

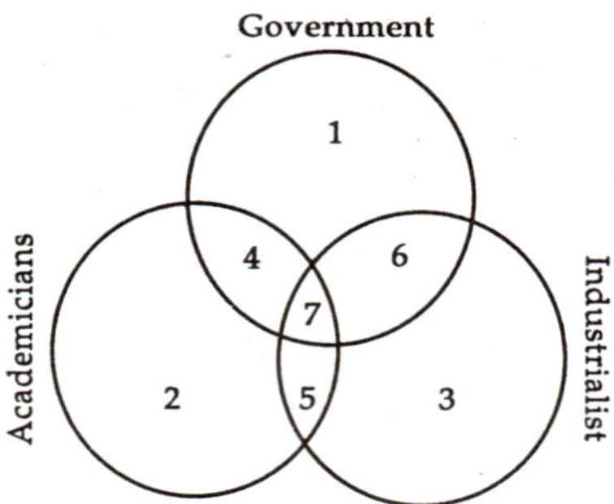

Fig. 32. 3: Covalency among responsibilities

1. Global statistics, news, issues solution to issues, theory vs. practices, waterfalls, accounts learning, 15 years schedule not required.

2. Distributed networking data and application skills and business communication and corporate culture skills.

3. Technically enabled education as video-tele-conferencing virtual classes covers the entire gamut of the excellent opportunities worldwide *Tel-education.* Methodologies for taking practical and theory exams, assessing the students answer sheets must be changed or reconsidered. Syllabi improvements committee should involve the tech youngsters, industrial experts and international or national level competitiveness into consideration. There should be paper of current technical advancements and researches in the last three - four months published in so—so national international journals or monthly magazines. In place of traditional routine viva exams there should be some technical quiz type 50 marks in the university syllabi for which the teachers should widen his knowledge. Methodology, need tie up.

4. State based logistic, hand held compact tools as Basic and Computer like operational skills.

Table—32.2 Academic Roles

Roles of Management	Roles of Principal	Roles of Teachers
1	2	3
Providing and having clear vision and mission.	To implement Vision and Academic Mission in practice.	Excellent learner, guide and watch man.
Creating 3-D environment: Teaching, Learning, Research.	Ensuring all activities geared to the benefit of primary customers as students.	Collaborate closely with student to map abilities shortcomings with view to unlock the former and remedy the latter.
Resource collection to foster a culture of excellence.	Harnessing human potential to building effective team.	Pursue mainstream research to provide solutions to improving tech quality life.
Neutrality in feedback through students or others.	Willingness to employ academic freedom for experiments and innovations without being deterred by failures.	Conversion of teaching learning process into an active intellectual engagement through intensified clarity towards knowledge.
Periodic evaluation conduction of academic practices.	Be open to ideas, suggestions even criticism insofar as its acceptance is in the best interests of-the Institution.	Honestly evaluate the student review and feedback for appropriate intervention and quality enhancement.
Clean single minded motto	Work to eliminate-remove artificial barriers within institute.	Integrate classroom teaching and education with work experience.
Fair and unbiased rules for faculty promotions and appointments.	Network with peer institutes to adopt 'best academic and governance' practices.	Perform social responsibilities by inspiring-motivating learners to become productive national citizens.

(Contd...)

1	2	3
Zero political backing as far as tech education is concerned.	Create a family bonding among students, parents, teachers and supporting staff.	Adopt diversity in teaching methods with liberal use of case studies and real time projects.
Make continuous quality improvement in centre stage of all activities and cater to varying aptitude with tailor approaches.	Open, transparent and fair in making judgments and decision making.	Be responsive with open eyes to demands of changing curricula, making theoretical knowledge applicable. Work for evaluation reform by developing new methods for screening the level of knowledge absorption of learner.
Constant and continuous boost back up to institute members through various meetings and gatherings.	Personal and professional integrity: Ideal academic head, efficient educational administrator and continuous learner.	Use new educational technology and learning aids to prepare new educational material to broaden horizon of learning for students
Facility providing like medical, sports, cultural and religious holidays, loans...	Develop appropriate mechanisms for success monitoring and evaluation.	Maintain a high level of professional efficiency by upgrading visible transmission in domain knowledge.

5. TTT exam as successful implementation as live on hand interaction with real experiments instead of laboratory demonstrations, Behavioral skills, Communication skills, Personality development, Customer-relationship management skills.
6. Identification of reasons man machine money utilize time, proud to academicians, inform.
7. Syllabi.

REFERENCES

1. APJ Abdul Kalam with A. Sivathanu Pillai, *Envisioning an Empowered Nation Technology for Societal Transformation*, Tata McGraw-Hill Publishing Company Limited, New Delhi, 2004.
2. David Kushner, *Let Us Entertain You*, IEEE SPECTRUM, February 2004, pp. 51-52.
3. M. Aruchami, *Quality Imperatives in Higher Education*, University News–a Weekly Journal for Higher Education, Vol. 42, No. 05, February 02-08, 2004, pp. 01-05.
4. Prof. Deshpande, Modak and Askhedkar, Creation of Research and Development Culture in Self Financed Technical Institutions, The Indian Journal of Technical Education, Vol. 26, No. 4, Oct-Dec 2003, pp. 13-16.
5. S V Chindhade, *Impact of Privatisation on Education in India: Some Stray Thoughts*, University News–A Weekly Journal for Higher Education, Vol. 42, No. 07, February 16-22, 2004, pp. 160-162.
6. Jalaja V. and Deshan Koovakkai, *The Problems of Digital Divide Among the Academic Community*, University News—A Weekly Journal for Higher Education, Vol. 42, No. 03, Jan 19-25, 2004, pp. 08-09.

33

Role of Knowledge Management in Technical Manpower Development

*K.Chandra Sekaran**
*V.Vijaya Kumar***

ABSTRACT

Building and running corporate-wide knowledge management systems in the domain of technical manpower development has been practised in our ancient days in India. However, a modern approach with formalisms are required to meet the current challenges. This idea is now gaining widespread attention as it strives more to implement effective manpower development methods. The new dimension of adding knowledge management in manpower development enables the mechanisms to handle both explicit and tacit knowledge in order to broaden the scope of manpower development. This chapter examines the knowledge management and its contribution to manpower development with set of technological solutions.

Key Words: Knowledge Base, Knowledge Management, Knowledge Transfer, Learning Organization.

* **Dept. of Computer Engineering, NITK Surathkal, Srinivasnagar– 575 025, Karnataka State.**

** **School of I.T., IPGSR, JNTU, Hyderabad– 500 072.**

INTRODUCTION

In the fast moving area of manpower development, which is characterized by rapid technological change and uncertainty, the most successful way that would systematically and continuously create more potential mechanism in its measure is to use 'knowledge management'. While technical manpower is of paramount importance for success in all high-tech and service domains, its development practice does not always live up to this challenge and requires tremendous efforts to increase its maturity. The need for further development practices of manpower adds to the demand for systematic knowledge management based approaches. Building and running corporate-wide knowledge management systems in the domain of technical manpower development has been practised in our ancient days in India. However, a modern approach with formalisms are required to meet the current challenges. This idea is now gaining widespread attention as it strives more to implement effective manpower development methods. The new dimension of adding knowledge management in manpower development enables the mechanisms to handle both explicit and tacit knowledge in order to broaden the scope of manpower development.

Knowledge is considered a crucial resource of each organization and, therefore needs to be managed carefully[1]. Systematic management of knowledge is of particular importance in fast changing knowledge-intensive application areas such as Technical Manpower Development. Knowledge is a mandatory source of success in this area as this country witnessed potential teachers of old era and their role in manpower development with the help of which only the good old universities and technical institutes are surviving even today. Knowledge Management (KM) is the formal method[2] and management of knowledge for facilitating creation, access, reuse of knowledge and learning from its application, typically using advanced technologies. Knowledge is information combined with experience, context, interpretation and reflection. It is high-value form of information. It is possible to apply readily the decision making and action taking steps of manpower development using KM. It is argued in this chapter that sustained knowledge management is a prerequisite to maintaining a competitive advantage and continuous growth with quality in the area of technical manpower development.

CHALLENGES IN TECHNICAL MANPOWER DEVELOPMENT IN INDIA

Technical education forms one of the major components in the growth of our country as the part of education system and is being seen as one of the prestigious programme for employment and betterment of life. Besides equipping the manpower with new and relevant skills, technical education is expected to produce persons who can monitor technological trends, assess their relevance to country's prospects and help to develop an appropriate national level strategy for technical growth and compete in the creation of new knowledge. As we have adopted the policy of liberalization and globalization of our country India, we must know that these 'lizations' do demand higher competitiveness in every activity. But we have been witnessing no tangible progress and steps in technical manpower in terms of its role in engineering education across the country. It is because, the mushroom of technical institutes do not have the 'minimum common requirements' before they venture into technical education thereby manpower development. These drawbacks have been briefed here: Most of the technical institutes that have mushroomed up have literally failed to impart quality education to the masses as (a) they do not employ the quality faculty, (b) lack of proper infrastructure, and, (c) un-updated and non-industry oriented curriculum. In addition to these, the expectations from industries do bring challenges through improved and modernized techniques of doing work, efficient and effective methodologies to sustain suitably, are also need to be considered with respect to manpower development in India. Besides all these limitations, we need to remember one more important point, that is., imparting technical skills and knowledge are essential, but making the manpower, particularly the students of engineering education, as good human beings is also essentially required at this stage in our country.

KNOWLEDGE MANAGEMENT PROCESSES

The goal of KM in technical manpower development is to improve the overall skills of all levels of the organization ((individual: faculty, staff and students), (group: people in different specialization in departments or section), (division: groups in different levels and departments), and (organization itself)) by better usage of the resources of knowledge. It is an activity associated with knowledge and as such goal oriented, planned and monitored.

KM used to be simply the transfer of knowledge from one person to another, the result of which enables the recipient to benefit from the collected wisdom of the more experienced members of society. This activity of so called knowledge transfer, a component of KM, happens when the founder of the family business gives training to his sons and daughters to run the business; these people also learn many things from their surroundings and different happenings in the environment in order to run the business successfully with more latest methodologies and technological solutions. However, the modern approaches for using the KM requires strategic planning with modern technical support, particularly the need of information technology based solutions.

Knowledge Management at the organization (technical manpower development organization or commonly known as technical institute) level requires a clear definition in which context and for what purpose the knowledge is intended to be used. These so called knowledge goals are closely related to the organizational goals. These goals would reflect the global competition that the organization is interested in exhibiting and the liberalization that it wants use in its processes. The identification and representation of the knowledge goals requires a clear definition of the improvements that are planned using this knowledge. For instance this can be a new faculty, acquisition of new technologies or acquisition of alternative approaches to impart training in the organization in order to increase and complement existing knowledge in a specific field. An instrument to consolidate knowledge goals at the individual level is the definition of education and training plans for employees such as members of faculty in the technical manpower development.

The process deploying Knowledge Management in organizations requires the following seven core processes that can be identified at the individual and organizational levels[3]: (i) Knowledge identification, (ii) Knowledge acquisition (iii) Knowledge development (iv) Knowledge dissemination (v) Knowledge usage (vi) Knowledge preservation and, (vii) Knowledge evaluation. The detailed description of these core processes can be found in[3]. As a whole, these seven core processes signify that KM is a management task relating the management of the organization and the processes of managing the knowledge that the human base has gained from the experience in the past either within the organization or from the external world for its globalization and technical competence.

KNOWLEDGE MANAGEMENT AND ITS CONTRIBUTION TO TECHNICAL MANPOWER DEVELOPMENT

Basics of KM

Data is a set of discrete, objective facts about events. It says nothing about its own importance or irrelevance. It is essential raw material for the creation of information. Information can be described as a message, usually in the form of a document or an audible or visible communication. It has a sender and a receiver. Information is meant to change the way the receiver perceives something, to have an impact on his judgment and behaviour. Information moves within an organization through both hard and soft networks. Data becomes information when its creator or receiver adds meaning. Experience describes results from historical, controlled or observational experiments. Experiments can be devoted to any kind of method, technique or tool for any stage of the software development process.

Knowledge is information combined with experience, context, interpretation and reflection. It is a high-value form of information. It is ready to be applied in decision making and action taking. Knowledge can be classified along a spectrum from tacit to explicit, ranging from knowledge the holder might not even be aware of to knowledge s/he is very well aware of (i.e., has a structured view onto this knowledge) or has even made available through writing, graphs, models etc. Tacit knowledge is personal knowledge embedded in personal experience and is shared and exchanged through direct, face-to-face contact. Subjective insights, intuitions, and hunches fall into this category of knowledge. It is hard to formalize and is generally in the heads of individuals and teams. On the other side, it is often assumed to be the most valuable and untapped knowledge. Explicit knowledge is formal or semi-formal knowledge that can be packaged as information. It can be found in the documents of an organization: reports, articles, manuals, models, lessons learned. It can also be found in the representations that an organization has of itself: organizational charts, process models, mission statements, domains of expertise.

Knowledge Management (KM) is the formal management of knowledge for facilitating creation, access, reuse of knowledge, and learning from its application, typically using advanced technology. KM deals with tacit as well as explicit knowledge. A very broad definition of KM also includes human resources related management activities, such as hiring new staff or to train staff in order to increase the company's capacities. We will use the term KM for handling both knowledge and experience.

Knowledge Needed for Technical Manpower Development

Here, we describe the knowledge needed to support the activities in the technical manpower development. In order to do that, we need to define who needs the knowledge we are talking about. First of all, this includes the promoters of the manpower development organizations themselves and their administrators, supporting personnel such as faculty and staff, and finally the students or the actual manpower of India. Furthermore, the customer of these organizations, (i.e., the potential parents of the Indian society, whose wards would become the technical manpower) often require knowledge about these manpower development activities that are being practised.

The knowledge needed includes the following: (a) *Overview of processes used*: First of all, every one involved in the technical manpower development need to know the processes or stages involved in it. This describes the type of life cycle used as well as the phases in the life cycle together with their main goals, activities and results. While for some groups, such as the students, this may be all the knowledge needed about the learning process that is the special step in manpower development, most others will need the overview to identify where their own piece of work fits in, which interfaces to other people or groups they have in the manpower development process, to set priorities in case of conflict, etc. (b) *Description of tasks and artifacts*: This is the core part of the manpower development support process and includes templates for the various artifacts (such as project plan, faculty recruitment, industry oriented projects for students) to be developed as well as descriptions of the steps to be performed for a task, and checklist to ensure completeness of the tasks. (c) *Description of steps and artifacts*: The description of steps to be performed and the artifacts produced is the central part of manpower development. The description typically includes the methods used, any sub-steps, and templates for the artifacts produced. Usage of these descriptions of steps and artifacts can vary a lot between the organizations which involve in the process of manpower development. Depending on the experience of own or the experience gained from others, the organization may follow the process described step-by-step, or they just get the template filled for the artifact needed. (d) *Development method used*: The development method can also be described as a collection of tasks and artifacts at macro level. (e) *Best practices used and lessons learned*: This involves the knowledge about approaches, techniques etc that have proven useful in other or similar contexts of manpower development, and might therefore be helpful for the organization to know about these. Best practices can also come from within the own organization, i.e., may be from other units of it (f) *General manpower development knowledge*: This includes the knowledge in understanding the target for the products after manpower development, measuring the success of this development process, developer skills at a minimum required level which must be satisfied in order to get the desired results and thereby giving a level of success as a measure, typical problems encountered in the past, and market data about the organization.

IMPLEMENTING KNOWLEDGE MANAGEMENT FOR TECHNICAL MANPOWER DEVELOPMENT

Knowledge management, as it is spelled out and explained in the above sections is a systematic and technology oriented approach in the organization that focuses upon the usage and delivery of strategically useful knowledge and expertise. The availability of such a system in place facilitates effective and timely schedule of different activities in manpower development including decision making. It is also true that the strategically literate people in a technical manpower development system such as an education institute, equipped with best and most up-to-date knowledge, deliver the required tasks in a timely manner, will produce work that results in more satisfied customers, in our case it is none other than our students with increased success and corporate value.

Traditionally and historically in the Indian scenario, the knowledge in any organization would be available on paper (partly, in the form of written documents), and, (another part) in people's minds. Unfortunately, the paper based knowledge has limited accessibility and is difficult to update. On the other hand, the other part of knowledge that is in the minds of various people across the organization will not be available fully, as people tend to behave differently in different situation and therefore making use of their knowledge becomes very difficult, and, people may also leave the organization if the situation forces, and in which case the experience or knowledge that the people have will be totally lost to the organizational growth. Hence, there must be an approach to use and implement KM in a technology oriented manner in organizations. In this context, it worth to recall the following technological innovations in this IT and Internet era: Data Warehouse and Data Mining, Knowledge Warehouse and Knowledge Mining, Data and Knowledge Bases, Ontologies and other allied concepts[4]. Details of these technologies is beyond the scope of this chapter, and can be obtained from different web sites.

Technical manpower development organizations that are looking ahead to become knowledge enabled, start off their initiative by becoming a 'learning organization'. It means that the organization should not look at the technological aspects (listed in the above paragraph) of implementing KM, and rather they should enable a mechanism in which the users or customers centric approach has been focused which is vital to the success of any KM initiative. The development and deployment of KM starts with understanding the need and objectives of the manpower development along with the strong commitment from the top management of the organization which intends to provide the technical manpower development process in the society. The information and knowledge gaps within the organization should be felt with an intensive analysis on the objectives of the task in hand, followed by the infrastructure (includes both human and technical) requirement before identifying concrete steps that could be considered in order to leverage and build a KM for the organization. Once these steps are completed, an organization can line up with the following stags of implementing and deploying KM for it: (a) *Awakening phase* – in this stage, review of vision and mission statements and analysis of infrastructure need are taking place along with the linkages of business strategy with KM. (b) *Actionable phase* – in this stage, knowledge audit, i.e., identifying what kind of knowledge and to what level is required for this organization, KM team formulation, KM architecture required for the manpower development derived from the above awakening phase, that is in line with the seven core processes (See knowledge Management Process) while looking at the typical knowledge needed (Please refer knowledge needed for Technical Manpower Development) for the organization, (c) *Implementation phase* – this stage involves the selection and implementation of a pilot project of KM and then a revised, full-fledged KM in place which would completely satisfy the goals of the manpower development organization. (d) *Maintenance and measurement phase*— this stage includes the measuring of the returns of the effort as well as the process of measuring the manpower development impact of KM using a set of appropriate metrics; this phase also includes the planning as well as conduct of periodic knowledge audits for the proper functioning of the system.

CONCLUSION

Knowledge Management in technical manpower development consists of activities focused on gaining knowledge from experiences of own and from other sources, and on the judicious application of that knowledge to fulfill the mission of the organization, which in our case is a technical institution. These activities are executed by amalgamating the organizational goals, structures, technological solutions and cognitive based strategies to raise the yield of existing knowledge and produce new knowledge. The long term effect of a KM system is that each entity in the manpower development process is constantly and consistently learning while enjoying the benefits and becoming more valuable to the society.

REFERENCES

1. Nonaka I and Takeuchi H, *The Knowledge Creating Company: How Japanese Companies Create the Dynamics of Innovation*, OUP, 1995.
2. D.E. O'Leary, *Enterprise Knowledge Management, IEEE Computer*, March 1998, pp. 54-61.
3. G.Ruhe, *Learning Software Organization, Handbook of Software Engineering and Knowledge Engineering*, Vol.1 Fundamentals. Readings, World Scientific Publications, pp. 663-667.
4. Sudhir Warier E., *Knowledge Management, Readings*, Vikas Publications, 2003.

34

Building Technical Manpower

The Character Way

*G. Divakar**

*Kalyani Divakar***

*M. Kiran Reddy****

ABSTRACT

Character is property. It is the noblest of possessions. "No man is bound to be rich or great—No nor to be wise; but every man is bound to be honest. Without principles, a man is like a ship without rudder or compass, left to drift hither and thither with every wind that blows.

Character is formed by a variety of minute circumstance, more or less under the regulation and control of the individual. Not even a day passes without its discipline, whether for good or for evil. Every action every thought, every feeling, contributes to the education of the temper, the habits, and the understanding, and exercises an inevitable influence upon all the acts of our future life. Thus character is undergoing constant change, for better or for worse either being elevated on the one hand, or degraded on the other.

*** Acharya & B.M. Reddy College of Pharmacy, Soladevanahalli, Chikkabanawara Post, Bangalore– 560 090, Email: divakargoli@yahoo.com**

**** Acharya & B.M. Reddy College of Pharmacy, Soladevanahalli, Chikkabanawara post, Bangalore– 560 090, E-mail: kalyanidivakar@yahoo.co.in**

***** Acharya Institute of Management and Sciences, Peenya, Bangalore– 560 058**

INTRODUCTION

Character is the foundation of the future of mankind. Robbers can break open and rob everything in the world, but not character. When we have lost everything but not character, we have not really lost anything. With character we can fearlessly face and conquer any kind of present and future. Without it, we have neither the present nor the future.

Education is hardly edifying without provision for character. Character-transmission is the essential mission of education.[1]

One can build one's own character. One can also lose one's character, even after building it. Character needs perpetual tending, like breathing every moment, for living.

There are varying needs of various individuals, societies, and nations. They are worked for in different ways, not un-often in indifferent ways, prejudicial to the advancement of others. But, there is one universal need of all individuals, societies and countries—the need of enough character. Given enough character, man becomes a true man. A true man alone can solve his own problems and help solve those of others.

Confucious said: 'One who is not a true man cannot, long stand poverty, nor can he stand prosperity for long'.[2] How true! Poverty brutalizes and affluence barbarizes man if he does not have enough character. When we do not have enough character our places of worship will become commercial houses, and temples of learning just factories.

When we do not have enough character, as students we will not devote our time to hard study, we will be more interested in extra-curricular activity than in curricular activity, and we will busy ourselves with thoughts and occupations which misshape our budding lives and we will wither away before blossoming. When we have to face the struggle for existence we shall find that we are nowhere in the grade. Then we will shamelessly live on somebody else's earning and dream of the coming revolution!

When we do not have enough character, our knowledge will be used for the undoing of man in a sophisticated manner; we will use real intelligence for doing small things and our high endeavours will then produce low results.

When we do not have enough character right thinking will be impossible for us. And from wrong thinking, how can we ensure desirable results? When we do not have enough character, in democracy such people will wield power that people will cry, 'Ah, When shall we have a dictator!'

When we do not have enough character ugliness will reign everywhere, our faces will lose luster, there will be no light in our eyes, hope in our heart, power of conviction in our mind, and joy in our soul.

Granted enough character, our strength will be more than our weaknesses, fortunes greater than misfortunes, woes less than weal, our present and future more glorious than our past. Granted, enough character, our places of worship will be holy sanctuaries for refreshing the soul; our temples of learning will be places of pilgrimage where man-making education is received.

Granted enough character, as students we will have the intelligence to see that the real issue on hand for us as students is to conserve energy, study well, build up our physical, mental and spiritual strength and fully equip ourselves for the struggle for existence. We will then easily see through the game of people trying to use us for their purpose at the cost of our life's interest.

If we want these things to happen to us— and who would not want- we have to do one simple thing—build our character. Man himself is the central theme. He is the end. He is more valuable than any possession in the universe. He must be salvaged, augmented and liberated in his own being. The way is to build character.

HOW TO BUILD CHARACTER

Character is what a person truly is, and his reputation is what he is supposed to be. The Greek word for character means to engrave one's mode of being in the world. History is made by character.

Character is defined as qualities or features by which a person or a thing is distinguished from another; the aggregate of distinguishing mental and moral qualities of an individual or a race as a whole; the stamp of individuality impressed by nature, education or habit; that which a person or a thing really is.[1]

Swami Vivekananda Says: "What you want is character, strengthening of the will. Continue to exercise your will and it will take you higher. This will is almighty. It is character that cleaves through adamantine walls of difficulties."[3]

And he proceeds to define character in this manner: The character of any man is but the aggregate of his tendencies, the sum total of the bent of his mind. We are what our thoughts have made us. Thoughts live; they travel far. And so take care of what you think. Every work that we do, every movement of the body, every thought that we think, bears an impression on the mind-stuff. What we are every moment is determined by the sum total of these impressions on the mind. Every man's character is determined by the sum total of these impressions. If good impressions prevail, the character becomes good, if bad, it becomes bad.

Character is so important for life that to have to live without it will be worse than not living at all. Character holds the key to any riddle of life. It can break each and every vicious circle. There is no mystery character cannot unravel. There is no wound it cannot heal, no want it cannot fill, and no loss it cannot make good. Hence, the most important thing among all creative endeavours of life is to know how to build one's own character and help build the character of others with whom one associates.

As Hindu psychology would bear it out, the character of the child begins to get formed even in its prenatal state. Thoughts of the parents some way impress the yet unformed personality-stuff of the child. The family is the first training ground for the building of the child's character. The parents, knowingly or unknowingly mould the character of the child by their thoughts and actions. The child catches passively, to begin with, all behavioural contagion, good or bad, without being able to discriminate or resist.

When the child is able to watch consciously, it begins to build its own character by seeing, watching and imitating its parents. Character building depends much on what kind of food for its mind the parents, supply to the growing child. In the family again, mother's influence in moulding the character of the child is incalculable. Only those parents, who throughout their life continue to gradually build up their own character, can truly build the character of their children.

Next to parents, comes teachers' influence in molding the character of children. That is why education in ancient India was entrusted in the hands of men of ideal character, the sages; to be instructed by them was a benediction.

HELPFUL DISCIPLINER FOR BUILDING

There are several disciplines for building character, which can be knowingly cultivated. These are:

1. Acquiring knowledge and training of the physical and mental systems in an integrated manner;
2. Practice of the three austerities of body, speech and mind as taught by Sri Krishna in the Bhagavad-Gita;
3. Training in acquirement of divine treasure;
4. Cultivation of approved or ethical conduct;
5. Commitment to the higher scheme of values;
6. Developing the powers of discrimination, concentration detachment and will power;
7. Training in developing the five powers of the true learner.

Worship of gods, of the twice-born, of teachers, and of the wise, cleanliness, uprightness, continence and non-violence – these are said to be the austerity of body.

Words that do not give offence and that are truthful, pleasant, and beneficial, and also the regular recitation of the Vedas –these are said to be the austerity of the speech.

Serenity of the mind, greatness silences self-control and purity of heart—these constitute the austerity of the mind.

These three-fold austerities are basically prescriptions for attaining psychophysical efficiency for being able to effectively line a higher life. Through successful practice of these, a person will develop a greater character as a by-product, which will enable him to obtain all round well being in the world.

Fearlessness, purity of heart, steadfastness in knowledge and yoga, charity, self-control, and sacrifice; study of scriptures, austerity and uprightness. Non-violence, truth and freedom from anger, renunciation, tranquility and aversion to slander, compassion to beings and freedom from covetousness; gentleness, modesty and absence of fickleness. Courage forgiveness, and fortitude; purity, freedom from malice and over weaning pride—these belong to him who is born with divine treasure.

Most of us may not have been born with divine treasure. Even then, this can be acquired. How? First we have to develop an insight into the inner meaning of these words through repeated deep thinking. By continuing to do so, an earnest desire will spontaneously grow within us to acquire this treasure.

Then our inner struggle will begin. This struggle must be faced and gone through without being nervous and despondent. Our own acquired past tendencies particularly the evil ones will put up stiff resistance but if we are well convinced that without the acquisition of the divine treasure, life cannot but be abominable; and are inflexibly determined to acquire it, and then through required struggle by God's grace, it can be obtained. Whoever succeeds in obtaining it, will have a great, but a divine character. Here is a challenge, which can be successfully taken up only up by the vigorous and intelligent among the youth. Who have not only an indomitable spirit of adventure in the inner world, but also courage, dedication, and an invincible faith in themselves.

CULTIVATION OF THE FIVE POWERS OF A LEARNER

In the Anguttara Nikaya, Buddha teachers his disciples to cultivate five powers of a learner. Cultivation of these five powers will endow any one with a character which cannot be destroyed either from within or from without.

1. *The power of faith:* The true learner has faith in his teacher and believes in his enlightenment and his ability to teach the Supreme Truth.

2. *The power of conscientiousness:* The true learner is naturally conscientious and has qualms of conscience when acting wrongly in thought, word or deed.

3. *The power of fear:* The true learner is afraid of the blame that comes from acting wrongly is thought, word or deed.

4. *The power of energy:* The true learner has an abiding energy to discard all wrong things and adopt the right ones.

5. *The power of insight:* The true learner has an insight into the real nature of things and he sees the decay inherent in growth and thereby prepares himself to destroy the root cause of sorrow.

If one wants to destroy sorrow and abide in the supreme truth, one must cultivate the powers of faith, conscientiousness, fear, energy, and insight, which are the powers of a true learner.[4]

THE SECRET OF CHARACTER: A WELL REGULATED LIFE

We have discussed some ideas known in human thought, which are open-ended and unlimited; these ideas can became reality only by a well-disciplined life. Only through such a life lived from day-to-day can these grand ideas be reduced to habit patterns, which, as a matter of course, become character. Those who live well-regulated, temperate and balanced life shall see the end of all sorrows.

No one living a haphazard and chaotic life will be able to build character, for the simple reason that only through repeated practices of authentic disciplines can one would one's yet unformed stuff of being in the cast of a worthy character.

Tiruvalluvar Said: Discipline of life is more precious than life itself, for it is out of that discipline that life derives value. One may study many philosophies and clear his doubts but it is the well-regulated life that ultimately avails and nothing else. Therefore, guard it whatever may be the difficulty involved.

The well-regulated life ennobles every rank of life. Where this fails, good or noble parentage will not save the man. A well-regulated life brings honour. Neglect of it will lead to disgrace.

The learned really betray ignorance when in spite of their learning they fail to regulate their lives in accordance with principle of social co-operation.[5]

As Tiruvalluvar emphasized, discipline of life is more precious than life itself, for it is out of that discipline that life derives values. It is these derived valued that formulate the sinews of our character. When we fail to regulate our lives in accordance with the high principles, we not only fail in social co-operation, but we also personally disintegrate from within. Therefore, all great teachers laid more emphasis on practice than on more theoretical knowledge.

Sri Ramakrisha Said: 'Sacred books only point out the way to God, Once you have known the way what is the use of books? Sacred books tell us only the way to God, i.e., of the means for the realization of God. That way being known, the next step is to work one's way to the goal. Realization is the goal.[6]

What is most important for us is to work our way to the goal of building character for all times.

CHARACTER AND CONDUCT

We can always better understand and appreciate a man's real character by the manner in which he conducts himself towards those who are the most nearly related to him, and by transaction of the seemingly commonplace details of daily duty, than his public exhibition of himself as an author an orator, or a statesman etc. Character in good part is conduct. You behave as you are. You cannot behave better for any length of time unless you are better. How do you become better than yourself? This can be done by deliberately practising approved or ethical conduct. What is to be considered approved conduct should not be decided impulsively according to one's fancy, but learnt from scriptures. Apastamba-Dharma-sutra (22.14) enjoins:

Absence of anger, elation, indignation, avarice, delusion, vanity and enmity; speaking truth; moderation in eating; refraining from exposing others weak points; freedom from jealousy; sharing one's good things with others; sacrifice; straight forwardness; gentleness; quietude; self-control; friendliness with all beings; absence of cruelty; contentment,- these form the approved conduct for men of all stations of life. By observing them duly one becomes universally benevolent.

It is to be particularly noticed how disciplines of self-chastening and other–regard are dovetailed in approved or ethical conduct.

But ethical conduct cannot stand the strain of various trying situations of life for any length of time unless we have a cultivated firm commitment to a sound scheme of values which takes care of the totality of the human personality and its fulfillment. Indian scheme of values— names four in the list; pleasures of life, wealth, righteousness and attainment of spiritual illumination. The psychology of the person is to be so trained that he finds meaning in pursuing the pleasures of life and wealth through righteousness and he discovers an increasing purpose of righteousness in spiritual illumination.

A man with a sound sense of values alone can find reason and meaning in building up character. Others find little sense in it.

Character building is initiated through a well-regulated struggle within oneself by way of habituating discrimination between the true and the untrue, discarding what is untrue and concentrating with love and tenacity on truth. Cultivation of the powers of concentration and detachment must go hand in hand. The secret of success in all worthwhile undertaking is the development of the will power. By loving to do what we ought do, we can develop will power.

Though there is much to learn as to how we should conduct ourselves in various situations of life, it is hardly possible to design right conduct for all occasions and times. Premeditated right conduct may prove to be artificial, our good intentions not withstanding.

Truly, right conduct has the delicate fragrance of the just blossomed flower. It is what spontaneously emanates from within the person who has done his homework for bringing himself up, under no outer compulsion, but by the propulsion of his own self-chosen ideals of life.

REFERENCES

1. Swami Budhananda, *How to Build Character*, Advaita Ashrama, Calcutta, 2000.
2. Ibid, Chapter '*Aphorisms of Confucius*', p 833.
3. *Swami Vivekananda on India and Her Problems*, Advaita Ashrama, Calcutta, 1976.
4. Sudhakar Dikshit, *Sermons and Sayings of the Budha*, Chetana, Bombay.
5. Rajagopalachari C., *Kural, The Great Book of Tiruvalluvar*, Bharatiya Vidya Bhavan, Bombay, 1964.
6. *Sayings of Sri Ramakrishna*, Sri Ramakrishna Math, Madras.

35

Technical Manpower Development
The HAL Approach

*S. Raghunathan**

INTRODUCTION

Hindustan Aeronautics Limited (HAL) is today the largest Defence Public Sector undertaking, and an MOU Company. It has also been declared as a "Mini Ratna", Category-1 Company. Since its inception in 1940 at Bangalore by a Private entrepreneur Shri Walchand Hirachand, it has grown progressively into a vertically integrated Aeronautical Production Organisation and is the largest in Asia with a noticeable presence in the international aviation arena. *HAL's major customers* are, Indian Air Force, Indian Army, Indian Navy, Indian Coast Guard, Border Security Force and Department of Space. To improve its share in international market, the company has formulated a new mission Statement as given below:

> "To become a globally competitive aerospace industry while working as an instrument for achieving self-reliance in design manufacture and maintenance of aerospace defence equipment and diversifying to related areas, managing the business on commercial lines in a climate of growing Professional competence."

* **General Manager, Foundry and Forge Division, Hindustan Aeronautics Limited, Bangalore– 560 017, Email: sraghunathan@halfoundryforge.com**

MANUFACTURING ACTIVITIES

Today HAL has got 16 production units and 9 Research and Development Centres spread out in 7 different locations in India. Its product track record consists of 12 types of aircraft from in house R & D and 13 types by license production. *HAL has so far produced over 3300 aircraft, 3400 Aeroengines and overhauled over 7700 aircraft and 26000 engines.*

R & D Initiatives

HAL has engaged and succeeded in number of R & D programmes for both the military and civil aviation sectors. Substantial progress has been made in the current projects like Dhruv—Advanced Light Helicopter (ALH), Tejas-Light Combat Aircraft (LCA), Intermediate Jet Trainer (IJT) and various military and civil upgrades. The deliveries of Dhruv were effected to Indian Army, Navy, Air Force and Coast Guard in March 2002, in its first year of production which is a unique achievement.

Space Programmes

HAL has played a significant role in India's space programmes in the manufacturing of satellite launch vehicles like PSLV (Polar Satellite Launch Vehicle), GSLV (Geo Stationary Launch Vehicle), IRS (Indian Remote Satellite) and INSAT (Indian National Satellite).

Joint Ventures

HAL has also two joint venture companies, BAeHAL Software Limited and Indo- Russian Aviation Limited (IRAL). Apart from the two, other major diversification projects are Industrial Marine Gas Turbine and Airport Services. Several co-production and joint ventures with international participation are under consideration.

Customers

HAL's supplies/services are mainly to Indian Defence Services, Coast Guard and Border Security Force. Transport aircraft and Helicopters have also been supplied to Airlines as well as State Governments of India. The Company has also achieved a foothold in export in more than 30 countries, having demonstrated its quality and price competitiveness.

Award and Recognition

HAL, has won several International and National Awards for achievements in R&D, Technology, managerial performance, exports, energy conservation, quality and fulfillment of social responsibilities.

Global Competition

The other key thrust area is to become globally competitive so that HAL can participate in the international aeronautical programmes. In this direction, company has already taken steps to establish "Centre of Excellence" progressively in various manufacturing fields i.e. Machining of Airframe Components, Composite Manufacturing, Sheet Metal working, machining of engine components, etc. These Centres will ensure highest quality products at competitive price.

HAL has taken another major step towards encouraging private industries, having necessary infrastructure and capability to become subcontractors for outsourcing. All assistance is extended to such industries to absorb the technology and quality standard required in aeronautical components/assemblies. These efforts will bear fruit in reducing the cost of our product and rationalization of manpower and infrastructure. This venture of HAL will also improve the industrial base of the country.

Human Resources

In tune with the company's Mission Statement and aligning the manufacturing activities to meet the changing environment and rapid technological and global competition, it is imperative to have a vibrant, skilled, committed and qualitatively excellent workforce to meet the challenges characterized by paradigm shift from license production to R&D based production duly balanced with co-development/co-production, technological upgradation, demanding customer requirements, focused diversification to civilian and export markets.

Accordingly in the HRD area, the following are the Vision, Mission and Objectives:

Vision

"To make HAL a dynamic, vibrant, value based learning organisation with human resources exceptionally skilled, highly motivated and committed to meet the current and future challenges. This will be driven by core values of the Company fully embedded in the culture of the organisation."

Mission

To enable all those working for HAL to give out their best to ensure their all round growth as well as that of the organization.

Objective

- Ensure availability of Total Quality People to meet the organizational goals and objectives;
- Continuous improvement in Knowledge, Skill and Competence (Managerial, Behavioural and Technical);
- Promote a Culture of Achievement and Excellence, with emphasis on Integrity, Credibility and Quality;
- Maintain a motivated workforce through empowerment of Individual and Team building;
- Enhance Organizational Learning;
- Human Resource to play a pivotal role directly and significantly to Productivity enhancement, Profitability and improve Quality of Work Life.

Strategy

- To be in total alignment with Corporate Strategy;
- Maintain Human Resource at optimum level to meet the objectives and goals of the Company;
- Competence Mapping, Gap Analysis and Upgradation of Knowledge and Skills through Training, Retraining, Multi Skilling etc.;
- Create Leadership with Shared Vision at various levels in the Organization;

- Focused Development of Core Competence in High-Tech areas;
- Building Cross functional Teams;
- Bring Company wide awareness of Mission, Values and Organizational Goals;
- Personnel policies on performance based criteria, ensuring Growth, Rewards, Recognition and Motivation.

FOCUS OF HUMAN RESOURCE POLICY

- Competence Building;
- Commitment;
- Motivation;
- Employee Relations.

In the backdrop of the above, focus of Human Resource Development initiatives at HAL emphasize on the following:

1. Manpower Planning

- Outsourcing of low tech and medium tech jobs;
- Fresh induction only in critical/highly specialized areas based on requirements due to increase in workload and super-annuation profile . In the Workmen Cadre, induction will be mainly in Direct Workmen category;
- Improving the existing qualification profile by focusing on induction of professionally qualified personnel and diploma holders.

Hence focus of recruitment would be to recruit people with combination of knowledge, skill, experience and attitude in line with organisational requirements through appropriate manpower plan ,both short term and long term recruitment programme.

2. Training and Development

Training is one of the most important interventions for developing human resource. Hence, identification of training competency profile in terms of vision, mission of the Company would be the focal point of the training and development strategy of the Company. The following objective has been set in this regard:

- To provide training to all employees at regular interval in a pian period of 5 years;
- Training to become an integral component of individual professional evolution by:
  - updating knowledge to avoid obsolescence;
  - enhancing professional creativity;
  - enabling employees to shoulder higher responsibility;
  - to create a business bias and strategic thinking to take up new business challenges (creation of Centre of Excellence, etc.).

The goals of training will be to progressively achieve 7 days training per employee per year.

Keeping the organisational requirement and the above goals and objective of training, the following has been identified as the key focus areas of training:

- Technology;
- Tooling;
- Quality;
- Information Technology.

Furthermore, to facilitate development of soft skills (change of mind set, managerial development etc.) training would be imparted on continuous basis. Tie-ups with Centre of Excellence like IITs, NDC, FIAS France etc. for training would be given prime importance.

3. Performance Appraisal

Appraising people for meeting Company's goal would be the prime focus of performance assessment. The new Performance Appraisal System based on work planning and commitment (mutually agreed tasks) , self review and performance analysis, performance review and feedback would ensure that the focus would be on value adding activities rather than on routine activities which bear no relationship with organisational goals and objectives.

Priority is given to identification of *low performers* and resultant corrective action throughout the company. Similarly, faster career growth opportunity is also provided to *high performers*.

4. Reward System

Focus of the reward system in the Company would be to promote team work and culture of achievement and excellence in the organisation. In addition to the mechanism of individual reward for making exemplary contribution in the key thrust area of the Company for overall excellence and for desirable attributes like creativity and innovation. Coupled with above, schemes like "Inter Divisional Competition" and proposed "Profit Sharing Schemes" etc. has been institutionalised in the Company for team reward.

5. Scheme for Learning and Certification for Executives

A "Learning Organisation" is essential for survival in the present era of Liberalisation, Privatisation and Globalisation. Therefore, "Knowledge" is the only Core Competence of Organisations for coping with changes. Since, individual knowledge is the starting point for organizational knowledge, it is only the employees who can convert knowledge into efficient actions.

In line with the above philosophy, among other initiative like institutionalising Learning Centres in Divisions etc., HAL has also introduced the Scheme for Learning and Certification for executives as a process for building individual knowledge. The Scheme inter-alia provides opportunity for the Junior and Middle Management Cadre Executives to broaden their perspective by not only learning about all functions and procedure in their respective disciplines but also in related areas and overall knowledge about the organization and its environment. It is proposed to expand the coverage of this Scheme further, if required, by linking the Scheme to some kind of Reward mechanism.

Lastly, HRD Plan will also include time-to-time Organisational Development(OD) Interventions to address specific requirements of the Company.

Training Schemes

In order to have an excellent workforce and people with Leadership Skill and Managerial Excellence various training Schemes for newly inducted personnel being currently operated, emanating from the company's Mission Statement are as follows:

1. Management Trainee Scheme;
2. Executive Trainee Scheme;
3. Diploma Trainee Scheme;
4. Technician Trainee Scheme;
5. Trade Apprentices.

Apprentices Trainee Scheme

Training Scheme for Trade Apprentices

Training Scheme for Graduate Engineers

Training Scheme for Diploma Holders

CENTRES OF EXCELLENCE IN TRAINING

Employee Training and Development is one of the most vital activity at HAL. Training activities undertaken may be classified as under:

- Programmes conducted at HAL Management Academy(HMA)—exclusively meant for executives at Senior Management Level and Middle Management Level;
- Programmes conducted at Divisional Training Centres–meant for Junior Executives and Workmen;
- Programmes conducted at Divisional Learning Centres/HRD Cells;
- Training conducted by external agencies within the country;
- Training abroad.

Management Development Programmes

The Programmes conducted at HMA are broadly categorized into general, functional and modular Programmes that are structured to ensure holistic development of individuals to excel in performance. Certain programmes, like Neuro Linguistic Programming, provide opportunity for experiential learning to manage oneself and others. Action learning is imparted in the wilderness through outbound training.

Some Programme Themes

- Visionary Thinking through Ethics and Values;
- Transformational Leadership to influence Organizational Culture and Corporate Governance based on Indian ethos;
- Knowledge Management for Competitive Advantage in the dynamic Environment;
- Creativity and Innovation for Corporate Excellence;
- Supply Chain Analysis and Restructuring for Value Addition;
- Patenting and Intellectual Property Rights;
- QFD and Designing for Manufacturability;
- Lean Management;
- Six Sigma Breakthrough Business Strategy for Sustained Success;
- Influencing the Outcome of Situations Through Application of NLP;
- Financial Engineering;
- Managing in the IT Age.

Methodology

HMA continuously reviews and modernizes its knowledge delivery systems to add value to the services offered by it. A balanced mix of training methods are used in the Programmes. Interactive learning is supplemented with case studies, syndicate work, role plays, management games, computer simulated business experiences, outbound training, book reviews, panel discussions and project work. Through project work, the participants gain experiential learning that they can transfer to workplace. Outbound training provides them opportunities for transformation to become effective leaders and team players.

Tools for Training Effectiveness

Diagnostics, experience sharing, action planning and learning diary help in enhancing the effectiveness of learning. Diagnostics exercise enables participants to identify difficulties faced in the work-place and helps them to look for solutions during the programme. The Learning Diary helps participants identify key learning points. Individual and group action plans are the means for transferring learning from the classroom to the workplace.

Faculty

In addition to highly qualified and experienced in-house faculty, HMA brings in expert visiting faculty from Indian Institutes of Management, Indian Statistical Institute, Administrative Staff College of India, Indian Institutes of Technology, Indian Institute of Science and other reputed management development organizations in the country. Practising line managers from HAL and other industries as well as other trainers/consultants are also invited as visiting faculty.

Trainees

In addition to middle and senior management development, HMA also handles the full 52 week training of Management Trainees. These young engineers are put through inputs on Balance of PEMS (Physical, Emotional, Mental and Spiritual) through sessions on Yoga, Naturopathy, Acupressure, Good Behaviour and are also exposed to spiritual counsels.

Infrastructure

Well equipped Classrooms, Library, Auditorium and fully furnished accommodation for residential programme have been provided.

HISTORY GROWTH AND ACTIVITIES OF TRAINING DEPARTMENT

The Training Department of Hindustan Aeronautics Limited was in 1950 to cater to the in-house needs. This requirement was met under the scheme 'Aeronautical Trade Apprentices" where fresh Engineering Diploma holders were given the required training. Subsequently to meet skilled manpower requirements, another scheme christened " HAL Trade Apprenticeship" was introduced. Under this scheme, bright young matriculates were inducted and trained. The training was for a period of three years. This scheme was continued till the Apprentice Training came under the preview of Apprentice Act 1961. The first batch for Training under the Apprentices Act started in 1963. Since then the training scheme is in operation. Today training is imparted in 10 designed Trades and the strength at any instant of time is around 400 apprentices. With the introduction of the Apprentices Amendment Act 1973 the Apprentice training activities were expanded to cover engineering degree and Diploma holders to around 450 trainees at any time.

In 1969, parallel to Apprentices training, the need to develop Managerial skills in both Officers in Grade I and II and employees in supervisory level was envisaged. This resulted in the introduction of Junior Management Development Programmes which provides inputs in current Management Practices/ techniques. Over a period of time, this scheme has had a substantial growth. A variety of Programmes in General Management, Functional areas, Interactive, Specialized and other need based areas are now included under the ambit of this scheme to cover all Workmen as well as Officers.

Presently apart for the Training Department at Bangalore, HAL has Training Departments in the other Divisions located at Nasik, Koraput, Lucknow, Kanpur, Korwa and Hyderabad.

Training Activities

The broad classification of the training activities conducted over the years is as shown below:

(a) Conduct of HRD Programmes for Junior Executive and employees and staff;

(b) Training of Trade Apprentices, Technicians (Diploma holders) and Eng. Graduates under the provisions of the Apprentices Act 1961 and Amendment 1973. Around 2500 apprentices are being maintained at any given point of time;

(c) Training of Executive Trainees (Tech);

(d) Remustering training for employees of HAL, Bangalore;

(e) Training of Retiring defence personnel;

(f) Training of Technician Trainees;

(g) Training of Engineering Diploma Trainees;

(h) Training on charge basis, to external Customers;

(i) Conduct of Literacy examination for the employees of HAL, Bangalore;

(j) Programmes on Do's and Don'ts;

(k) Refresher Training Programmes for First and Second line Supervisors in technical and non-technical modules;

(l) Special programmes as and when projected by the Divisions.

Infrastructure

Well equipped Classrooms, Library have been provided for conducting Training Sessions.

Other Efforts

In additional the above initiative efforts towards organizational excellence is achieved through the following HR interventions:

- Quality Circles/TQM;
- Suggestion Schemes;
- Cellular Manufacturing;
- Lean Manufacturing.

CONCLUSION

HAL being a High Tech industry is exposed to high Global Competition. It becomes essential to have a highly motivated and dedicated workforce and Managers with excellent leadership qualities and dynamism. Constant HR interventions of the above nature become the theme for the success of the organization.